In Search of Cider

Cider and Cider Makers in Cornwall, Devon, Dorset and Somerset

Published in 2012 by

somersethistory.co.uk

10 Society Road, Shepton Mallet, Somerset BA4 5GF

Printed by Remous,Wyvern Buildings, Glovers Close, Milborne Port, Sherborne, Dorset DT9 5EP

ISBN 978-0-9572611-0-5

Cover design Nigel Reece, Cognique, 8 Leigh Road, Street

Foreword

By Anthony Gibson OBE
former South-West regional director of the NFU and one-time CAMRA cider correspondent!

I first started taking an interest in cider in the mid 1970s, when I was the Regional Information Officer for the NFU in the South-West. Born and brought up in South Devon, I had always been aware of the region's cider tradition, but by a curious twist of fate, it was actually the Government decision to impose excise duty on cider in the 1976 Budget which turned a passing interest into a consuming one.

The NFU was naturally opposed to the tax and lobbied against it. I played my part by compiling as exhaustive a list as I could manage of the cider-makers in the South-West, so that they could be rallied to the cause. Our efforts didn't make much difference to the outcome (although we did manage to save Horace Lancaster a bill for many thousands of pounds in back-tax, when Customs and Excise tested his cider and discovered it was so strong it counted as wine!), but they did provide me with a check list of cider farms that I could visit in the course of my duties, armed with my two gallon Whiteways stone jar.

Rather like Alan Stone, my journeys of cider discovery took me to some strange and fascinating places, and I certainly experienced just as many navigational difficulties armed with my one inch Ordnance Survey maps as he appears to have encountered with his Google maps! Many of the names in this admirably comprehensive guide

All of which means that the modern day cider enthusiast can be guaranteed just as much variety and interest if he embarks on a pilgrimage around the region as I enjoyed all of those years ago, especially if he is armed with this guide. But do not get the impression that this is just a gazetteer. Besides all of the information that you need to track down the cider-makers, fascinating accounts of the idiosyncrasies of their businesses and some highly amusing accounts of Alan's own experiences when going off in search of them, this book contains much wisdom and colour on the history of cider, and the traditions and techniques associated with it.

One of the issues which he discusses, and which must have been aired in arguments in public bars a thousand times, is the essential difference between Somerset and Devon ciders. With the expert endorsement of Liz Copas, Alan puts it down to the predominance of tannin-heavy bittersweet apple varieties in Somerset, whereas in Devon, they have tended to favour the bittersharp, and sometimes slightly sweeter apples. In my own experience, Devon ciders tend to be slightly sharper and more acidic; Somerset's to be more mellow and structured. But don't take my word for it, or Alan's for that matter. Put this book in your pocket and find out for yourself.

The cider-making tradition isn't quite as strong in our other two South-Western counties, although both Cornwall and, especially, Dorset are now fast making up for lost time. I shall certainly be making a detour through the lanes to St. Veep when next I'm in the Duchy, while the Powerstock Cider Festival in West Dorset is a gathering of the cider clans never to be missed. And if you are visiting the Royal Bath and West Show, make a bee-line for the Orchards and Cider section, which is one of the best features at any farming show anywhere in the country. The selection of ciders is second to none, and the chances are that you'll find Alan there, ready as ever for a chat about his favourite subject.

Cider is one of the West Country's abiding glories. It offers history, folklore, tradition, variety and pleasure unconfined. This book is your passport to an Aladdin's cave of cidrous riches. Good searching, and good drinking!

Contents

Apologies and Thanks

Firstly a big apology to any cider producer I have missed. I have made a considerable effort over 18 months to search out as many commercial producers as possible but I am sure there are more out there. Part of the problem is the rapidly expanding number, another is that some of the smaller ones do not really want to put their head above the parapit. Anyway it leaves more to search for in the future.

I also appologise for any mistakes in information or opinion. This is a personal search and I have tried to be as thourough as I could. In most cases the producers have verified and approved their own entry though not all have replied to emails. If visiting a producer please do not rely on the information in this book - most have web sites and for others I have tried to include telephone numbers.

Thanks - now to the more positive! This book would not be what it is without a lot of help from a number of people. Liz Copas has been wonderfully generous with her time and help and I have clearly credited her contributions in the text. Other cider experts like Keith Goverd and Andrew Lea have also helped. In the counties Andy Atkinson for Cornwall, Chris Cole, Nick Pring and Mark Venton for Devon and Nick Poole for Dorset have been particularly helpful. From SWECA I would like to thank Neil Worley, Alex Hill, John Perry and in particular Bob Chaplin who is such a big help in so many ways to so many of us.

I would like to sincerely thank my family who, as always, have had to put up with me dashing off here and there. I notice there are photo's from both sons, Richard and James in the book. Richard proofed and commented on all the sections as I was writing them and my wife Christine has done the third proof read. Any errors and typo's that remain are entirely my fault - though I might use dyslexia as an excuse!

And of course thanks to the very many cider makers who have given me so much of their time. They are a wonderful and diverse bunch united by their passion for cider. I hope readers will repay their efforts by searching them out themselves.

Alan Stone, Shepton Mallet, 5th May 2012

Introduction

This book is a report on a journey of discovery. It aims to do what it says on the tin. It genuinely is a search for cider and cider makers in the four south western counties of Cornwall, Devon, Dorset and Somerset.

It does not claim to be a 100% listing of all cider producers in the area. If I had an intention of doing that it has proved impossible, it is a moving feast and that is one of the reasons why researching this book has been so interesting. The book probably contains mentions of at least 95% of cider producers in the area at the time of going to print. The vast majority of these have been visited and interviewed and have included an individual article about each of them. At the end of each county section, though, I have also mentioned a number of other cider makers who I have heard reference to and who may be worth searching out for yourself. The reason that this cannot guarantee to be a 100% accurate listing is that these are exciting times for cider and cider makers. Many new businesses are setting up whilst others are winding down. Some of the new businesses are of a rather transitory nature and it remains to be seen how many of them can establish themselves long term.

It is little over three years ago that I wrote my Somerset Cider Handbook in which I identified 37 cider makers selling cider in the county. Some people have asked me why I am repeating the exercise so soon. Once I had 'finished' Somerset I spent some time gradually meeting cider makers in Devon who really deserve a book of their own. I also found that there is an exciting cider revolution going on in Dorset and Cornwall is now beginning to discover that it is not only about selling rough cider to tourists but it too has a genuine cider tradition stretching back centuries. These were things I wanted to cover and encourage people to look out for. As for Somerset, I have discovered at least 10 new producers! Nearly all of these have set up in the last four years.

The one criteria for a cider maker used in this book is that they have to be registered with HMRC to sell cider. This in itself is a slight problem in that there is a culture of unlicensed cider 'sheds' and clubs across the region. Often communal efforts where friends get together to make and drink some copious quantities of cider. There are also still a considerable number of farmers and other amateurs making cider on old presses on farms for their own consumption. I do refer to a few of these in the text, they are a very vital part of our cider heritage, however I try to make it clear where they are not selling to the public. Even some of the smaller makers who are registered are only officially allowed to sell wholesale. I do not want to get anyone into trouble with HMRC.

One of the interesting challenges has been identifying the separate history and heritage of cider in each of the four counties. Although much is overlapping it has been possible to discover some interesting county traits and in particular differences in the varieties of apples used. This has been fascinating to discover and for each county different people have provided me with very substantial help; in Cornwall Andy Atkinson and Keith Goverd; in Devon Mark Venton and Chris Coles; in Dorset Nick Poole and over a whole region the totally invaluable help of Liz Copas the former Long Ashton expert and author of The Somerset Pomona some of whose comments I have included verbatum. Discussing our cider heritage with these and many others has helped me reach a new level of understanding about how the character of ciders is determined and the difference in our regional tastes. This is still very much a work in progress and ideas are still evolving but it has added another aspect to my 'search' which I feel enriches it considerably.

Another aspect of the search has been around the different types of cider that are being made. The previous 'golden age' of cider was in the 17th and 18th centuries but it is almost certain that that level of both quality and variety has been surpassed in the last few years. The starting level is the traditional farmhouse 'rough' cider which used to be produced on nearly every farm throughout most of this region. This is the fermented juice of apples harvested and pressed in the autumn fermented in barrels and drunk the following summer, particularly around haymaking and harvest time. However some farmers were always better at making cider than others. Selection of apples, cleanliness of equipment, timings of racking and different storage methods can make huge differences and some farmers developed skills around these. This straightforward 'honest' cider is still what you will find with the majority of producers in this book.

However some try to make premium products and utilise different techniques - many of these techniques dating from the 'golden age' over three hundred years ago. Some produce ciders fortified up to greater strengths, some 'keeve' their cider to give natural sweetness. Others go through the laborious processes of bottle conditioning to produce ciders that will compete with the most expensive continental sparkling wines. Most producers will now sweeten most of their cider to cater for modern tastes and modern taste again drives a perceived modern need to carbonate ciders to satisfy the palate's desire for fizz. As you will read there are techniques to achieve both of these things with natural methods but those really are the reserve of the specialist craft makers and will necessitate a premium price. Cider has to respond to its market and in the past few years many, even small cider makers, have started to bottle a considerable proportion of their produce both to meet the market and to extend shelf life to ensure it arrives with the consumer in the state they want it drunk. Others have reacted to the government's plea for sensible drinking by concocting products which only have a 4% ABV whereas cider naturally is likely to be in the range of 6% - 8%.

There is also an interesting recent fashion for adding some fruit or other flavourings to ciders. In fact this was also common during the 'golden age' and my son Richard, with me as labourer, has experimented with a lot of different ideas - some of which have tasted very good. Unfortunately, there are a few problems currently to be worked out with this. Although beers can have any flavour added, the regulations set out by HMRC do not allow anything to be added to cider - if they do it is classified as 'made wine' and subjected to crippling tax duties. In practice this means that many of the craft producers cannot sell flavoured products. There is an additional issue in that some of the more commercial producers are making fruit 'ciders' where the taste is very overpowering or synthetic in flavour using some heavy duty industrial fruit concentrate and possibly less than desirable quantities of apple juice.

The amount of apple juice in a cider is an interesting debate. Most people would assume it is close to 100% fermented apple juice - and indeed for the majority of producers featured in this book it usually is. However, even some traditional makers have always either watered down or produced a second pressing of slightly weaker ciders. Industrial producers are likely to have lower levels and to be legally cider it now has to contain a minimum of 33% apple juice. Because of a mathematical formula applied this can actually be as low as 19% apple juice and it is believed that some supermarket own-brand ciders struggle to meet even this low requirement.

Cider producers themselves differ in their backgrounds and aims. They range from rustic old characters to young farmers sons, from scruffy 'peasants' to smart business executives, from placid laid-back lifestylers to thrusting commercial entrepreneurs. There are still a good number of places where the cider making is part of a genuine mixed farm business. I wouldn't like to work out the exact sums but over the past few years it is quite possible that the long term decline in farmer makers has actually been reversed. Farm diversification and the need to employ sons is one driver but perhaps more significantly is the decision of some of the major cider makers to grow their own orchards and stop taking apples from their existing farmer suppliers - a number of whom have responded by starting to make their own cider or sell the apples to other new producers.

The majority of cider makers however, are now specialists in just that - either full or part-time, whatever system they follow or products they make. They of course are making cider for a living and there seems to be a graduated scale from a craft cider maker to some very industrial set ups. Most of them are very much linked to apples and orchards - either their own or through very strong relationships with them. Even the biggest producers in this area Thatcher's and the Shepton Cider Mill are very well known for their interest in growing the apples. One has to be a little suspicious of those where there is no strong tie-up.

This book will try not to be too judgemental about what is a 'good' or 'bad' cider and certainly not about what a 'real' cider is. For those of us who also like a pint of Real Ale and have grown up with the very excellent work that CAMRA have done to perpetuate and promote our local ales it is sad that so many people think the same sort of criteria can be made to apply to cider. I have been involved in some very lively and sometimes acrimonious online debates on this topic. CAMRA make judgements and offer a set of criteria for what they think a real cider is that even the genuine craft makers think is totally unworkable. They just do not understand cider and work on a mistaken premise that like beer it has to be a product with live yeast - missing the point that cider is formed by the yeast dying and in many types of cider live yeast can be seriously detrimental to the stability and quality of the product.

However defining what a 'real' cider is remains a challenge. I think as well as some of the technical aspects it is also related to the relationship of the producer with his apples and has as much to do with the attitude of the maker and his ideals as any exact recipe. You 'know' a real cider when you understand it. In this book we will not be judgemental on what is 'real' and will largely try to provide the information for the reader to decide what is 'good' or 'bad' by themselves. I know what I like but would encourage the reader to search out cider so they can make their own self-informed ethical decisions. I certainly do not subscribe to the school that the smaller and more rustic the cidermaker the 'better' their cider is going to be.

This search for cider has been very enjoyable. Quite expensive, with the increased costs of petrol travelling around the South West has not been cheap. Quite frustrating wrestling with the often very misleading output of Google Maps which was accentuated by wrongly typed postcodes and human error on my part. But it has been a constant joy to meet so many interesting cider makers who almost without exception have really enjoyed a chance to talk about what they do.

I certainly hope this book encourages you to get out and meet as many of them as you can yourself.

South West England Cidermakers Association SWECA. www.sweca.org.uk

This book has been written with the encouragement and support the South West England Cider makers Association.

SWECA is an organisation which groups nearly 60 South West cider makers together. It is one of four regional associations across England, Wales and Ireland who co-operate with the National Association of Cider Makers NACM.

Of these organisations SWECA possibly has the best blend of cider makers including those of all shapes and sizes ranging from large national producers such as Thatchers and Shepton Cider Mill, right the way down the scale to new start ups-businesses. The condition of membership is that a producer should be producing a minimum of 1,000 gallons, though there are other associate membership   categories for others involved in cider.

One of the things that fascinates me about cider makers is their friendliness and willingness to talk to one another about cider, how to grow the apples, how to make it and how to sell it. It is difficult to imagine another industry where large and small all get on so well with one another. Meetings are held two or three times a year where a number of relevant topics are discussed. There is often a focus on HMRC regulations and Food Hygiene and Health and Safey matters - here the link up with NACM is vital with national experts like Nick Bradstock coming along to inform members. There is often a focus on the cider market and marketing. Orchards and their cider apple varieties are either talked about or walked around. There have been tours around members' production facilities and tasting sessions to compare ciders.

One of the big activities of the year is running the bar in the wonderful Cider Marquee at the Bath and West Show where one of the widest selections of regional ciders ever assembled is available for the public to drink. The stand is mainly manned by SWECA members and it offers another chance for members to socialise.

Many noteable cider makers have served on the SWECA committee. The current chairman is Alex Hill who runs Bollhayes Cider, though he is probably better known for founding and running Vigo - the premier supplier of equipment to small and medium-sized cider makers based in the Blackdown Hills. The Immediate past Chairman is John Perry from the Ilminster produced cider maker. However the most important person beyond doubt is Bob Chaplin who for many years has been the secretary who holds the whole thing together. Bob has worked for the Shepton Cider Mill through all its various guises, thick and thin, for nearly 40 years and is a real servant to the industry. His current role is orcharding manager - looking after both their own orchards and those of their growers. He is a fount of knowledge about people in the industry.

In this book I have included, as far as I can see, all the current SWECA members and have put the initials SWECA after their address details. It is not a badge of assurance - but at least you know these are people who take their cider seriously. Membership is focused on the four counties covered in this book though in recent years a few from outside the region have joined to take advantage. For the sake of completeness these are listed below:

146 Cider Company, Southampton, Hampshire 07738 823867

Orchards Cider And Perry Company, Brockweir, Lower Wye Valley, Forest Of Dean 01291 689536

Out Of The Orchard, Pershore, Worcestershire 01386 552324

Rocquette Cider, Guernsey, 01481 234111

Upton Cider Company, Didcot, Oxfordshire, 01235 850808

Wessex Cider, Fifield Bavant, Nr Salisbury, Wiltshire 01722 718742

Whin Hill Cider, Wells-next-the-Sea, Norfolk 07769 571423

Section 1
Cornwall

Andy Atkinson of Cornish Orchards

Cornish Cider Heritage

"There is no heritage of cider in Cornwall - they just make a bit of scrumpy to sell to the tourists"

So I was told by a friend and ardent Cornishman when telling him I was investigating the subject. To be honest it seems to be a pretty widely held view amongst many - even in the cider fraternity. However, it is not actually the case and it gradually became clear to me that Cornwall has a considerable cider heritage, vestiges of which can still be found and in the current cider revival some are indeed being rekindled.

To start with I was aware of little other than the two most prominent cider producers, Healy's Cornish Cider Farm, which dates back only about 25 years, and Cornish Orchards with little more than a decade to its existence. However it is when visiting the latter and talking to Andy Atkinson in particular that I began to discover that there had been many producers before.

Having been an Economic and Social History student my academic discipline likes to back up any suggestion with fact. I therefore return to one of my favourite set of statistics. The agricultural returns for orchards (tree fruit of any kind) for the year 1883.

The total for orchards in the UK was 185,782 acres.

Herefordshire	27,081
Devon	26,348
Somerset	23,407
Kent	17,417
Worcester	16,804
Gloucestershire	14,926
Cornwall	4,869
Dorset	4,073
Monmouth	3,919
Salop	3,718
Middlesex	3,467

The balance split between 39 other counties.

It should be noted that this includes all fruit orchards which obviously to a large degree explains the acreage for Kent and Middlesex and it should be remembered that Worcestershire (Vale of Evesham) and Gloucestershire were also considerable top fruit growing counties particularly for cherry and plum. In general though it will be seen that the vast bulk of orchards were in the three main cider counties and those counties adjoining them, of which Cornwall was one of the more significant.

Another clue came with the historical re-enactment series 'The Edwardian Farm' shown in early 2011 where they had a go at making traditional cider from orchards on both sides of the Tamar Valley.

I went to talk to Andy Atkinson to get an understanding of Cornish Cider from him. When setting up his Cornish Orchards business he had based it very much on just that - Cornish orchards. He found many small run-down apple orchards on his own farm and near to where he farmed. At the same time the Cornwall County Council were taking an interest in their local apple varieties and encouraging identification, propagation and planting.

Andy reckons that even 70 years ago there would have been at least 100 farmers and cottagers making cider in Cornwall and going back further many more than that. Indeed a cider making tradition very close to that in Devon. However, physical distance from the rest of England and the scarcity of population in the county meant that no significant commercial producers developed in the late 19th century as they did in the other cider counties and with changing patterns of farming and taxation the heritage faded away during the 20th century.

He feels that another factor which held back commercial development is that the orchards tended to be a lot smaller in Cornwall. For obvious reasons orchards tend to be limited to locations with protection from the elements in valleys where land is at a premium. He suggests that smallholders or cottagers usually had orchards as small as up to one and a half acres and even on farms orchards would seem to have been most frequently only up to only two and a half acres in size. There was not the land or the market for more cider than could be produced from this. He also suggests that there was a co-operative element. He has found three round granite crushing mills in barns on farms local to him. These were quite expensive and substantial peices of equipment and he feels it is most likely that smallholders would have bought their apples to the local farm to mill.

Although it needs a lot of further investigation it may be possible to push the heritage of Cornish cider back further. Elsewhere in this book I have explored the tradition of cider in South Devon and the 17th, 18th and early 19th century commercialisation of cider to be shipped to the London market and for use by crews on board ships. There is evidence of cider being shipped from many small ports around the Devon coast and I suspect if the Coastal Port Books for Cornwall were examined we would find similar evidence there. The investment in stone crushing mills is also very similar to Devon and could well indicate a purpose other than self consumption behind early Cornish cider making. This trade would possibly have withered away with the decline of coastal shipping and the spread of railways in the mid 19th century which facilitated trade from inland areas.

Another piece of evidence for a Cornish Cider past came to light recently when I was in the office of Chris Riddle the Chief Executive of the Royal Cornwall Show. On the wall was an old poster, framed and hung for posterity. It is a notice of the Cornwall Farmers Society dated 1803 setting out the classes for the show of that year. One of them is:

'Orchards, To the person who shall be the Occupier of an orchard in Cornwall (not less than one Acre) well stocked with Cyder Fruit, in the best state of Improvement and Cultivation'

The prize for this class was a very significant five guineas. Chris also gave me a copy of his book on the history of the show and it would appear that in 1800 there was also a five guinea prize for the production of an essay which would *'shew, from actual Experiment, the best Method of making Cyder'* The prime role of the Society at that time was for the improvement in agriculture and this clearly shows an active interest in cider in Cornwall at that time.

The picture that emerges is of orchards and cider mainly restricted to the valleys and inlets of south Cornwall. Much of the evidence seen so far comes from the Valleys of the Tamar and the Fowey. This could explain why my friend referred to in the opening quotation was not aware of the heritage - he is from the north of the county where the landscape is much harsher and less suited to orchards. However I am not convinced that it was totally restricted to southern valleys. One of the most renowned Cornish apples for cider is the variety Tommy Knights and new plantings of this are being encouraged. The 1993 'Book of Apples' comments that this is an apple local to St Agnes which as far as my limited geography is aware is in the wild far west of Cornwall.

Is there a distinctive 'Cornish cider'? Again Andy Atkinson has some ideas on this. As there were largely small orchards on smallholdings and farms they very much tended to be mixed orchards that grew apples for consumption, desserts and cookers, as well as apples for cider. Indeed the evidence, such as we have, very strongly suggests a lot of dual purpose apples like Tommy Knights or Tom Putt would have been used. This would most likely have produced a sharper ciders, perhaps with a more wine like taste than the tannin laden ciders of the main cider making counties

- but not the slightly bland tastes of the 'eastern style' ciders which are largely reliant on dessert cull apples. The evidence of my tasting of cider from Hayne Farm would appear to support this and Andy Atkinson's aspirations for his Cornish Orchard ciders seem to very much reflect this tradition.

There is also the tradition of 'large houses' in Cornwall, some of which are now owned by the National Trust. From Victorian times there had extensive landscaped gardens which built collections of and propagated apple varieties. Collections of tags and tales from old gardeners still abound and have fortunately been retained by a number of TV documentaries. This tradition, although not directly cider focused, is very much linked in to the heritage.

Another person who has been helping with Cornish apples is the former Long Ashton scientist and consultant Keith Goverd. In recent years Keith has spent a fair bit of time in Cornwall and has seen a lot of apple trees being planted out, both bittersweet and traditional Cornish varieties. It includes a Cornish collection to act as mother stock for propagation, grafting and budding, and he is hoping for a second project of this nature. He has done some consultancy work for potential new producers in Cornwall and also for the National Trust Estate at Trelissick. He feels that some of the orchards and new producers are still very much below the horizon and that the next few years will start to see both the apples and the products emerge. His view is that in the 20th century Cornish cider tended to suffer because of the relative scarcity of apple trees. Anything that tasted decent went to be eaten and that it was only the worst of apples left that went for cider. He feels that this is about to change.

On a more historical note Keith points out that there has been a thriving apple growing industry on the Lizard both historically and recently and that cider was produced there as well. He also points out that there were links between Cornwall and Brittany which involved both export of apples from Cornwall to Brittany and vice versa. There are apples grown in Cornwall that have a distinctly French character in their name. Even in recent years there was liaison between Cornish and French apple growers.

There is scope for a lot more research of records and on the ground investigation looking for more evidence of the heritage of cider in Cornwall. All I hope to have done here is give people a push to look for more. However, there is already enough Cornish cider around today to make it well worth the effort of looking out for and visiting the county.

Cornish Orchards

Andy Atkinson Dole, nr Liskeard, Cornwall. www.cornishorchards.co.uk. 01278 751593 **SWECA**

There is a sense of integrity about the cider of Cornish Orchards that sets it apart from most other ciders on the market.

Much of the juice comes from traditional Cornish apple varieties from either old or newly planted Cornish Orchards. Much of it is back sweetened with natural apple juice from the same orchards. And all of it is of a consistent high quality.

But at the same time it is a commercial operation, big enough to be making own brand 'Press Gang' keg cider for the famed Cornish brewer Skinners and 'Orchard Cider' for the even more famous Sharp's Brewery, as well as having an extensive penetration for their own products throughout the county and indeed the country.

When you meet the man behind it, Andy Atkinson, it all makes sense. The quietly spoken former farmer comes across as a sound entrepreneur with that same sense of integrity that permeates his business.

I had met Andy a few times before going to visit him, at the Royal Cornwall Show where they have an excellent stand, at a food and cider event at Darts Farm near Exeter and at a SWECA meeting. I was really looking forward to a deeper conversation. The first thing I did was to dispel the myth I had been fed that he was a northern incomer. True he was born in Yorkshire but his mother was from the South Hams just across the border in Devon and his formative years were spent there including his student years at Seale Hayne Agricultural College near Newton Abbot where his education included the famed Cider Bar in the town.

He became a farmer at the age of 23, first farming in Dorset and Devon before coming to Cornwall in 1978. In 1992 he took on the tenancy of the Duchy farm where he still is. For the first decade it was nearly all about dairy farming. However dairy farming went on a roller coaster ride. Firstly, the national Milk Marketing Board was broken up by the government in its drive to bring competition into the market. The Milk Marketing Board had existed since the 1930's and, although it had its critics, had ensured that dairy farming maintained a basic level of profitability. At first it looked as if the free market would bring in a golden age as the milk buyers competed to attract farmers. Prices rose from around 19p to 26p per litre. However, then the combined influences of the big milk dairies and the growing pressure from the supermarket giants put the squeeze on and by 2000 the milk price had crashed down to 16p. This was just as Foot and Mouth struck the farming community to its

very heart when it was already struggling with TB and BSE. Andy says he got sick of seeing about farming crisis on TV and he wondered what the outlook was. As an entrepreneurial young farmer he could not get enthusiastic about anyway forward - disillusion, disappointment and frustration were three words he used to describe his thoughts. He obviously was thinking of farm diversification which was then all the rage. He pondered on producing cheese or yoghurt but decided he had had enough of dairying - another option was beginning to emerge.

When first on the farm in 1992 the Cornwall County Council were encouraging local farmers with grants to plant out orchards with traditional varieties. The environmentally conscious Andy, with a foresight he would not pretend to, took advantage and started replanting a former orchard and planting new. In the first instance he bought 200 trees of 17 varieties and has budded these on and within five years had planted out 15 acres. In 1998 his daughter received a wedding gift of some natural apple juice from Cheshire. It set Andy wondering if he could produce his own from the orchard he had already planted. Nowadays we take cloudy natural apple juice for granted but in the 1990s it was still a 'new product.'

The apple juice proved a big hit at local farmers markets and Andy began to see its potential. He planted more apples and encouraged friends to do the same. As a former hobby home brewer and wine maker it was only natural after two years to try making cider. 2002 was the year that he first tried to sell cider and the year that the dairy cows went. Although it has always been a livestock farm, for the past six years he has very much gone down the cider route.

He examined old maps and went out and found traditional orchards. He now sources apples from all over the county, some from orchards over 100 years old. Because of the level of production he is achieving he also sources apples from Devon. He is particularly pleased with some apples he is getting from the traditional cider apples which supplied Whiteway's the former giant of Devon commercial cider.

Of the traditional Cornish varieties his favourite is Tommy Knight and he also rates Hockins Green highly. Others include Lord of the Isles a big cooker / cider apple; Ben's Red an eater and Tan Harvey a good bittersharp; Collogate Pippin is a massive Tamar Valley apple which is so large and juicy that if you hit it against a tree juice starts to seep out.

He first made a traditional high strength cider in oak barrels with treacle added to increase the strength and sold it like a wine at near 8% proof. He discovered that there was little market for this type of product. He has been one of the pioneers of making good socially responsible ciders closer to 4%. Back sweetening with apple juice helps them to retain body and flavour. Most of his cider is also gently carbonated. The purist fans of traditional cider may feel this is a sacrilege but Andy points out that if he is to grow his business he has to produce ciders that people want to buy.

At the same time he feels it would be pointless to try to compete with the giant industrial cider makers with their glucose and concentrate packed products with low levels of juice content. He is treading the fine line between artisan and commercial. He has recently rebranded their products to strongly bring out the Cornish heritage. His Cornish Gold is a major seller and his biggest seller is their Orchard Draught. About 50% of their production is sold draught and 50% bottles. Last year production exceeded 100,000 gallons.

He finds there are too many pitfalls to marketing through the supermarkets and have tended to plough his own furrow to outlets where quality matters. He sells to hotel and pub chains and restaurants with chefs such as Rick Stein and he sells through the top of market tourist attractions like the National Trust visitor centres and the Eden Project. Outside Cornwall he does export to three European countries but the bulk of his exports go to places such as Bristol, Bath and London.

You can also go to the farm where during the summer season he has a nice little farm shop where you can taste the products. When I visited he had just introduced an alcoholic ginger beer which he is producing - very good.

I like Andy Atkinson and Cornish Orchards. His product may not please a small minority of the purists but we all want cider to improve its image and reputation. Andy, as a man of marketing integrity, is making a real and innovative contribution to that process.

Haye Farm

Nigel and Alix Vincent, Haye Farm, St Veep, Lerryn, Cornwall. 07811 442512 wwwhayefarmcider.co.uk

In all my searching for cider in the four counties whilst putting this book together visiting Haye Farm has to be one of the highlights. This is probably because the contrast between what I was expecting and what I found was so great - but a friendly welcome and a really nice cider certainly helped as well.

I was driving down to Cornwall to go to the Taste of the West Awards which in 2011 were being held at the Eden Project - in a four hour lunch in one of the biodomes. Old Mill, the company I work in for my day job, was sponsoring a category and imagine my delight when this was won by Perry's Cider from Dowlish Wake in South Somerset - I had the pleasure of sitting next to John and Liz Perry during the meal. However I am getting ahead of myself, back to Haye Farm.

Seeing on the map that Haye Farm was only about seven miles from the Eden Project I left a bit early to fit in an investigative visit on the way. I had come across the cider at the Royal Cornwall Show where a Cornish food wholesaler had a few pre-poured containers on their stand - to be honest it was only okay, but this was not the ideal way of storing. Over the summer there had been comments on the internet forums that Haye Farm had been sold following the death of the farmer in 2009, and lamentations that cider making had ceased. However, I thought I had better check it out for myself - I am certainly glad I did.

It was damp underfoot but a sunny morning as I made my way down increasingly narrow Cornish lanes south of Restmorel, through Lerryn and on towards St Veep. My spirits rose as I spotted a sign for Cider Sales and went down an even narrower lane and in the bottom of the valley was a small farm. The sign said to toot my horn so I did. There was also a mobile number to phone and I was about to when I heard someone coming up through the farmyard and was greeted by a very cheerful young woman who later amazed me when I discovered she had been married for 17 years and had teenage children. She had been down in the orchard picking up apples and when I said I was looking for cider took me into a shed with an old press

*Alix Vincent
by the press
as Haye Farm*

at the back and poured me a taster out of a wooden barrel. Nectar - it took just one mouthful to reveal an extremely good cider with some residual sweetness and the almost wine like flavour of some interesting apples.

I decided to say who I was and my purpose in visiting "Aren't you the farm that was for sale and was stopping cider making?" I blurted out with my usual want of tack. She agreed that is was but said they had had some very good news which had only got sorted in the fortnight prior to my visit. Her husband Nigel was the son of the previous owner and he and she had been offered the tenancy of the farm by the new owners Bill and Anna Coles. Even better of all the people who looked at the farm they were the one potential buyer who had been interested in the cider making aspect and were keen for them to carry on making!

I began to ask more about the history of cider making on the farm and it became clear that this was the holy grail - a true traditional Cornish Farmhouse cider maker - that is not meant to be in any way derogatory to the other very good makers and in particular to Andy Atkinson who is doing so much to maintain the tradition. But here we had a farm where the same family had been making cider in the same way for many years. Nigel is at least the 4th generation of his family to farm at Haye. His grandfather, great uncle and father preceded him. It is believed that cider has been made here since the 13th century. The farm is in the right location for a traditional Cornish cider farm. It is near the banks of the Fowey and Polrunan Creek, the next major valley along from the Tamar and as previously mentioned the link between these valleys and the possibility of export to London or for ships crews was probably a key part of the Cornish Cider tradition as it was in South Devon.

They have three local orchards at Haye, St.Cadix and South Lerryn and the selection of apple varieties is amazing. The Duchy Nurseries have been helping to identify 30 different varieties of mixed dessert, cooking and cider apples including many local and one or two unique to the farm. Alix highlights Golden Noble as a particular favourite and the list includes the like of Alfriston, Gaul, Red Bramley, John Standish, John Broad (aka Captian Broad), Lord of the Isle, Pigs Snout, Patagonia, Parsons Plate, Strawberry Pippen, Tregonna King and Winter Stubbins - all new to me! In recent years Alix has been planting some more traditional mainly Cornish varieties in her orchard at South Lerryn including Tommy Knight, Cornish Gillyflower (which I happen to know makes an exceptional apple juice), Queenie, Cornish Aromatic, the Rattler, Pigs Nose, Manaccan Primrose, Pear apple, King Byard and Box apple.

The method of cider production is traditional as well. They have a large old twin screw press which holds two and a half tonnes of apples per pressing. As all the apples are picked up by hand this equates to between 90 and 100 sacks. And they aim to do 15 pressings a year - talk about back-breaking! Alix was in the process of picking up when I arrived and apparently Nigel and their children, other relatives and friends are persuaded to help. The apples are milled in an old electric mill, though they used to have an old mill powered by two men. Over each weekend they build a cheese on the bed of their press with straw holding the pommace in place. When I arrived on Tuesday morning that week's pressing was just about finished and the pomace would be fed to their beef and sheep.

The juice from the press is pumped into wooden barrels and Nigel makes a point of keeping these barrels topped up with juice as the fermentation progresses. The barrels are mainly 100 gallon hogshead or 117 gallon pipes and there is a second shed with a row of barrels. Nigel makes a very big point of getting the barrels very clean. Just about the most modern equipment on display is two boilers in which he heats the water for cleaning which includes rolling the barrels with a chain inside. Such attention to cleanliness is essential if traditional methods are to produce a consistent result. Most years they have been selling out of cider during the season and Alix says that most of the cider they sell is quite young and still has a bit of natural fizz in it. I suspect I was rather lucky to come across such a fine, matured cider - I think there had been some mix up over labelling - I would certainly recommend they mislabel some barrels again!

One of the charms of Haye Farm is that they have carried on making cider in the same way for many years without reference to other cider makers. Their methods are as they always have been and they are charmingly modest about their efforts. Alix says that over the summer they went to a cider festival in Launceston just to taste some other ciders and came away thinking that there own was not half bad. I hope as the new arrangements on the farm settle down and evolve that their cider will be available to more cider drinkers.

I bought a gallon of cider and back in Somerset that evening when I eventually got home I tasted it again - just to reassure myself that it was as good as I thought. It was and Richie, my son, backed this up - one mouth full and he asked what on earth it was, a really good complex taste - sublime was the word that sprang to both our minds and although we taste a rather wide variety of ciders I can assure you it is not and adjective we use at all often.

Healey's Cornish Cyder Farm

Callistock Cider Farm, Truro, Cornwall TR4 9LW www.thecornishciderfarm.co.uk
SWECA

I really enjoyed my visit to the Cornish Cyder Farm. I had not been quite sure what I would find - was it just a tourist trap with the addition of a national commercial brand? Or was there more of the traditional of cider maker lurking underneath? I am very glad to say it was the latter, though with a modern, forward looking approach, and the bottle the Special Reserve Cyder which my son and I drank that night was a really excellent drop.

I had been to the Cyder Farm on a number of times over the years and had seen it grow and develop. The business started about 30 years ago when David Healey was running the Post Office in Mevagissy, which compared to many makers these day makes him a bit of an old hand. He had brought in cider from local producers but realised he could do it himself. He brought a small farm and started planting apples - then about 25 years ago he bought the much larger farm where they are today and converted it into a cider farm. They planted 25 acres of cider orchards, mainly with Bitter Sweet cider varieties like Harry Masters Jersey, Dabinet and Yarlington Mill. Nearly from the start it was open to the public and now around half a million visitors a year come to the farm and are able to discover a wealth of cider heritage.

I think my first visit must have been nearly 20 years ago. The children were quite young and the animals around the farmyard would still have been the major attraction for them. I remember the tractor pulled trip around the orchards and we purchased a poster with a bucolic smiling yokel which adorned our wall for many years - and to my surprise as I look to my left at the bookcase now whilst typing this there is one of their attractively shaped bottles with a candle stuck in it. As a family we visited at least once more on our occasional Cornish holidays and I had visited to buy some cider on a few occasions whilst visiting Cornwall for work.

As an

attraction and cider heritage centre it has continued to develop. The shop has grown over the years and there is now a massive restaurant. However, there is more than that. As well as still doing the trips around the orchard, there is an extensive museum of old cider equipment which has been collected by David Healey. It has become one of the more extensive collections I have seen, attractively displayed in cellars below the barns. There is also the Cornish Distillery which for the past 10 years has been making cider brandy and is now branching out into whisky. The product may be a little on the pricey side but I am fully in support of the recent growth of interest in craft niche spirits that we are seeing across the country. Visitors can also view the 'craft cider' bottling line and the modern belt mill where apples are crushed. There is the jam making factory - and of course there are still the essential animals around the farm yard. And most importantly this is all for free! The money is made by the sales in the shop - why oh why is there not a cider attraction as good as this in Somerset or Devon!

A slight aside, but one which I found extremely interesting, is a display board in the shop which explains the history of David's Grandfather Donald Healey 1898 - 1988. He seems to have been an engineer with incredible energy and as part of his extensive CV was the Healey of the legendery Austin Healey sports car of the 1950's. The distinctive shape of this the grill of this has been subtly incorporated into the design on the label of the Special Reserve Range - a touch of marketing class. Donald retired back to Cornwall in 1976 and at the age of 78 started to get involved in wind turbines and renewable energy generation. A man with a vision.

Healey's are probably best known now for their Rattler brand. David Healey's two sons, Sam and Joe are in their 20s and are part of the Perranporth beach surfing set. They came up with a brand and cider that was suited to their generation. It is now one of the leading national brands considering it is not from one of the big five manufacturers. A keg cider with a refreshing sharpness about it, unlike the cloying sweetness of some off the other brands aimed at the younger generation. There are now also the inevitable pear cider and berry cider versions as well.

I was interested when manager John James showed me the original prototype label for Rattler. The iconic rattlesnake head was not present - in fact it used the traditional Cornish Cider Farm label with just the wording changed to Rattler. The name, as stated in an advertising standard hearing in 2009, comes from an old variety of Cornish apple, The Rattler. Presumably this is one of those varieties where the pips rattle inside the apple when ripe. Anyway it is now known for the snake caricature drawing which is on the pumps in the many pubs that now serve it. On my way out of Cornwall I stopped at Jamaica Inn - amazingly this is a very pleasant pub out of season when you can turn a blind eye to all the tourist hype - and had an excellent pint of Rattler. What I had not spotted before was that the snake has disappeared from the main labels on the bottles of the product. Apparently the snake image was too appealing to children! Which led to the 2009 hearing. Our mad politically correct age strikes again. It has been replaced with some great surfing designs - which is where the product came from anyway.

Yes, Healeys Cornish Cider Farm is not your ordinary old farmer making cider in pressed straw. It is a commercial cider business which actually was probably a bit ahead of the trends and has been one of the cider producers who have been able to capitalise on the 'Magners' revolution. It may have been started to capitalise on the many tourists in the area, but it was done with proper cider orchards making cider in the same way as many other traditional producers. I will be interested to see how they grow and develop over coming years - and I will certainly be popping in to pick up another bottle of Special Reserve next time I am down in Cornwall.

Polgoon Vineyard and Orchard

Kim Caulson, Polgoon Vineyard and Orchard, Rosehill, Penzance Cornwall TR20 8TE. 01736 33346 www.polgoon.co.uk

I first met Kim at a Taste of the West trade fair two or three years ago. I think I may have slightly got hold of the wrong end of the stick at that time. She had provided a very drinkable bottled 'cider' for the exhibitor's reception. Although it was very pleasant, I went back for another glass a few times!, I was not sure how much it was

Kim and John inspecting the blossom at Polgoon

a cider - especially as I picked up the impression that they were only making it as their vineyard had suffered a poor harvest of grapes so they were making this cider with desert apple apples to fill the gap.

I think their product has now stood the test of time and when I reconnected with Kim by email and phone I was delighted with her friendly response and answer to my question as to how much cider making was a part of their business. I take the unusual step of quoting her reply.

'The cider part of Polgoon is essential to our solvency! It started very much by accident when 2 years in a row we had a poor grape harvest because of bad weather in the summer months. The sparkling wine equipment used to make our wonderful sparking wines wasn't being used so following the same traditional method but using apple juice 'Aval' was created(Cornish for Apple). The original Aval was picked up by Fortnum & Masons, Rick Stein's and some London Michelin restaurants. The Raspberry Aval that followed was initially considered by John (husband winemaker) as too gimicky to show to serious sommeliers but we couldn't have been more wrong as It is now our biggest seller, pink and sparkling, well balanced and fruity but dry, its a fantastic aperitif and often used as a dessert wine, most notably at the Gilbert Scott, Marcus Wareings resturant in St Pancreas. This has recently been joined by a Blackcurrant Aval which will I think be equally popular.'

They are using the genuine bottle conditioned *methode traditionale* including all the bottle turning and disgorging the sediment, leaving a naturally sparkling product - a process which I explain in more detail in the Ashbridge Cider feature in the Devon section of this book.

They also now make a range of Cornish Ciders in the three flavours. This is made from the same selection of apples but is fermented using more traditional cider making methods and is lightly carbonated. Unusually they bottle this in small 330ml bottles. I thought I had better taste some and got a bottle from the excellent Green Valley at Dart's Farm, Exeter. I still have the taste in my mouth as I write this. It fully justifies the description on its label as a light, fresh, crisp and fruity cider which I would imagine would be appreciated by many who like a more refined cider.

Polgoon has an excellent website - with online sales - and there is a shop now open seven days a week on their vineyard and orchard which also holds frequent events and tours. The Polgoon ciders are a million miles from farmhouse scrumpy but are a quality option in today's vibrant and varied cider market place. I will certainly be visiting when I next get a trip to Cornwall.

Penpol Cider

Keith Langmaid, Middle Penpol Farm, St Veep Cornwall PL22 0NG 01208 872017

When I was on my voyage of discovery to Haye Farm, Alix Vincent mentioned that there was another small cider maker just down the lanes. This was confirmed as I drove out and found a sign in the hedge pointing away from St Veep. Unfortunately I was on a very tight schedule and couldn't spare any time to explore further.

However, when I was mentioning this in conversation I discovered that a friend of mine, Nancy Norman, had in fact been there earlier in the year and tasted the cider. Now Nancy is of good Somerset farming stock and from one of the classic cider apple growing areas around Baltonsbourgh and Pennard though she now lives up the hill at Cannards Grave, so we can place a bit of faith that she knows something about it. She had been on a short holiday down that way and on the way back decided they should call in. Husband Chris, retired farmer, was driving so did not really need any cider and he stayed in the car. Nancy felt however they really should try it.

She says she met the elderly farmer cider maker who took her into his barns where there were many old barrels in a really traditional looking operation. She tried a couple and selected one to buy a small container of to bring home with them. She did however baulk at the cider made in whisky barrels.

From her report it certainly sounds as if I should make sure I drop in on Penpol cider next time I am down that way!

Skreach Cider

Hugh Chapman St Buryan,
Cornwall, 01736 811090
www.skreach.co.uk

I first came across a sample of
Skreach Cider when I was at Nick
Poole's in Dorset, interviewing him
for this book. He had a sample of the
cider someone had given him. Nick
phoned up Hugh and invited him to
bring a barrel of his cider to the
Powerstock Cider Festival where I
enjoyed tasting it again - though at the
Powerstock Cider Festival you end up
enjoying tasting everything!

Skreach must be the most far flung cider maker featured in this book, St Buryan
being right down the far end of Cornwall between Penzance and Lands End.
Unfortunately my travels have not in the past year taken me down that far - however I had a chat and took a picture of Hugh at Powerstock.

He has been making cider now for six years and is gradually expanding. He has
imported a mobile press from France which certainly looks an intriguing piece of
kit. He uses a mixture of bittersweet fruit such as Dabinet and some local Cornish
varieties. He is aiming to produce a drinkable high quality cider for selling around
the many gastro pubs down that far end of the peninsula. He sells most of his cider
wholesale in nine gallon casks and occasionally in bag in the box or 5 gallon barrels
for events.

From the evidence of my two tastings I would have said it is a clean dry cider with
quite a dark colour. Nothing wrong with that of course and it is certainly nice to see
a new craft cider producer in Cornwall making his cider in the traditional way.

One thing that has slightly fascinated me looking at his website is that he has a range
of Skreach cider clothing, tea shirts and fleeces. Surely he must be the smallest cider
maker to go down that route!

Other Cornish Ciders

In this short section for each county I will round up the remainder of names which my search, and the limitations of time, have not enabled me to find out more about. In the case of Cornwall this is so far a rather short section.

Halford Creek Cyder, Mudgeon Vean, Nr Helson TR12 6DB. 01362 231341 www.helfordcreek.co.uk
Right down the end of Cornwall not far from the Cornish Seal Sanctury, which I visited on many occasions when my children were small, is Halford Creek Cyder. Although it doesn't appear to have a shop their products are said, by their very good website, to be available in tourist attractions and shops throughout Cornwall and the West County and in some restaurants in London.

The apples come from orchards they have planted on a 55 acre small farm on the slopes about Helford Creek. Their range is very much apple juice orientated but they do make a Helford Creek Cyder. A very natural product matured in oak barrels and interestingly they say is made from old Cornish apple varieties. It is available in either 75cl or 500ml bottles.

The Lizard Cider Barn Predannack, The Lizard, Cornwall - TR12 7AU www.chy-cor.co.uk
This tourist attraction is right down on the Lizard peninsula, about as far south as you can go in England. As far as I can understand it the Lizard Cider Barn sells a selection of ciders including a small amount of its own making. A web reference lists Cornish Blacksmiths Cider and Vintage Cider.

I believe Keith Goverd did some consultancy work with them to encourage them to expand their cider making but he is not sure if they actually acted on it. A SWECA leaflet of two years ago lists them as members, strangely with an address in Somerton, Somerset. I am not sure that they are still members.

Davards Cider and Apples, Trevilla, Linkinhorne, Callington Cornwall PL17 8QP 07816 577952
Two websites, one a food from Cornwall website and the UKcider website list David Pritchard of Davards Cider as a producer of cider and apples in North Cornwall

Skinners Brewery, Riverside, Newham Road, Truro TR1 2DP 01872 271885 www.skinersbrewery.com.
This is the first, but not the last, mention in this book of good regional brewers who have teamed up with a local cider maker for their 'own brand cider.' Skinners are best known for their beer 'Betty Stoggs' but they also sell Press Gang Cornish Cider a very pleasant 4.8% ABV cider which I have drunk many times, especially in their bar at the Royal Cornwall Show. As their web site says this cider is 'created for us by our friends at Cornish Orchards.'

St Ives Cider, David Berwick, The Old Mushroom Farm, Halsetown, St Ives TR26 3LZ. Only spotted this one on a list of prospective SWECA members a few days before going to print. Website investigation suggests ir is part of the St Ives Brewery and their first cider is only just about ready

Others

I suspect there are a number of other small producers selling very locally to the immense tourist market in Cornwall. As they never need to stick their head above the horizon they are incredibly hard to spot. As Keith Goverd says, things are beginning to happen for cider in Cornwall and it could well be that in a few years time the list of producers will be a lot longer.

Apples at Polgoon

Section 2

Devon

Cider barrels in a 15th century barn at Brimblecombe Cider

In search of Devonshire cider

This search for cider in Devon was, at first, quite a daunting task. In Somerset I had spent over 20 years gradually getting to know the different ciders and it makers and had a comfortable start. Devon was a different proposition for me. Okay, over the years, I had drunk a number of Devon ciders and had met one or two producers but beyond that it was really a clean page on which to write.

There was also the impression that cider in Devon was not as important as cider in Somerset. The whole image of Somerset is rooted in cider - it is the major defining image of the county, followed by Cheddar cheese. For Devon clotted cream would be my first image but there would be many other things for a county which is so rooted in our 'tourist' knowledge of place. However, Devon had always featured in my reading about the history of cider. As shown in the introduction to the search in Cornwall, during the late 19th century Devon had the second most extensive fruit orchards to Hereford and nearly all of this must have been apples used for cider. It was also true to say that reading the cider classics revealed Devon along with Hereford and perhaps Worcester as being the intellectual home of cider in the 17th and 18th century. It was in these places that the great innovators and interested landowners lived. Devon was frequently mentioned whilst although it was clear that there was cider in Somerset it did not feature in the same terms.

It would be tempting to delve deeper into these early writers but this is not primarily a history book. For those interested I suggest 'The History and Virtues of Cyder' by R K French and I have been making to few suggestions to Ted Bruning who has just published 'Golden Fire' a fascinating narrative history of cider from the beginning up to the current day. I will also wait until the section on Hunt's Cider of Paignton as the proper place to develop an aspect of the history of Devon cider which I found on my travels. Suffice to say that in the early years of the 19th century cider was as important or maybe more important in Devon than it was in anywhere else in the country.

During the second half of the 19th century Devon cider seems to have suffered a relative decline which is perhaps more marked than in the other cider counties. This was as much a decline in reputation as it was in quantity. Devon cider that was going to London seems to have been used as a base product to produce false cheap wines whilst in the county itself it became the drink of the farm worker rather than the farmer. This was not just related to Devon. In the mid 19th century 'truck' where farm workers were paid part of their wages in cider was becoming a scandal for the attention of the social reformers. In 1857 The Bath and West Society published a paper by Richard Dawes, Dean of Hereford in which he observes of cider drinking workers.

It is a well known fact that the labourer loses his physical strength at a very early period of life, and I know it has been stated on medical authority that idiocy prevails to a greater extent in the cider counties than any other part of England.

Cider was undergoing a lowering of social status as a drink and in Devon this was intensified by the phenomenon of Devon Colic. At the times of year of high cider consumption, particularly haymaking and harvest, labourers were being struck down with intense stomach pains which were incapacitating and could even lead to death. With the slow pace of medical research at that time diagnosis was slow and there is still not total agreement. However, it is now widely believed that the cider was being poisoned by lead being used in the caulking in the cider barrels. On top of this there is information from Lyme Regis, just on the border with Dorset, of a 'lead sugars' being used to sweeten sour cider. Despite these problems, cider remained an essential part of the agricultural scene and in many areas of the county farmers would have considered it essential to supply his labourers with cider and to ensure he got the best labourers he would have had the incentive to produce a 'nice drop'.

Towards the end of the 19th century there was a second wave of industrialisation in cider making and firms, some already long established, like Gaymers in Norfolk and Bulmers and Westons in Hereford, began to grow. In Devon that firm was Whiteway's of Whimple near Exeter who were established in 1891. The history of this illustrious cider making company has been charted in a company history by EVM Whiteway published in 1990. In the first half of the 20th century Whiteway's became a national force with very progressive marketing and entrepreneurial business skills. From early years they had focused on having their own distribution centre in London and their markets even extended to operations in America. Their advertising always included great play on the fact their products were made with apples from Devon and frequently claimed health giving properties that we would not be allowed to claim today. They also diversified their range into Cydrax, a non-alcoholic fizzy drink, and even Sanatogen Tonic.

To increase their production capacity they took over a number of other Devon cider producers, including Hunts of Paignton who themselves had storage capacity for 450,000 gallons of cider. In 1959 they carried out a merger with Showering Brothers in Shepton Mallet who on the back of the immense wealth from their Babycham product had already acquired Coates Cider and were soon to acquire Gaymers from Norfolk. Showerings became, along with Bulmers, one of the two cider producers who still dominate our market 50 years later. Showerings in turn was taken over by Allied Breweries which became Allied Domeque, was then sold to Matthew Clark and then Constellation Europe and in 2009 to C and C Brands thus coming under the same umbrella as the Irish Magners. Production at Whiteways continued until 1989 when just two years short of its century it came to its end.

However, Whiteway's has left a very considerable legacy on the cider scene in Devon. It was so dominant that it seems to have rather stifled the development of other commercial producers. In Somerset there were a number of medium sized producers that came into being over the years. Some farms that continued to grow, some like Coates and Showerings were more industrial from the start. In Devon too there were a number of smaller commercial producers. Some, like Henley's of Newton Abbot and Symonds Cider even predating Whiteways. The three H's, Hunts, Henleys and Hills of Staverton, together surprisingly with Schweppes Cider at Hele were all absorbed into Whisteways whilst we believe that Howels at Stoke Canon was absorbed by Taunton Cider. The only commercial scale survivor until nearly the end of the century was Inch's of Winkleigh whose history can be read about in the section on Winkleigh Cider. There have always been smaller farm based cider businesses in Devon. Some like Churchward's of Paignton and Farmer John at Newton Poppleford have sadly gone but others featured in the coming pages are still going strong. Gray's of Tedburn St Mary is worthy of note as it is almost certainly the county's longest operating farmhouse cider maker.

The most direct legacy of Whiteway's was Green Valley Cyder which is covered in a separate section, but the more important legacy was in the orchards. A producer of the scale of Whiteway's requires a considerable tonnage of apples, 16,000 tonnes is quoted for the 1930s, and a good proportion of 20th century Devon cider orchards will have supplied them. Once Whiteway's closed some of these apples from the bigger commercial orchards went straight to the factory at Shepton Mallet. I can remember one lunch hour collecting apples from the large orchards of the late Raymond Burroughs at Whimple, Michelin and Dabinett I think for one of my many unsuccessful attempts at home cider making. For the smaller, more traditional, orchards supplying Shepton was not a real option. Some orchards would have been ripped out, many others just left to decay, grazed by animals with only sporadic harvesting of the apples for which there was little market. Some farmers who had previously made cider but had given up to supply Whiteway's started producing again in a small way - there are a number of examples of this in the coming pages. However as interest in artisan cider making revived during the first years of this century, new people looked to make cider and many of these have sourced their apples from former Whiteway's orchards. It is mentioned a number of times in these pages and probably forms the most significant lasting legacy.

When I come to answer the tricky question as to what makes a Devon cider different from a Somerset one, or one from elsewhere I believe there is another legacy in the nature of the traditional orchards Whiteway's left behind. The taste of cider is very much determined by both the apples that go into it and the land on which they are grown. Given the diversity of land types in both Devon and Somerset it is not likely that there is any one defining taste from each county. Spotting difference from different orchards is a highly skilled task. Having drunk a lot of varied ciders I don't count myself up to the task but it is one of the things that makes searching out individual ciders such an interesting hobby; you never know when you are going to come across pure nectar.

The Gaymers Connoisseur range of ciders includes a 'Somerset Cider' and a 'Devon Cider'. The major difference between the two is that the Devon cider is slightly sweeter (by the way both these excellent bottled ciders are well worth trying). This reinforces one popular belief that Devon ciders are sweeter than Somerset ones, although I have also come across many who believe Devon ciders ar sharper. I think both views too much much of a generalisation. However, I am picking up that there are differences in the apples grown. The commercial orchards in both Somerset and Devon reflect the Long Ashton Research Station varieties, selected as the vintage varieties in the 1930s and 1950s. In fact very few orchards predate this time. They include the standard high tannin Yarlington Mill, Harry Masters Jersey, Michelin, Bulmers Norman, Dabinett, Redstreak and a limited range of up to about 20 other varieties selected for their tannins and reliability in cropping. In Somerset where the influence of Long Ashton was closer and there were more commercial producers of cider it is quite rare, though not impossible, to find many orchards with other traditional varieties. In Devon the commercial orchards follow the same pattern but in many of the smaller orchards I get the feeling there is a more diverse selection. I asked pomologist Liz Copas if she could help and she came up with the following about Devon varieties.

Looking through the old lists of Devon varieties, I find it hard to spot anything reliably bittersweet. Not since Royal Wildling! '

Hugh Staffordwrote in the eighteenth century in a letter to friend on the importance of South Hams [Teign and Dart] 'By end of C17, every valley filled with cider orchards, SHARP & SWEET" which is characteristic to this day.

I have a list of acres/hogsheads/varieties listed in Devon in 1757. There were some trees called 'bittersweets' but in the main the varieties were either sharps or sweets. More recent lists of varieties that we can associate a taste with the name, include mostly sharps or dual purpose if you like, usually called Natural, for example Halstow Natural. The rest are usually something Sweet, eg Bluey Sweet, Then there is the more modern list of survivors from the Devon past, eg, Woodbine, Slack-Ma-Girdle, Northwood, all sweets. And sharps Fair Maid of Devon, Colemans Seedling, Ponsford etc.'

On top of this it has been suggested by James Crowden and others that Devon used more dual purpose apples; Tom Putt was propagated in Devon. Other non bitter-sweet apples also featured in recent years such the sharp Browns Apple and the famed Court Royal a pure sweet. These would bring extra tastes and flavours and a bit more acid into the blend of apples, perhaps giving a bit more of a complex rich wine flavour. It is this I think I can detect in the ciders of people like Mark Venton and others and it could be interpreted as 'sweet' as against the high tannin 'chewy' ciders of Somerset. Generalisation is highly dangerous and there are Devon varieties like Major that definitely give a high tannin 'farmyard' flavoured cider. I personally think it is not down to identifying a distinctive county flavour - but recognition that there are more tastes in cider than commercial producers have been focusing on for the past half century.

Again according to Liz there are a few areas of Devon which may have had a more distinctive local flavour.

'There are a few notable areas where things grew a bit more easily and cider may have developed a bit more local character. The South Hams being one and also the area around Exeter and Crediton, sheltered in the shadow of Dartmoor with excellent soils. Colemans Seedling comes from here. I remember when I was doing a planting survey for Inch's cider back in the 1990s that there were plenty of good orchards around with many Devon varieties still flourishing.'

With the advent of new producers Devon is now slowly shaking off its image of 'scrumpy' ciders fit for only the farm labourer or the tourist which seems to have predominated the farmhouse end of production through the entire 20th century. For new producer Mark Venton this can't come soon enough. He is one of the few who are trying to make a real quality traditional product by traditional methods.

When I set out on my search for Devon cider I did not know what I was going to find. The truth is if I had done it ten or even five years ago I would have discovered considerably less and what I would have found would have been a lot less interesting. However, the new producers are not only being innovative, but some are capturing what is best of the past and bringing it back into operation.

Sitting with Chris Coles of Green Valley, and researching on the internet I identified roughly around 40 makers at the beginning of 2011. A few of these have since disappeared - short lived enthusiasms, and I have discovered others starting out. It is impossible to keep track of them all, and I hope part of what I am doing is not providing all the answers but encouraging others to do their own 'searches for cider'. I have visited and talked to as many cider makers as I could and at the same time have discovered far more about a county I erroneously thought I knew. Devon is a massive county where postcodes cover extensive areas and Googlemaps has repeatedly proved fallible at locating cider farms. Still it has been a lot of fun so far - and I look forward to trying to complete the task!

Ashridge Cider

Jason Mitchell, Barkingdon Farm TQ9 6AN www.ashridgecider.com **SWECA**

One of the problems with Google maps is that if you put the wrong postcode in you don't know where you are going to end up. The difference between TQ9 6AN and TQ9 8AN turned out to be about 8 miles - including driving through Totnes. I was in plenty of time for the appointment but after driving up and down a narrow Devon lane with absolutely no buildings on it and realising that a dog walking lady genuinely had no idea where Ashridge Cider was I had to resort to the mobile phone and retrace my steps to near Buckfast Abbey.

I had met Jason a number of times before, particularly at the Taste of the West Trade Show. Always in smart, casual dress he projects a very different image to your typical cider maker. However, his image fits his product - a quality top end cider. I eventually found him at the unit he rents on a small farm industrial park in the hills above the Buckfast to Totnes road. Everything is very well organised though this is not a premises open to the public. Jason says he comes from a scientific background and was living on and running a timber business at an Ashridge Farm in South Devon in the early 1990s. When his market for timber dried up he turned his attention to the six or seven acres of cider orchard on the farm. He now sources apples from some of the many traditional local Devon orchards around him. Varieties like Ellis Bitter, Sercombe Natural and Tremletts Bitter are important to his mix. And the sharp/ bittersharp Browns Apple which was first identified by cider maker Edwin Hill in an orchard just down the road at Staverton. He says Browns are important in a mix to counteract the problem of too many mild fruits.

At that time draught cider still had very much a 'yokel image' which did not appeal to him. From the start he was looking at the top end of the market and was making a champagne method cider. He got in touch with the pioneer of this type of cider in Britain, James Lane from Hazelmere in Surrey and learnt all he could from him. For the first seven years he produced up to the duty threshold limit by producing 10,000 bottles a year. Eventually he decided to increase production and take on the burden of the very high rate of duty on this type of product - £1.75 per bottle. In the 1990s when he had few competitors he was able to get £7.50 a bottle. Now 15 years later, despite the price rises in the meantime and the addition of paying the levy he often struggles to achieve a pricing of £9.50. Increased competition both from other cider

Stack of bottle conditioned cider bottles at Ashridge Cider

makers and from cheap Cava wines put a cap on the price achievable.

He deserves every penny he can get for his cider. His process involves handling each bottle a minimum of 24 times. The cider is left at least twelve months to mature before bottling into champagne style bottles along with a spot of sugar, champagne yeast and bentonite as a fining agent. It is then left for another two years to allow the yeast autolysis and breaking down which he says gives the excellence of the flavour. After 18 months he begins to process of disgorging the yeast. The bottles are placed in especially made racks called pupitres. Here they are twisted daily and the shape of the rack is used to gradually alter the angle they are kept at and the remaining yeast and sediment gradually collects to become a plug in the neck of the bottle.

The bottles are then chilled right down to 4 degrees centigrade and a special unit freezes a two inch section of the bottle neck. The cap is removed and a plug of ice containing the yeast sediment is shot out and the bottle is now properly corked. The whole process is done by hand. As the cider is by now bone dry another little shot of sugar is added for the Vintage Cider at this stage. He also makes another high quality bottle conditioned product 'Devon Blush' which now has a shot of blackberry syrup as well as a small shot of sugar added. The adding of flavours at this stage is something that the French have long carried out but when Jason first made the Devon Blush in 2005 he was one of the first in this country to try it commercially. He has maintained his production level of his bottle conditioned ciders at 10,000 bottles a year but also has other strings to his bow.

For the past three years he has been making a 500ml bottled cider. This is a really good bottled cider with a rich, mature and complex taste. Bottling and gentle carbonation is carried out by Perry's at Dowlish Wake. This is one of a limited number of bottled ciders I would recommend people make a point of looking out for. On top of this Jason is making a range of organic sparkling soft drinks and has set up carbonation and pasteurising equipment specifically for this.

For the future he likes the idea of producing a lower alcohol keg cider, it fits his pattern of looking for niches in the cider market place.

Brimblecombe Cider

Ron Barter, Farrants Farm, Dunsford 01647 252783 **SWECA**

Googlemaps totally let me down when trying to find Brimblecombe - it took me miles from anywhere. I suspect the published postcode I had was not the right one! Great thanks go to the landlord of the Teign House Inn at Christow who twice put me on the right road. This pub by the way is certainly worth a visit - excellent beers, a wonderful ham, egg and chips and they had even had a cider festival a few weeks previously.

For the record I eventually found Brimblecombe at the delightfully named Nogsland, a name that doesn't seem to appear on the maps. It is on the B road from Exeter to Mortonhamstead before you get to Dunsford and is well worth the visit.

Both Brimblecombe Cider and its owner, Ron Barter, are bursting with character. Ron, a former engineer, bought the business about 15 years ago from a local farming cider maker who was retiring. I first met him three or four years ago when he had a cider stall at a Beef and Sheep Show in rather remote Hatherley. It was not the remoteness that led to very few farmers turning up, more the weather which produced the first sunny, dry day in a protracted wet spell and farmers had a lot better things to do. I was delighted to find Ron and his stand which provided a worthy distraction to waiting for farmers. With long silver hair and bushy silver beard he is certainly one of the most instantly recognised cider makers.

I knew Ron was not going to be there on the day of my visit. He had told me on the phone the day before that he had to man a stand at a folk festival at Sidmouth but

The massive press at Brimblecombe Cider inside a former medieval manor house

his wife would be present. In fact she had gone with Ron and I met a friend who has been helping them out for nearly the entire 15 years they have had the business. Maggie is a chirpy little lady of advancing years who didn't seem to mind at all that I had disturbed her sitting reading The Telegraph in the sun. She took me through to the press room and I have to say that I was immediately gobsmacked. I was standing inside what was obviously the remains a 13th century manor house and in front of me was a huge screw press reputed to be 400 years old. Behind this was a range of 14th / 15th century barns which have been extended and adapted over the years in a natural way that made them appear more of an organic growth than buildings. These contain a large number of wooden barrels full of cider. It is a very traditional set up and one that really ought to be preserved for the nation as part of our rural heritage. Just thinking about the passage of time and the people who would have been through the building over the centuries made the visit worthwhile to me. Across the yard is another small barn in which some other old presses and cider making equipment which Ron has acquired are stored.

The actual cider is equally unique. Traditionally made and pressed through straw and then stored in old wooden barrels for a long time it develops a character which may not be to the taste of everyone accustomed to less challenging ciders. In the late summer of 2011 I was offered tastes from barrels from 2003 and 2004 and even 2002 - though I was warned that may have gone past its best! Personally I find that unless it has been kept very airtight most ciders do not really improve after two or three years but there are some people who love this sharper cider and Ron's stand is found at many events and the cider at many festivals.

I think the business tends to rely on passing tourists who it is assumed will only visit once - perhaps justifying a hefty price tag of £9 for 2 litres. It was also sad to report that the previous night they had had a break in and a number of barrels of cider they had had ready for a festival were stolen. Small cider makers do not deserve that. Old historic farm buildings are difficult to secure against determined thieves who were really getting very little for their criminal efforts - banks may make a more worth-while target.

Brimblecombe Cider is a must to visit for its history and heritage - I just hope you can find it without the diversions I had.

Bollhayes Cider and Vigo

Alex Hill, Dunkerswell, Honiton, EX14 4LF 01404 890262 www.vigopresses.co.uk
SWECA

On all my cider travels I don't think I have come across anyone quite like Alex Hill. A quietly spoken man, smartly dressed - without going to the extremes of a suit - he exudes an air of professionalism and steadiness. The sort of person you would trust to get things done. He has now just started a two year stint as chairman of the South West Cidermakers Association.

He is unique in the cider industry and probably never expected to find himself in a position where virtually every craft cider maker in the country would have had con-tact with his business Vigo. It is located in a modern industrial estate warehouse on the Dunkersfield Airfield. This has to be one of the most bizarrely located industri-al estates in the country. You find it on a windswept hilltop in the middle of the Blackdown Hills which straddle the Devon/Somerset border about a mile from the small disjointed village of Dunkerswell. One of the features of what is basically a land that time forgot is an appalling road infrastructure. Whatever direction you approach it from you seem to end up on narrow, winding single track lanes. It is not exactly where you would have expected to find an extensive industrial estate which would look more in place on the edge of one of the larger regional towns.

Alex is best known for founding and running Vigo. In 1984 he first imported some small cider presses from Hungary and started selling them. We will all have seen, and probably experimented with the iconic timber and cast iron basket presses, suitable for crushing a few litres of juice at a time. And we all will have turned the handle of one of the scatters which sit on the top and munch the apples down into a pulp pre-

pressing. Making these available has probably been the spark that reawakened the interest in small scale cider making. They still sell well and will be seen being operated at virtually every community cider event demonstration. I can name a number of small modern commercial cider makers who still have their original press which they let out to 'hobby' producers. I spent many years looking at them enviously on the Vigo stands at various shows. My early cider making efforts had been pre 1984 and I experimented with many cheap but unsatisfactory methods of trying to turn apples into juice - including burning out the wife's food blender. Once I saw them I knew they were what I wanted, but with the financial pressures of a young family could never justify the £500 or so to get set up.

However, as the business grew Alex developed a much wider range of equipment and products for cider producers of all sizes. In fact the business has been split into two. One supplying the smaller hobby cider and winemakers the other supplying commercial cider, wine and fruit juice producers. My son (Richie) and I have often found it confusing as to where the divide between the two comes - we assumed at first we were hobby makers - but discovered that some of the equipment and sundries we were buying classified us as commercial. My son's purchase record is now listed under commercial but when I arrived to interview Alex with a list of bits my son wanted me to purchase I had to go through the questions again!

Alex reckons that his client base includes the vast majority of cider makers with a turnover of under £1 million per annum and a very significant proportion of UK winemakers. This is not surprising as there are very few other places you can buy much of the equipment he supplies. However, in these days of internet shopping I have noticed a number of the younger cider makers trying to source supplies direct from the continent. I am not sure that they are gaining much advantage from this. Postage costs reduce the 'savings', plus I have heard of slow delivery and damage in transit and the need to translate instruction sheets and change the plugs. Alex on the other hand prides himself on the quality of service offered by Vigo and the level of advice they can give customers. I can confirm how helpful they are. They also have a team of engineers providing technical back up.

The fascinating Vigo catalogue is viewable online and has equipment for whatever your size of production. Presses range from the very, very small basket presses, through the Voran hydraulic rack and cloth presses right up to belt presses. I mistakenly commented that it was a shame the belt presses - those that wash, chop and press in one continuous process - were so expensive. Alex corrected me, pointing out that some of the smaller models had now come down in price to around £20,000! However, the good news is that Alex is convinced that the method of crushing apples is not crucial to the quality of the finished product. He is suspicious of the claims that some people make that rack and cloth has an advantage over belt presses - or that the American squeeze box has an advantage over either. The only thing that concerns him is pressing with straw and some of the impurities and off tastes that can be introduced there. For me the Vigo show room is a cornucopia of dreams, Richie has already managed to spend a couple of thousand pounds there.

My favourite piece of equipment that he has purchased is the Spiedel Mill. It is a bright yellow and black plastic construction mill for producing the pomace from the apples. It may looks like a glorified garden shredder but do not make that mistake. Garden shredders start at around £100 while this mill is about £700. In Richie's first year I persuaded him he could not afford the mill and to go for a garden shredder. It was agony. You virtually had to put the apples into the shredder one by one and frequently stop for de-blocking. This was after crucifying health and safety to make the entrance larger. And you end up with a pomace that was not fine enough to give up all its juice. With the Spiedel Mill you can literally pour the apples in and it will keep up with an excellently constituted pomace pouring out at the bottom. Your pace is determined by the speed of apples you can get in the top. Best invention since sliced bread.

There is equipment for bottling, pasturising, and carbonating. The latter would be very useful for the small-scale producer but is unfortunately rather expensive. Mind you there are bargins to be had at Vigo. Last summer Richie and I bought six second-hand 11 gallon plastic barrels for £6 apiece. They are ideal for storing some of our experimental batches in. I suspect these barrels were over 20 years old. They seem to have been made originally for Taunton Cider - but came with Thatcher's labels on them.

Dealing with so many artisan cider makers Alex reckons this industry is in fine shape at the moment. Craft cider making ticks so many of the boxes: local, healty, natural and with low food miles. He thinks that makers do have to respond to what the public are looking for. Although there is a market for dry ciders the public is more often now looking for a medium sweet with medium strength alcohol. For the smaller producer he feels this is best achieved by sweetening with apple juice and pasturising in bag in the box bags. Simple and effective - we will have to give it a try.

Bollhayes Cider
Alongside Vigo, Alex is a cider maker in his own right with Bollhayes Cider. He started this commercially in 1988 but has deliberately kept it small, under the 7,000 litre tax threshold. He has been asked by Her Majesty's Revenue and Custom how he knows that he is keeping below the limit and points to the three stainless steel fermenting tanks he uses - each holding 2,300 litres!

He is perhaps best known for his Champagne cider and he used to bottle the majority of this production but found this one heck of a lot of work especially when others were getting into the market. He now only produces a few hundred bottles of this a year - I tasted a bottle with a label commemorating the total eclipse a few years ago - and very good it is too.

The majority of his cider now is a straight farmhouse draught cider. He uses a blend of apples ensuring that he gets good quality cider apples, mainly late season varieties of bittersweets and bittersharps and he makes his cider between late October and early November. One third of the apples he grows himself the rest come from other selected local growers.

Most of his cider is sold through local Blackdown pubs. I had drunk it at the Culm Stock Inn but he says you have to ask for it specifically as the barman seems to prefer serving another Blackdown cider - a bit tricky that. It is a good traditional farmhouse cider with a clean taste. One of his main outlets is the Merry Harriers and you are likely to find it at the Candlelight Inn in Bishopswood, or the Half Moon at Clayhydon. However, with constantly changing landlords it is difficult to guarantee it at any one place. He also sells through the specialist cider wholesalers who source for many cider festivals around the country. The cider is also available for sale to callers at the Vigo warehouse though he makes it at his home.

Alex gave me a bottle of a carbonated cider to try - he had been experimenting with producing this the previous week. Possibly a touch on the too fizzy side - but how nice to be able to borrow a piece of kit from work to carry out such an experiment!

I really enjoyed meeting Alex and chatting with him added a new perspective to my view of the cider industry and he fully deserves the respect he is held in.

Chucklehead Cider

Mike Dinnage, South Hayne Farm, Shillingford EX16 BL www.chucklehead-cider.co.uk

You will mainly find Chucklehead Cider on some of the agricultural shows, that is their major outlet. I have seen them at the Bath and West, the Mid Devon, Dorchester, Melplash, Frome and probably quite a few more shows that I haven't yet been to. They and Nigel Stewart from Bridge Farm, Somerset are the two cider makers you are most likely to see at these West Country shows and they both always sell good clean ciders which are a credit to the craft and give an excellent impression to the public - praise I am afraid that can not be always given to all cider makers who sometimes use the captive public at shows to offload second best quality product.

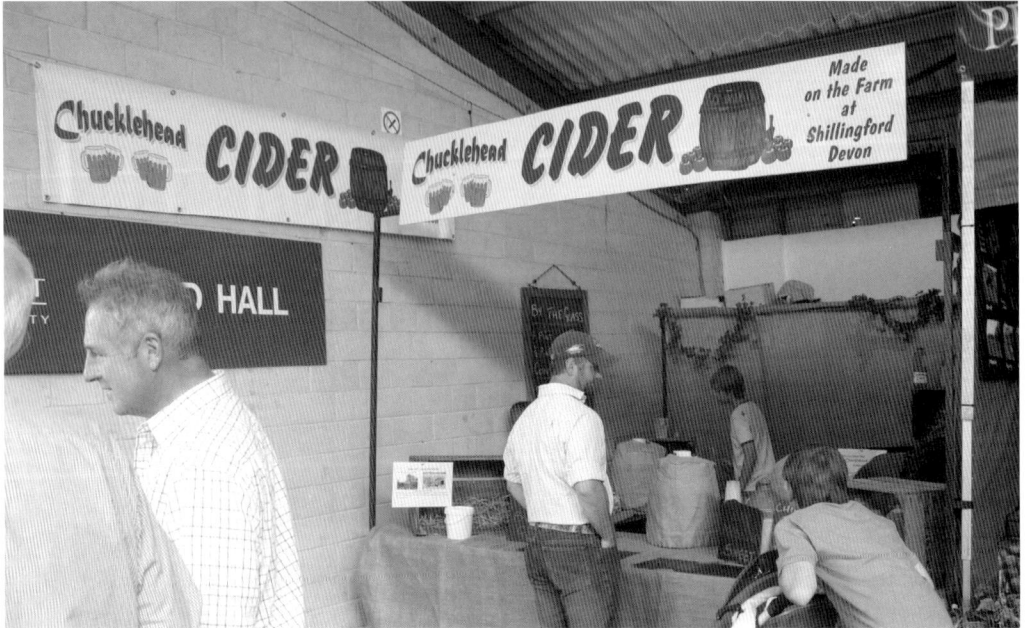

I must admit to being a little slow in coming to appreciate Chucklehead. Although they are on the edge of Exmoor they are on the Devon rather than Somerset side and my first book was restricted to Somerset. I was also slightly put off by the name. The dictionary definitions imply the chucklehead means 'numbskull. fool, jolter-head, bonehead, dolt' anyway a bit of a stupid person and I am not sure that is the greatest marketing stance. However,it has grown on me and I can see what they were getting at.

I have not been to the farm, visitors can only obtain cider from it by prior arrange-ment and that is too complicated for me on my very occasional trips up the North Devon link road. Much to my surprise my brother Chris has been there. He is a ministry farms inspector and got an instruction through work to visit. He rung the farmer up first and was told that there were no animals. It is a small farm of 50 odd acres and a larger surrounding neighbouring farmer just grazes his sheep across it. My brother still had to go and inspect to prove it!

Chucklehead is run by Mike and Liz Dinnage and according to their website they have been making cider since 1993. I think I am right is saying the farm is the home of Mike's father and they make their cider there, mainly from apples obtained from Devon and Somerset. The scene is further complicated by the fact that Liz and Mike actually live in Sussex where their teenage children go to school. It is only at the odd show like the Bath and West that you see them both on the stand. Quite often it is the cheerful and chatty Liz on her own; at other times it is friends of theirs who have been roped in for the day - one couple who I have talked to a few times coming across from Sussex for the day to man it.

Talking to Liz at the Dorchester Show last year I realised how difficult it can be to run a stand. Dorchester is a two day show on a Saturday and Sunday. I dislike two day weekend shows from my own working point of view, getting the accountants and financial planners to man the Old Mill stand which I organise is difficult enough at a weekend - but for two days! Anyway on the Saturday it had been their friends running the stand. Talking to Liz on the Sunday morning she said she had had phone calls about how quiet it was until the early afternoon when the phones went quiet. She arrived on the Sunday morning to find they had had massive sales in the late afternoon and she was unlikely to have enough stock to last the day.

It really fascinates me how much cider is now being drunk on these shows. It seems to be the thing to do and people who would never think of drinking cider at any other time take to it like ducks to water. I only hope that some of the show popularity sticks and helps build sustainable sales for good cider on other occasions.

Anyway, back to Chucklehead, look out for them on the shows and drink their very good product. If you aren't likely to be going to shows then you can order their cider through their online website where they offer a number of sizes of bag in box, I strongly suggest buying the larger sizes and they will last quite well.

Countryman Cider

Vernon and Teresa Shutte, Countryman Cider, Felldownhead, Milton Abbott, Tavistock, Devon PL19 0QR Tel: Milton Abbot 01822 870226 **SWECA**

Dangerously near the edge! I had to cross over into Cornwall to reach Felldownhead and meet Vernon and Teresa Shutler of Countryman Cider. I crossed back into Devon via an ancient 15th century bridge and drove up the steep hill on the other side of the valley. The small hamlet of Felldownhead owes its existence for the need (in previous centuries) to refresh the horses on their trip from Launceston to Tavistock in the days when horses were essential for transport.

Countryman Cider also owes its location to its position on that route. Cider had been made by the Lancaster family since 1858 on the Cornwall side of the river although this was mainly for on farm use. Their original 1858 equipment can be seen in the North Cornwall Museum at Camelford. In the early 1950s Horace Lancaster decided to go more commercial with his cider and moved the production across the border to another holding the family owned at Felldownhead where is was beside the road rather than down a dead end as it had been at Lawhitton. Mind you

Attractive display of stone jars - one of many bonuses at Countryman's cider

the road was moved to a lower level 50 years ago and since then has been downgraded from an A road to a B road so the location is hardly on a major route!

In 1972 Horace upgraded the business putting in new milling and pressing equipment, and a roadside silo - tailored to the available premises by Beares of Newton Abbot. This is number 231 of the hydraulic presses Beare's installed on farms over a 50 year period. Horace sold the business in the late 70s after the introduction of the double whammy of cider duty and VAT. It passed through a couple of owners until it was bought - by Vernon and Teresa in 1997.

Vernon had been an accountant in Poole, Dorset - he is now the Hon Auditor for SWECA - and had made cider with his grandfather in the New Forest - also helping at New Forest cider. He was looking to buy somewhere to make cider and when he saw an existing business for sale he thought it was an ideal opportunity. There is a courtyard of barns - one of which is converted into the house, so they live right in with the business. The growth of the business has been rather limited by the shortage of local cider apples but he makes a creditable 10,000 gallons a year. He has a bush orchard of his own, and harvests half of the apples used from local orchards - within a 20 mile radius. A few apples come from personal contacts in East Devon, other fruit is brought in local people from nearby villages.

He has a pretty large collecting pit (silo) which holds up to 25 tonnes of apples and as the whole system is geared towards larger batches he does not find it feasible to make single varieties - his cider is always a blend of varieties including a number that are local to the Tamar Valley. The sample I tried of his 'Gold Label' was really rather good with a fruity but sophisticated taste. My son and I looked at each other in appreciation as we supped some later that evening - very nice.

He sells his cider through a number of routes to market, no one of which is dominant - probably the best way to be. One outlet is Teresa's attractive small shop on site. There is a good collection of cider jars and a very attractive converted milking parlour which had been used as a store shed since cider production moved across here in the 1950s. Visitors to the shop are encouraged to wander around and look at the equipment and orchard - as many tourists find the "industrial heritage" aspects of the business of interest.

He also sells through local farmers markets - though like most producers has cut down on the number of these. Wholesalers come for his product to put in the many cider festivals and he has a good pub and local shop trade - through this is frustratingly tied to the holiday season. He also bottles in plastic PET bottles and sells through Mole Valley Stores - the agricultural merchant with branches across the South-West.

When I visited it was interesting to see his Beare's Press. The hydraulic ram was right up as he was in the process of changing the leather seals. These were two leather bands nearly an inch thick. It was interesting to see how mangled the old ones were - though he said the press had still been working efficiently!

I enjoyed meeting Vernon and seeing Countryman Cider. A pleasant business without too many aspirations - making a very good traditional Devon cider. He is open to the public Monday to Saturday 9.30 - 6.00pm all year around.

Gray's Devon Cider

Ben Gray, Halstrow, Tedburn St Mary EX6 6AN 01647 61236

The Grays have been at this Devon farm in the hills above the dual carriageway of the A30 west of Exeter since the 1660s and there is good reason to believe they have been making cider there ever since. Opposite the farmhouse on the north side of the farmyard is a long cider house which I was told was especially constructed for the purpose in the 1850s. It is on a similar scale to the one used by the Hunts at Paignton and is also built into the hill so that apples can be brought in at the higher level and gravity used to save labour through the system.

In these days of an ageing farming population I would think you could still refer to Ben as a younger farmer. This is very much a working mixed farm with cider just fitting in as one part of the farming calendar. These days the main emphasis is on the 500 ewes. They have a number of acres of orchard - the newest 8 acres dating from the 1980s which include the standard bittersweet favourites Dabinett, Yarlington Mill, Ashton's Bitter and Chesil Jersey. These complement a wider selection of varieties from their older orchards and fruit bought in by neighbours.

Against a hedge can be seen the remains of an old horse-powered circular stone crusher though it is many years since this was used. They now use a big electric powered mill and the cheese is built on a hydraulic rack press made by Beares of Newton Abbott and of the sort used by many of the larger West Country farmhouse cider makers. Ben is currently making between 10,000 and 12,000 gallons (50,000 litres). The amount had dipped slightly but seems to be building up again with the renewed interest in cider.

The juice is fermented in black plastic tanks and then when the previous year's supply has been sold it is blended into a marvellous rack of old oak barrels, hogsheads and pipes right along the lower level of the impressive cider house. He says they just take the apples as they come to produce a bulk, standard dry cider which, with one of the joys of cider making, can well vary from barrel to barrel. Where people require it they sweeten with saccharin. I asked about other sweeteners but Ben said his father had years ago bought a rather large supply of saccharin which will take most of the foreseeable future to use up!

Most of the cider is sold direct from the farm, which may be a bit of a surprise considering it's out of the way location. They have just put a new sign at the end of the

Ben Grey in his amazing 1850s cider house

farm track and any visitor will pull up in the tidy farm yard. The door to the cider house is nearly obscured by a large fig bush. Inside the pricing sign informed me that cider was £4 for 5 litres! Ben comments that he hadn't got around to updating it so I have probably prompted that - however I hardly think he is going to be that expensive.

Another major outlet is somewhat surprisingly through the Green Valley shop at Darts Farm. This dates back many years to when Darts Farm first started to develop their farm superstore. Before Green Valley started producing after the closure of Whiteway's during the 1990s the shop had always stocked Gray's cider and the Darts are a family who are extremely loyal to their suppliers. So Gray's cider still has almost equal prominence to Green Valley's own produce.

Ben says that the Devon County Show in May is another major outlet and they do supply a few local pubs and festivals. The National Cider Centre in Sussex regularly collect and wholesalers Merrylegs and John Hallam ensure it is well represented at many other festivals throughout the country. They do a little bottling but this is not really their scene at the moment.

It is good to see a cider business where it is genuinely a part of the traditional whole farm enterprise. Many cider businesses now, even if they started on a farm, seem divorced from it. Here the farm comes first. This is not backwards looking - Ben is currently investigating installing a wind turbine - it is fitting cider into the agri-business and with luck this model should be sustainable for another 350 years.

Green Valley Cyder

Chris Coles and Nick Pring, Green Valley Cider, Darts Farm, Topsham, Exeter
www.dartsfarm.co.uk *SWECA*

If you only go to one place to find out about Devon Cider, Green Valley Cyder is it. Green Valley is a unique combination of an artisan cider maker, cider and beer specialist off-licence, working in synergy with Darts Farm, one of the largest and best farm shops in the country.

Chris Coles and Nick Pring were managers at the former Whiteway's factory at nearby Whimple when Allied Domeque decided in 1989 to close that production facility and consolidate them elsewhere. Chris and Nick decided that they wanted to keep on making cider and found a location at a small farm shop near Topsham. They bought some of the old equipment, including some large old oak vats, moved in and started producing - becoming one of Devon's more significant producers.

Darts Farm Shop as it is now known, has altered beyond all recognition over the past 20 years. It now has the appearance of a massive superstore and being just outside Exeter and in a tourist area has been able to grow and grow. You can now find all sorts of franchises for clothing, household goods, Aga stoves, mountaineering equipment, giftware and an excellent fish and chip shop as the growth has been driven on by the three Dart brothers. However, it has remained very much a farm shop at heart selling the best of local product and it remains very loyal to both its suppliers and staff. I was at a dinner once and talked to Michael Dart as he introduced a lady member of his staff who they were taking out as she had been with them over 25 years. They are great ambassadors for local food and drink.

Green Valley Cider has grown along with the Darts Farm business. They have taken on the franchise of an off licence for local cider and beer. You now visit their part of the shop and are faced with a selection of over 150 West Country ciders, many from Devon. This has been my introduction to many local producers and Chris and Nick are always keen to give a chance to new local cider makers. We must not forget the beer either as they have an even bigger selection of excellent bottled beers from around the West Country.

But of course they also make their own ciders there. To one side of the off licence is a little hatch counter where either Chris, Nick or other members of staff are always willing to give you a tasting of their ciders. They sell a straight draught range and a range of bottled ciders including Stillwood premium quakity brand. If you are invited you can step straight out of the back of the shop to where they make cider. There is a hydraulic Stone's press which when I went in the autumn of 2010 had a gang of three working it. Food miles are zero! There is in fact now considerable pressure on space with the growth of both the shop and their own production.

Both Chris and Nick are very interesting people to talk to with a wealth of experience of the cider industry. I first met Nick at the Duchy College of Agriculture in Cornwall where he has done some lecturing and was attending a food industry conference at which I was speaking. I probably wouldn't have included photographs of old Somerset cider makers to illustrate my points on marketing if I had known he was attending! Chris is now one of the most influential people in the renaissance of Devon cider. It was to him I turned when I was first planning this book and together we pooled our resources to come up with the list of Devon producers - though I would not blame him for any I missed. Chris organises the cider supplies for the CAMRA run Ales from Devon tent at the Devon County Show which has draught cider from at least 12 Devon makers on offer. He is also an active member of SWECA.

From talking to them I get the impression that the early years for Green Valley were quite lean. Bulk draught cider in pubs was declining and although the switch to more quality bottled products and new markets had started for many makers it was not coming quite fast enough to match the bulk decline. That has changed in recent years and during the Noughties Green Valley found themselves running out of cider and having to up production significantly. They have also looked at the opportunities new markets offer. At the Devon County Show in 2011 they had their keg product on their stand and although like most expanding producers they had taken note of the government's 'drink aware' campaign and produced a lower alcohol cider they have managed to retain a proper cider taste. Some other new kegs products I have come across seem to have gone for safer, blander tastes. There is no need for keg products to lose taste as those of Green Valley and Sheppy's show.

They have also capitalised on the fashion for fruit flavours in cider. I first came across their strawberry cider at the Fire House, a truly excellent cider and real ale pub in the centre of Exeter. I must admit to viewing these products with some suspicion but as it has been reported that Green Valley supplied Wetherspoons pubs with nearly 900 20 litre bag in boxes of strawberry cider during October 2011 then somebody must be getting something right.

Anyway, whenever you drive down the M5 do pop into Green Valley. They are less than five minutes off the motorway. Follow the signs to Exmouth / Topsham and you will soon see the signs to Darts Farm. I can never resist picking up a bottle or two to try from their excellent and interesting range.

Heron Valley Organic

Natasha Green, Crannacombe Farm, Hazelwood, Loddiswell, Kingsbridge, Devon TQ7 4DX. 01458 820111 www.heronvalley.co.uk

Being a mere mortal male, well aware of my own inadequacies, I always get slightly alarmed by the image of the entrepreneurial woman business person. They always sound so driven, setting up business after a career in PR or something, they seem to be set on a course to rather challenge men.

From what I knew of Natasha Green of Heron Valley I was concerned before approaching her. University, career in clothing, bought out her parents and siblings to take over the family farm and business, running the business with an all female staff - I was nearly quaking in my boots! However, as usual my preconceptions were unfounded, as soon as I started talking to Natasha I felt totally relaxed and recognised someone with a considerable sense of humour - a quality I value above all others.

The business is basically, like so many others, a diversification of a family farm. They started making cider commercially 28 years ago, which I suppose makes them relative veterans for Devon producers. When Natasha started her own family she knew she wanted to come back to Devon and six years ago bought the business and took over running it.

This is not about rough farmhouse cider but making a natural cider that definitely veres towards the 'foodie' edge of the scale. I have drunk it on a number of occasions, usually from Green Valley at Dart's Farm, and find it extremely pleasant. I found a tasting note I made some time ago, '*Very nice cider with a fair amount of depth and character.*' As in the same tasting session another cider from someone else I gave the note, '*okay but not sure about the claimed subtle fragrances, rather a dirty sulphurous nose,*' you can see I don't always give such praise.

They get their hand picked apples either from their own orchards or from about 20 other local orchards. These supply various amounts from one sack upwards. They are very proud of the fact that they use a lot of local apple varieties. The list on their attractive bottle label mentions, Fair Maid of Devon, Hangy Down Cluster, Foxwhelp, Browns, Sheeps Nose, Ten Commandments, Slap me Girdle, Pig Snout, Dabinet and Kingston Black - a worthy list indeed and they only use varieties recognised as cider apples. They tend to press from single orchards and then do a lot of blending to get a consistent taste.

They make about 8,000 - 9,000 gallons a year - it is a bit confusing that the larger makers tend to refer to their production in gallons whilst the smaller makers more usually use litres. At about 4.5 litres to the gallon this puts them at over 40,000 litres - a serious maker. They also have an impressive range of apple juices, soft drinks and ginger beer - have a look at their award winning website to see the full range.

They have a hydraulic press which is really a bit small for their current requirements and they are looking to upgrade to a belt press soon. As mentioned they have an all female workforce which includes one of Natasha's sisters. Cleanliness of all things through production and bottling is of key importance to the consistent quality of their cider. In line with their creed of keeping everything natural they are one of the few sizeable cider makers who do not use sulphites at all. They ferment in large plastic tanks and then mature the product for at least three months in oak - which presumably helps to produce its rich colour. One touch I really like is that the apple pomace is fed back to their herd of the local organic South Devon Cattle that they keep on their farm.

Natasha says that each aak barrel produces a slightly different taste. It is the natural yeasts that build up within them and she definitely has her favourite barrels. She feels it is all part of the alchemy of the product which is something she really enjoys. What a wonderful word that is, alchemy. The dictionary says ' *1) the medieval fore-runner of chemistry….2) a seemingly magical process of transformation, creation or combination.'* It really does describe the process of making cider outside the industrial cider factories. Maybe instead of 'artisan' or 'craft' cider makers we should all be known as 'cider apple alchemists'.

They sell their cider bottled either as an organic still cider or lightly sparkling through carbonation. It is a medium, gently sweetened with organic cane sugar cider and then pasteurised. The bottled cider is at 5% ABV. They also do draught in bag in boxes at 6% and for local pubs they even keg some themselves. I gather this is quite a gentle kegging process, putting the cider in a 11 gallon barrel and adding a small amount of pressure. All the bottling and pasteurising is done in house - although it can be a bit labour intensive without advanced equipment.

They have quite a parochial approach to marketing. They do not sell from the farm but sell just about all their product in the South Hams itself or Exeter and Plymouth. It is sold through pubs, shops, bars and cafes. They believe in having a strong relationship with each of their customers and do not use wholesalers. They tend to keep the same customers only taking on a few new ones each year. Part of their joy of the cider is knowing they have a really good product and developing that relationship with their customers. Natasha was quite amused as she told me they had recently won the Esquire Magazines 'Best Cider in the World' award!

Natasha is not looking to take on the world; she is just very involved with her product. If you are not in a position to go to South Devon but are tempted to try their cider do not despair as they now have an online shop and are finding they are dispatching cider all across the country - order one day, delivery the next.

Hancock's Cider

Helen Hancock, Clapworthy, South Molton, Devon 01769 572513 www.hancockscider.co.uk

North Devon has a fascinating cider market which is quite unlike anything I have come across before. If you go into somewhere like Lynmouth and into one of the very numerous shops selling cheap gifts to the thousands of tourists you are quite likely to find as part of the range an extensive selection of bottled ciders. Of course cider to the tourists is nothing new and you are likely to find some on offer in any tourist spot in the West Country, but I can't think of anywhere else that you will find quite the same diversity in non specialist off licences, and often of ciders that you are unlikely to find anywhere else.

Palmerhayes, Ostlers and Winkleigh are important suppliers into this market but probably pride of place has to go to Hancock's Cider from nearby South Molten - well nearby in terms of the extensive nature of North Devon. The Hancock family have been making cider for around 150 years and in the recent past have been one of the bigger producers in the county.

Norman Hancock having all but retired from the business it is now run by his daughter Helen Hancock and they still make around 22,000 litres a year, though with the plentiful apples they made nearly 30,000 last season. Originally they would also have had a lot of local farm gate trade but with Helen looking after a young family as well as running the business that is no longer possible and they have shut their shop.

Helen does everything herself. She says she may get a bit of a hand from her husband or father during the pressing season but that is about it. Everything else is down to her including all the filtering, bottling and labelling. She does have a part time delivery driver and a wholesaler comes to collect once a week but I can imagine that during the summer season this must get a bit frantic.

Using Devon apples they have a large old hydrualic press and make a traditional cider. She now does very little as draught cider; it is nearly all in bottles. Mainly 500ml, or 1 litre in glass, Helen feels it keeps better in glass, or 2 litre PET bottles or 2.5 litre plastic flagons. She also does gift packs with a selection of bottles. She filters the cider to get clarity but it is basically a straightforward traditional cider. It is all still cider as they do not carbonate.

Their ciders can also be found in some of the Mole Valley Farmers shops, Mole Valley being a South Molton based company, and in 2010 Hancocks won a Taste of the West Gold Medal. Their simple effective website reflects the nature of the product and as long as the holidaymakers keep on coming what more can you want?

Hunts Cider

Richard Hunt, Higher Yalberton Farm, Yalberton, Paignton TQ4 7PE 01803 782309 www.huntscider.co.uk *SWECA*

It was only when I visited Richard Hunt that I began to get clear in my mind a distinctive heritage for Devon cider. Of course I already knew there were slight differences in taste to the Somerset cider that is so local to me but now I was to discover a distinct historic tradition which took commercial cider production back further than anything I had expected to come across.

For once Google Maps served me well in finding my way off the nightmare congestions of the main roads in Torbay. I did take one wrong turn right at the last minute but that was only a minor diversion and one I was glad I made. Although less than a mile out of the industrial estates along the main road between Paignton and Brixham I found myself in a delightful green valley full of small orchards with a healthy crop of ripening apples temptingly hanging from the trees. I had not been aware of this oasis of cider orchards in South Devon.

Richard Hunt is an impressive looking young man - well over six foot, he spent six years as a professional rugby player though it doesn't seem to have left a mark on him. Also impressive is that he had actually prepared for my visit and handed me some photocopied sheets of paper. And it was these that opened up a past I had not been aware of.

Hunt ancestors had allegedly been making cider since 1771 and formed N P Hunt and Son in 1805 as is shown on some surviving old bottles. They were one of a number of prominent cider making families in the Paignton area. There were three Hunts named in an application to Queen Victoria for the 'Paignton Harbour Company' to build a new dock. Amongst the items listed to be exported from this dock were apples and cider (per pipe). Further reading has shown that during the 18th and early 19th century there was a thriving trade exporting cider from the south Devon ports to in particular London but also elsewhere. Cider was also being sold to ships on longer voyages as medical science gradually realised that it help to prevent the dreaded scurvy amongst the crews and had reasonable keeping qualities on board.

Once I had started looking I have found a number of references to this trade. Exeter would seem to have been the biggest port for exports but as well as Paignton even small ports like Salcombe are mentioned as exporting considerable amounts. Other standard histories of cider refer to these London bound exports being bought by dealers who doctored them and sold them disguised as wines at a time when cider as itself was not in great fashion. Although there is scope for a lot more historic research it would appear that the South Devon trade tended to decline as the 19th century progressed. One reason may have been the scandal around lead poisoning in Devon cider - which I have covered elsewhere. It is probable that another contributory factor was the spread of the railways which led to a general decline of the relative advantages of costal shipping as a means of transporting goods. However, it revealed to me a commercial cider producing tradition on a scale I had not appreciated at a time when I had thought cider was still very much about small-scale farm production for local consumption.

N P Hunt and Son continued throughout the 19th century as a significant sized cider business. In the early 20th century it became a subsidiary of a Reading brewer, H & G Simonds, which I believe eventually became an important part of the brewing giant Courage. However, in 1934 it was sold on to the then rapidly expanding Devon cider maker Whiteway's Cyder Co who needed the production capacity and access to the Simond's London market. According to the history of Whiteway's *'This cider factory consisted of a number of buildings constructed from rough local granite with a large house and cottages, all with fine sea views about a mile inland between Paignton and Brixham, Devon. There was a large number of oak vats ranging from 1,000 gallons to 23,000 gallons with a total capacity of 450,000 gallons and within the buildings were the usual cider making plant comprising mills, hydraulic presses, filters, pumps and oil engines. The factory was set in 50 acres of orchard and pasture land, some of which was in demand for housing development. All this was sold to Whiteway's Cyder Co Ltd in December 1934 for £34,000.'*

Richard Hunt is the eighth generation cider makers in the family - though his direct line were more farmers who had diverged from the line of main cider making business. Richard's great-grandfather first came as a tenant farmer to Higher Yalberton Farm in 1915 and they have been making cider here ever since, though for the first 20 years or so they were mainly selling apples to Whiteway's. They were not even the only cider makers in the tight little valley as Churchward's Cider was another well known cider maker until they gave up about a decade ago. Unfortunately the name seems to have been polluted and lives on as a supermarket own brand made by the Aston Manor fizz factory near Birmingham.

Richard's grandfather expanded the cider making side of their farm in the post war period when he brought a new Beare hydraulic press from nearby Newton Abbot. He died in 1990 and Richard's father took over. During my visit I also met him, another tall imposing farmer, whose main concern was around running the farm. They were previously time a dairy farm though he told me that now they have 300 acres of single suckler beef and 9 acres of caravans. It is the caravans which are probably the main revenue earner these days.

Mr Hunt senior, Richard's father rather only paid lip service to the cider - producing whatever came out for sale to tourists. It wasn't until Richard came home to the farm in 2005 that more attention was paid to the cider. He was told 'here's a press - get on with it!'

In the past five years he has increased the production by 200% and is now up to around 12,000 gallons. He is also honest about the sharp learning curve he experienced in order to improve the quality of the cider. He has improved cleanliness of the barrels and is now experimenting with some bottles. 50% of their production is

Inside the 1812 cider 'factory' at Hunt's Cider Paignton

still sold at the farm to tourists. His grandmother sells it out of a window at the old farmhouse in various sized containers. Straight dry or medium - the medium now sweetened with sucralose. He has bought some bottling equipment and a small carbonator. He is looking into pasteurisation and experimenting with sales of bottled ciders to local shops. They also supply two local pubs and of course some cider goes out to cider festivals. Richard knows he has to take the business forward and has great plans.

Firstly however, we need to take a look at where he currently makes his cider. To me this was the most awe-inspiring aspect of my visit. Beside the road is what looks like a substantial barn. In fact it appears to be probably the earliest purpose-built cider factory I have discovered. The building is first mentioned in 1812. It is built into a bank so apples can be unloaded from above and has huge space for storing barrels.

The listed building record from 1993 includes:
Cider Barn belonging to Higher Yalberton Farmhouse, Yalberton Road. Early C19th. Local grey limestone rubble; corrugated-iron roof half hipped at W end......
HISTORY: The barn serves 6 orchards. Paignton was well-known for cider production in the early C19...... This purpose-built cider barn is of especial local interest, but it is also a rare survival in Devon, both larger and more mechanised than usual.

The barn and farm belonged to the Jackson's who were another local cider making family. They still own the farm though the Hunts have been tenants for approaching a century. It now looks as if this may be coming to an end. The Hunts have over the years being buying land of their own and now mainly farm about a mile up the lane. The elderly Mrs Jackson who is the current owner is looking at her family succesion. The farm buildings are being sold and are likely to become barn conversions as so many farm buildings have been over the past few decades. It seems very likely that this historic cider factory will become part of that process.

However Richard is looking to move forward. Richard drove me up the lane to their very smart caravan site and then walked us across the road to one of Richard's newer orchards. His orchards contain a significant amount of the commercial varieties - Dabinett and Michelin in particular but also quite a few older local varieties. One, Paignton Marigold, they believe is one of their own. He is currently planting out another 5 acre orchard in which he is intending to have 50% Devon varieties including in particular Brown's and Sweet Coppin.

Richard led us over to the corner of the orchard where he has a vision for a cider producing shed, storage and visitor shop. When this visit took place in late September 2011 he was just about to put in outline planning premising and hopes to be developing the site by the spring of 2012.

I wish him luck - he is really one of the only remnants of the historic South Devon tradition and even if things have to change it will be nice to see it continue.

Indicknowle Farm

Mark and Sue West, Indicknowle Farm, Combe Martin, EX34 0PA 01271 883980

It is absolutely delightful when you go on holiday and discover nearby an unsuspected cider farm. This happened to me a couple of years ago one autumn when we rented a cottage at Parracombe in the wilds of North Devon. A big sign in a field led me down to the farm where I discovered some more than acceptable cider.

Indicknowle Farm is very much a family farm. Mark and Sue West together with father Geoff West and their three sons run a small 100 or so acre farm which has found it needs to sell product direct to the public to make itself pay in the harsh economy of family farms of this scale. They have rebuilt the farm over the past 15 years, when they first came it was almost totally derelict. They have a farm shop which is basically open from 9am - 6pm from April to autumn and for longer hours in the summer. In the winter they will sell cider to people if they are there but ask people to remember that it is a working farm.

Their farm shop is very different to many I visit being focused almost solely on produce produced on their own farm. Beef from the beautiful Ruby Red Devon cattle, lamb from Suffolk cross sheep and pork from Middle White cross British Lop pigs, plus of course cider and apple juice. This selection of meat and cider is very popular for summer barbeques with campers at some of the nearby camp and caravan sites and they usually sell out of meat by the end of the season.

They have a considerable cider heritage. Father Geoff and son Mark have a Somerset background originating from near Street in Somerset where Geoff still has interests. Geoff's grandfather was a cider maker in Middle Leigh in the early 20th century and at that time was a bigger cider producer than the renowned Hecks in the same road. He also had links with Squire Neville Grenville at nearby Butleigh one of the key figures in the development of standards for cider production. Mark represents the fifth generation of cider makers.

They have a number of orchards around the farm. Some very old ones tucked away in steep valleys which Mark showed me on the large scale OS map of the farm and some more recently planted. They are planting out an interesting mixture of mainly sharps and sweets which would seem to be more traditional for Devon. Varieties planted include Cornish Gillyflower, Dunkerton Late Sweet, Slack Ma Gridle, Browns, Sweet Coppin, Sweet Alford. Cider Ladies Fingers and the modern Falstaff for apple juice. They also have a mystery variety of their own. Small, about

the size of a Browns Apple, but with a green orange hue when ripe and a russet streak it yields an incredibly sweet dark oak coloured juice. Mark took me to see the semi fallen surviving tree at the bottom of one of his very wet orchards - mud has been a feature of the 2011 cider making season in much of the South West whilst the rest of the country is grumbling about drought. He has taken cuttings and grafted twenty one onto rootstocks to try to conserve the variety, he reckons it makes a good single variety cider but so far no one has been able to identify it.

They have a large traditional screw press from Mark in Somerset for cider plus a modern Voran for producing apple juice. They currently produce less than the 7,000 litre duty threshold and also crush for other local cider makers. The cider is matured in oak barrels and is straight as it comes off the press - it is not further blended at all to give a very natural product; every barrel has its own character. From my limited experience of two visits they make a good, fruity, clean cider with plenty of character and some residual sweetness. Mark makes a point of cleanliness with his wooden barrels - getting a chain in to ensure that the entire residue is got out of the barrels - something that you cannot be too fussy over.

Geoff took to me into the cellar to taste some of his 'special' ciders. These are not for the public consumption but for his own enjoyment. He feeds the cider over a period of years with extra sugars and more fresh juice to get the alcohol level up. We tasted his 'sherry' which he guesses is around 12% alcohol and his 'maderia' which he thinks is around 16%. He learnt a lot of his cider making from his grandfather who he started to help to build the cheeses when he was only nine years old. His grandfather used to make a 'gin' where the cider was fermented out very dry with the addition of juniper berries. For the home cider maker there were plenty of ideas to try and the ciders did seem to certainly warrant their lofty descriptions.

Currently just about all their sales are from the farm gate although some has found its way to the odd local folk festival and wassail. I don't think Mark is looking to significantly change that. I think this family farm type set up selling good farm produce direct to the public is a very worthy enterprise and more in line with our traditional rural roots than perhaps any other cider maker I came across - if only they made their own cheese as well!

Killerton Estate Cider

Killerton Estate, The National Trust, Killerton, Broad Clyst, Exeter EX5 3LE 01392 881912

When I visited the National Trust's Killerton Estate in Devon, following help from shop manager Hilary Sluman, I was really lucky to meet Ed Nicholson who as Area Warden - Forester I gathered was one of those busy people who loves to be out and about. He is certainly very enthusiastic about his work.

He has worked for the estate for eight years and defines his job as managing habitats for the enjoyment of the public and ensuring they can experience them. Orchards are one of those habitats and one that offers huge potential to fill this role. The cider and juice is a by-product of that core function but one that fits in extremely well. The money from sales of cider helping to make the habitat sustainable - a word which he says is often abused but works well here. The cider orchards are also a brilliant basis for telling other stories to the public including blossom and bees for the honey which is made on the estate. The sward is also used for grazing by sheep and making hay later in the season when it becomes an old fashioned hay meadow.

The estate contains around 50 acres of orchards, mainly traditional but including some new plantings by tenants. They estimate that the orchards contain over 100 different varieties of apple including many standard commercial bittersweet apples but also some specialities of their own. Both Killerton Sweet and Killerton Sharp are from the estate whilst Star of Devon came from one of their orchards in Broadclyst.

They only make about 6,000 litres of cider a year, partly to ensure they keep within the duty threshold and partly as they like to leave 50% of all the apples for wildlife over the winter - he terms this as 'habitat reasons'. The National Trust at Barrington Court in Somerset follows a similar practice.

In the autumn they use volunteer labour to pick up the apples and crush them. Apparently people are very keen to pay £100 a week for board and lodgings to submit themselves to this quite arduous and back-breaking work. I can only imagine the reaction I would get from my son Richard were I to suggest this! They press the apples on a big 18th century press, but they now use a modern mill - the old one with a standing engine and belts was getting a bit frightening health and safety wise. The cider is fermented in 1,000 litre IBCs and racked twice during the spring before being sent out to be sheet filtered and pasteurised and put in 75cl wine type bottles.

The vast majority of the cider is sold in their shop and they are quite happy sticking to the scale they are at. However they are thinking of looking to sell in a few local shops and pubs and they have also experimented with about 1600 litres of apple juice. They find the apple juice very easy to sell but they are quite short of suitable apple varieties for juicing. The cider itself is a very nice clean straightforward cider - possibly best chilled but definitely very drinkable.

It is really good to see the National Trust looking after this now quite rare type of habitat - it is an essential part of the cider picture and public awareness of cider heritage.

Lyme Bay Cider

Lyme Bay Winery, Shute, Axminster, Devon EX13 7PW www.lymebaywinery.co.uk

Lyme Bay Cider has come a long way since I first knew it probably 20 years ago. From vague recollections I believe back then it was a traditional cider maker in a barn / shed just off the coast road on a bend as you went down a hill somewhere near Seaton with a view out to sea. I know I went back more than once so it must have been good stuff. But then it disappeared.

A few years later I saw signs to it off the road at Musbury pointing across the river and up into the hills. That is where you will find it today. But it has changed quite considerably with cider now not the prime driver of the business. They still make very good cider though.

Most of the cider is sold under the Jack Ratt brand named after the early 19th century Devon / Dorset smuggler Jack Rattenbury who operated in the tricky expanse of Lyme Bay - now better known as the Jurassic coast. They obtain their juice from Julian Temperley's excellent and extensive orchards at Burrow Hill Cider across the border in Somerset. He crushes the apples before the juice is sent to Lyme Bay for fermenting and finishing. The cider is a clean traditional cider which it is a pleasure to drink when you find it at some of the country shows - although I didn't see it at quite so many during 2011. The cider is a frequent award winner at foodie type event's notably Jack Ratt Scrumpy won Best Speciality Product in the South West 2009 and 3 gold stars at The Great Taste Awards.

The business now focusses on what I would term as 'gift drinks'; fruit wines, sparkling fruit wines, fruit liqueurs, sloe gin etc now form the bulk of the range. It can be seen all over the country - most notably in the gift shops at the many English Heritage sites. It can be quite disconcerting in the Yorkshire Dales to be asked to sample a wine from Dorset.

It is interesting in the context of this study to see how a cider business has evolved. Using some of our native fruits is as worthy as using our local apples. Although I may not be personally enthusiastic I do make a drop of sloe gin and my son and I have experimented with many of the hedgerow fruits in cider for our own consumption. I think they do have a shop at their factory open during working hours Monday to Friday - and the cider is certainly worth hunting out - and long may Lyme Bay Cider feature in Devon.

Milltop

Peter Webb, Milltop Orchards Combeinteignhead Nr Newton Abbot. 01626 870881 www.milltoporchard.co.uk

Milltop was one of those names that kept on coming up on lists of Devon cider makers which I could never pin down. It seemed to be also a homebrew beer business and I was told it was no longer making cider. However, at the Taste of the West Trade Show in April 2011 I was informed that it certainly did exist so I thought I had better track it down.

Somewhere up a long track between the madly named Combeinteignhead and Stokeinteignhead I eventually met Peter Webb, a forthright and busy former vet who is very much the businessman. He had bought the Milltop orchards from their previous owner in the autumn of 2010 and is dragging it up to standard with big plans for the future. Basically it is an apple juice company with only 5% of its production currently cider. They have quite an extensive acreage of dessert apples plus some cider varieties such as Dabinet, Michelin and Browns. However, the cider apples may be under threat as the trees do not perform as well as the modern dessert varieties.

He points out a couple of fields on a hill the other side of the valley where he has the potential to plant out up to another 45 acres of orchard - this could be a pretty big business. As it was autumn they were crushing apples when I arrived in the first commercial scale 'bladder' press I have seen. After milling the pomace is put in a bladder where water poured into the outer chamber squeezes the juice out. They seemed to be getting efficiencies comparable to most more conventional cider presses.

They have a very well provided bottling room with a good range of equipment and bottle in a variety of sizes. When I visited they were doing a batch of juice in five litre boxes for a particular customer. Peter says they sell their product mainly locally currently mainly through Farmers Markets, farm shops and pubs. However he is looking to increase his markets and is talking to a café group. I suggested that with Torquay on his doorstep he must have a massive potential with all the tourists. He grimly informed me that anywhere else in South Devon yes, but in Torquay there is no market for quality food or drink products!

Although for now apple juice is the emphasis the business could evolve. They are growing a few raspberries and may look at other fruit. He is also not ruling out expansion of the cider element but wants to understand more about it first. He has booked himself onto a Peter Mitchell cider making course and it will be interesting to see how he feels after that.

Ostlers Cider Mill

Peter Hartnoll, Ostlers Cider Mill, Goodleigh, Barnstable EX32 7NR 01271 321241 www.ostlerscidermill.co.uk

Ostlers Cider Mill was something very different as far as cider makers go. In this search for cider I had many places that were hard to find and some epic struggles with Googlemaps UK but I think this one beat the lot. After entering the postcode Ostlers Cider Mill was quite clearly marked in an estate on the eastern edge of Barnstaple. When I was on the estate I realised that there was no road through to the location marked on the map so I went on an elaborate journey to try to find a way to the other side of the estate. I eventually did this only to find nothing. In the end I phoned up and was told to find the village of Goodleigh and phone from there. Only trouble was I could not get a phone signal in Goodleigh and had to drive back nearly to Barnstable from where I got instructions, went back to Goodleigh and set out from there up some narrow lanes, then onto about half a mile of unmetailised farm tracks eventually ending up in a steep valley surrounded by a pleasant orchard. There seemed to be absolutely no relationship by a number of miles to the Google Map I had printed out. It may be a challenge but this is not really one for others to find - there are no sales from the premises.

There is also not a lot of cider. Although about 15,000 gallons are made each year this is nearly all turned into and sold as cider vinegar. I was absolutely delighted to eventually meet the owner Peter Hartnoll, a real character. Now in his 60's he was seriously injured in an accident as a teenager and is partially paralysed down one side and the strain of this on his body has led to more recent problems with hips so he is only semi mobile. He for many years ran an off-licence in Lynton about 20 miles away on the North Devon coast where a lot of trade was selling cider to summer tourists. He bought this eight acre orchard in Goodleigh which he says is historically the premier fruit growing parish in North Devon and where he can trace his family in the parish record back to 1530. He started making his own cider to sell to the tourists who, he says, wanted it as sharp and sour as possible. He poured me a glass to try saying he wouldn't be offended if I didn't like it. In fact it was fine, a very traditional cider but I could see that with pouring into containers for tourists and storing in shop windows it was very likely to turn into the acetic product that he has a bit of a reputation for.

However it was this that proved his salvation in more ways than one. He heard about the healthy properties of Cider Vinegar and found he had a barrel which had developed the 'mother' and had turned into vinegar. He started taking two tablespoons morning and night at a time he was wheelchair bound and on 12 painkilling tablets a day. It may seem a very good sales pitch but within three weeks he was off all pain killers and within five he was out of his wheelchair.

That was 15 years ago and he eventually found running his shop too much for himself and moved down to his orchard. He has now virtually given up trying to sell any of his cider; there are four or five shops in the North Devon towns which take it for selling to tourists. But his business has grown and flourished selling cider vinegar. He has recently been joined in the business by his daughter Becky who can look after the IT side. As well using five wholesalers they sell throughout the world via mail order on the internet. His interesting leaflet is full of client testimonials which he says he receives almost daily from people who have benefited from Cider Vinegar - or whose livestock have benefitted, quite a bit gets sold to horse owners and farmers. Peter walked me around his production premises where he has a large Voran press and stores a huge amount of cider in black plastic 1,500 litre tanks. The cider has to be stored for three years until it has developed into mature vinegar. Everything is natural from the apples to the yeast and vinegar culture.

Peter is also a fascinating man with an interesting outlook on life. He has a strong belief in astrology and astrologers and believes they have been able to predict his course in life. Having eventually found his delightful orchard and home, I have to say it was a real pleasure meeting Peter who has triumphed so far over adversity.

Palmershayes Cider

Aubrey Greenslade, Palmershayes Farm, Calverleigh, Tiverton, Tiverton EX16 8BA
01884 254579 *SWECA*

The Greenslades are a lovely, very traditional, farming family who have lived on Palmershayes Farm since 1905. I met Aubrey who is 70, his welcoming wife, daughter Wendy who is very much involved in the cider making and John, Aubrey's elder brother who at 80 still seems actively involved as well. Aubrey says he was first given cider as a three year old and has been making it all his life. Times have changed - he now says he didn't give cider to his grandsons until they were 4 or 5, only a drop mind you!

The farm is now on a minor B road out of Tiverton and was effectively bypassed when the North Devon Link road was built about 20 years ago. Not surprisingly this led to a huge drop in their sales from passing trade of cider, but they insist that these are now picking up again. A bit surprisingly maybe as there is not a sign on the gate at all - 'we need to get another one made sometime'! They are in fact open for cider sales at any reasonable hour as long as there is someone around.

Beautifull orchard at Palmershayes Farm

They gave up milking about 10 years ago but Palmershayes is still an active farm of around 200 acres. They have about 60 cattle but most is now turned over to arable - and of course about 4 acres of traditional cider orchard around the house. I went for a walk up through the delightful orchard with Aubrey, the trees were laden with cider apples of all hues and a push along apple harvester had already made a start on collecting the season's crop. Many of the trees are up to 60 years old. Cider used to be a bigger part of the business; he can remember the days when they used to take 18 gallon barrels into the pubs of Tiverton. They miss the regular trade they used to have. One family called Fox used to take 30 gallons a week whilst there were many regulars who used to have five gallons every 7 - 10 days, if they didn't come they knew there was something wrong.

They make about 7,000 gallons most years and some years up to 9,000 gallons. In an old building they have a large hydraulic press and most importantly a bottling line - which seems to be the domain of Wendy. The main outlet for their cider is in the tourist orientated off-licences in North Devon and they bottle much of their output in attractively shaped one litre jars, the ideal gift of Devon cider to take home from your holiday. Two and a half litre bottles also sell well and they seem to bottle in all shapes and sizes of glass and plastic. All their cider is still and unpasteurised though they do run it through a filter. They sweeten with saccharin which effectively hides a quite sharp authentic dry taste beneath. I get the impression that most cider is well over a year old before bottling meaning it is a very stable product. They have recently produced a new label for cider vinegar which they have been surprised at a good demand for. Mind you Aubrey informs me they have tanks around the

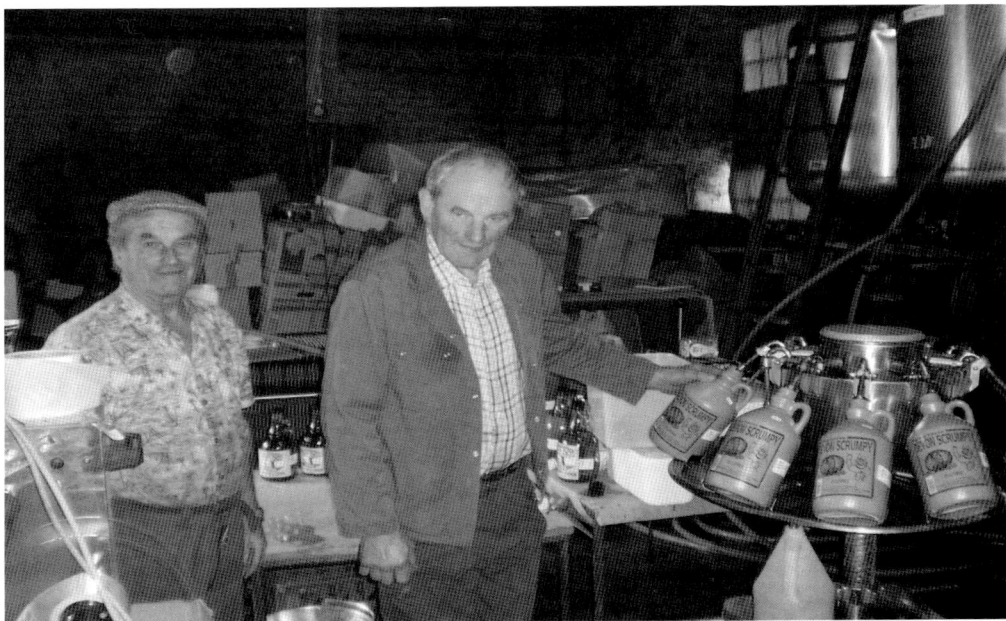

back with 10,000 gallons of vinegar if I knew anyone who wanted any - they aren't going to run out for a while.

It is well worth making the effort to visit the Greenslade's, there are not that many truly traditional farmhouse operations left in Devon - they are a part of our Rural heritage which it is good to see still thriving.

Reddaway's Cider

Tom and John Reddaway, Lower Rixdale Farm, Luton, Chudleigh TQ13 0BN

Tom Reddaway is possibly the youngest cider maker featured in this search for cider, though his father John is very much still involved. For location Lower Rixdale Farm has to be one of the most scenic I came across in Devon. A minor road off of the A380 winds through the small, picturesque villages of Ideford and Luton and past more horses than I think I have seen out on the road than anywhere else in the country. In two trips each way along the lane I think journey time was more than trebled by the need to wait for horses, whose riders at least always waved politely.

From Luton a no-through road runs for almost a mile up an attractive green valley towards the farm. You realise that you are on the right road because on one side of the road are the cider orchards. However once I had arrived at the farm it was a good job there were a couple of five gallon plastic barrels waiting for collection as there were no other notices about cider - although Tom does say they are open for cider sales at any reasonable time as long as there is someone around.

I found John, the farmer before I found Tom. He was moving some of his large golden haired South Devon beef cattle - the local breed - which they farm along with the early lambing Dorset sheep on this good pasture land. Apparently it was John's father who first made cider on the farm but he died nearly 30 years ago. They stopped making cider and sold the apples to Whiteway's, planting a second orchard and for a while the sale of apples covered the farm rent. However, when Whiteway's shut they started making some cider again, but always keeping under the 1,500 gallon threshold.

Tom has now started taking a more active interest in the cider and they have a website and attractively designed label for their new bottles. Most cider is still sold as draught either to local pubs and shops or to callers at the farm with a bit going to festivals. Most of their sales have come from a word of mouth following and they have not felt the need to go in for much marketing. They have a Voran double bed rack and cloth press and below the farmhouse is an excellent cider cellar with rows of wooden oak barrels. Tom says that the most important element of their cider making is the cleanliness of the barrels for which they have a steam cleaner - it certainly results in a clearer, fresher cider than oak barrels sometimes do. He is experimenting with storing in whiskey and rum barrels, getting a couple of new barrels each year.

Tom is doing the bottling himself. He describes it as 'raditional with a modern twist.' His draught cider is filtered for clarity, slightly sweetened with sucrelose and then carbonated with his own small twin head carbonator. It makes a very nice fresh cider drink and doing it himself certainly maintains the margins that getting it contract bottled would decimate. He bottles relatively small batches at a time, as needed, so he doesn't need to pasteurise. These bottles are a lot easier to sell into local shops and places like Dart's Farm which is not many miles away.

Tom is keen to gently grow his business but also seems keen to stay under the duty threshold. He feels his next development may be to experiment with apple juice for which there appears to be a ready market.

David Rowe - Berry Farm

David Rowe. www.berryfarmcider.co.uk **SWECA**

Nigel and David on sacks of apples in the converted dairy

In Clyst St Lawrence, the very attractive village hidden down narrow Devon lanes there is a Berry Farm and just down the road is Clapp Mill where Nick Millman, the lively and interested farm manager, lives. Working for him is young cider enthusiast David Rowe who, as part of his job, looks after the orchards, some gardening and horticulture and makes the cider. David now lives with his wife and two young children a few miles away in Whimple. It a bit confusing as David had previously lived in Clyst St Lawrence and had even for a while lived in Clapp Mill Farm which at that time was owned by his in laws who were selling up as retiring farmers. At some point he was working in a pub in nearby Broadclyst - isn't 'clyst' such a wonderful Devonian sounding name - who were selling some 'Berry Farm cider'. He went along to find out more about the cider making and to see if he could do it better. The first commercial outcome of his endeavours was in 2011 and at their first attempt they won the Champion Cider at the Devon County Show which has since been followed up by two seconds at the Mid Somerset Show where I helped David out by rescuing his demijohns for him.

They have converted the emptied out milking parlour at Clapp Mill Farm to make a cider production and bottling area and it makes an excellent setting. They have replaced their original small Vigo screw press, more suitable for the home cider maker, with a P2 Voran hydraulic rack and cloth press which seems to be the standard for small commercial producers. In their first year (2010) they produced only around 1,500 litres and in the autumn of 2011 hope to have taken this up to 7,000 litres. They have sold product both in bulk and bottled as 'Berry Farm Cider Organic Traditional Devon Cider'. This is sold through Darts Farm and a couple of very local pubs including the New Inn in Broad Clyst and the Five Bells in Clyst Hydon. They have also sold quite impressive quantities through the English National Cider Farm in Sussex.

David takes a rather different approach to cider making to Mark Venton, the other excellent cider maker in this small village. Where Mark is determined to make the traditional systems work David is keen to take the more scientific and 'modern' approach. Like my son Richie, he has been on the Peter Mitchell training courses and very much believes in making cider making clean and safe and avoids all risk of spoilage. Whether this will end up clashing with the organic aspirations of the owners remains to be seen. But it shouldn't, some of the very best organic producers certainly use modern science. David is carrying on his learning experience both in work and off his own back in his garage at home.

Their apples come from the traditional certified organic orchards on the two farms which Nick describes as being in need of plenty of TLC, and this is part of David's task. They have not yet been able to identify all the varieties but there would seem to be a good blend of traditional Devon apples and the more commercial vintage cider apples required by the former Whiteway's operation. It is quite probable that the blend of local apples has a lot to do with the competition success of both Mark Venton and Berry Farm in competitions.

As you can probably tell Berry Farm Cider is very much a work in progress and the biggest ongoing project is quite exciting. One of the disused buildings at Clatt's Mill Farm is the former 'Poundhouse'. I have not looked in detail yet but this may well have been the location for threshing. Anyway during the 20th century it was used for cider making and formerly held a big old cider press. David's parents in law can remember that around the Second World War they used the press to get the juice from apples in the local orchards and this was then sent as juice to Whiteway's who could not press enough on their own.

Anyway Nick located on another farm in South Devon a very big old twin screw press which had not been used for many years but shut up in a shed that was falling down around it. Although it took some time he managed to persuade the owner that it wasn't doing the press any good and to sell it to him. With considerable effort it was dismantled and brought back to Clapp Mill where restoration is ongoing with a target of having the press working by the harvest of 2012. The project has thrown up a number of problems with broken pieces of wrought iron and the screws seemingly permanently stuck. A local foundry has become involved and the workers are as excited about the project as Nick. Oil has been poured down through the screw and after a week of so of soaking Nick got an exultant phone call when they got the first screw loose.

I very much hope to be making many more visits to Clapp Mill Farm both to see the progress with the cider making and with their heritage project - both of which are very worthwhile.

Sandford Courtney Cider

James McIlwraith, Solland Farm Sampford Courtney Devon EX20 3QT *SWECA*

I met young Matt McIlwraith, a giant of a lad, at the SWECA AGM and made a loose arrangement to visit him the following week. When I managed to connect a road sign for Solland together with the rather vague Googlemaps PostCode location I arrived at the farm to find he wasn't there. However, there was another giant of a man who I correctly assumed was his father, and I quickly discovered that James McIlwraith was not only a giant of a man but also a giant of the cider industry.

I had been aware of pieces of various stories but had never been able to put them

James McIlwraith beside the large vats he is erecting at Solland Farm

all together, but now I was to hear it from the horse's mouth. I had first come across Sandford Courtney Cider at the 2010 Bath and West Show. I had checked that it was not Barny Butterworth's Sandford Orchards and seeing only 'posh bottles' when there is so much else on offer at the show I didn't pay it much attention. Later in the year talking to Chris Cole at Green Valley he mentioned a chap who had been involved in a number of very commercial cider businesses but was now making some really good cider. As it was cider flavoured with elderberry and other ingredients, something my son was experimenting with, I bought a couple of the distinctive flip-top stopper glass bottles and found it was a very pleasant and sophisticated drink.

James, I discovered, has been involved in cider for 30 years - all his career I would imagine as he looks younger than me. His background was in Plant Biology and microbiology. He started helping cider maker Vernon Bland at Oldbury near Bristol being friendly with Vernon's son. Since then he has been involved in the setting up of a number of cider companies. He moved on to the Frampton Cider Company at Frampton on Severn and from there on to Symonds in Herefordshire. Whilst at Symonds, Greenall Whitney wanted a strong cider brand for selling through their pubs. James's wife Alison was responsible for brand and going through a box of old labels came across a pair - Scrumpy Jack and Scrumpy Jill. Scrumpy Jack has since become one of the major national brands and largely because of it Symonds was sold to Bulmers. The directors had tried to form a management buy out but could not manage it.

James decided to buy his own company and obtained the legendary Devon cider maker Inch's from Sam Inch in Winkleigh in 1989 which he ran for 10 years before the advent of alchopops and the pressures of Venture Capital meant this too was sold to Bulmers. James, who by now had bought his farm at Sampford Courtney in Devon, went off to Guernsey to form the Guernsey Cider Company. This has now evolved into the Rocquette Cider Company run by the son of James's former business partner, James Meller, who James has a high regard for. He still has a nominal share holding but is not actively involved. James strongly recommends I go to Guernsey to look at this company and I met James Meller at the SWECA AGM. One day, but probably not in the scope of this book!

James then bought a former Whitbread factory in Tiverton and with the help of others formed the Devon Cider Company. I must admit at the time I had very mixed views about their products which I saw as a more akin to alcopops. Time now suggests that they were just ahead of the game. They made a whole range of fruit ciders, such as blackberry, strawberry, elderberry etc. As the excise regard these as 'made wines' rather than ciders they were made to about 4% - 4.5% ABV, hardly promising territory for a cider fan. They had a quite active promotions policy and I saw them one year at the Bath and West and again at a Taste of the West Trade Show. Here a young member of staff rather irritated me when offering tastings by treating with contempt my request for a cider flavoured cider. Actually the blackberry cider I did taste was quite pleasant but that was not the point. Anyway Devon Cider became a rather spectacular financial failure and James sounded quite bitter that some of the investors appear to have made a lot of money from it and I get the impression they left him holding the baby and the blame.

However James does not strike me as someone to be down for long and Sampford Courtney Cider looks to be a very constructive project. This time it is a family venture including his wife Alison, son Matt and daughter Alice. They had planted out 50 acres of orchard about 12 years ago with standard cider varieties such as Dabinett, Michelin, Bulmers Norman and local Devon variety Ellis Bitter, plus some Bramley to act as an acidifier. The rest of the farm has been run by Alison for breeding horses but a back injury has led to a reduction of that side of the business. James says that he appears to have had a fortunate foresight when he built the main building including an acid proof floor and good drains. This makes it ideal for the conversion to cider production which it is now undergoing. The latest move is the instillation of some large oak storage tanks which Green Valley no longer had space for as they need to be under cover. You can still see where each stave has been carefully numbered so they can be put back together.

The philosophy of Sandford Courtney Cider is that they are making and selling a wine so they do not chaptelise (add sugars to take the strength up). The result of this is a high quality and natural product to which they can add their syrups to flavour. In the case of their leading seller Elderflower a Waitrose video on Youtube

Upmarket range from Sandford Courtney

shows James and Alice collecting the elderflowers from the hedgerows around the farm and making their own syrups. Also in the range I am pleased to say is a very high quality vintage cider.

Very clever and attractive packaging makes this an ideal up market product. Not one for the festivals and cider bars but for the restaurants and top end supermarkets and delicatessens. In the case of all flavoured ciders I think it is important that the added flavours add to the cider flavour rather than swamp it, but Sampford Courtney Cider seems very much along the right lines. I look forward to tasting some more of it.

Sandford Orchards

Barny Butterfield. Lower Park Farm, Crediton, Devon, EX17 3PR 01363 777822 www.sandfordorchards.co.uk **SWECA**

Barney Butterfield is one of the busiest people I have ever met. He is always doing something else. In fact I could have called this book 'In Search of Barny Butterfield'.

The first time I didn't meet him was when he was running his stand at the Taste of the West Trade show a few years ago. I went to his stand and he was not there, instead there was a pleasant young woman sat on the floor behind the stand with her back supported by the wall reading a book. I discovered she was Marie, Barney's girlfriend or maybe by then already his wife - she helped me to tastings of some pretty decent cider. A few years later they now have two children.

I met Marie again a couple of months later at a farming conference where she was interested in our speaker's talk on helping young farmers by using the tax and benefits structure. Somewhere I did meet Barney, young and enthusiastic, and arranged to visit him at his farm during a golf day I was helping organise at the nearby Downes Golf Club, Crediton. He was not there. The signs to cider sales were rather rudimentary at that time and I had to search the buildings to check I was in the right place. I was still not convinced as apart from a couple of half filled IBC's, a half pallet of empty bottles and what looked like part of a dismantled bottling line there was not much sign - though newly planted apple trees in the bottom of the valley did look promising. I later discovered that they had only just moved into this council farm from the village of Sandford.

Over the years at many shows and exhibitions or on his stall in Exeter or at cider meetings I must have met Barney at least a dozen more times - but have still to succeed in the meeting where I can sit down and talk to him to find out what drives him. Each time he is not only busy but also dashing off somewhere or doing something. I think there have been three more appointments to meet him at the farm - for the most recent one I saw him put the appointment into his diary - but when I arrived I found he had dashed off to Vigo to collect some urgently needed part. Another time I cannot blame him as weights and measures had arrived and were inspecting his procedures, not a time you would want to talk to anyone.

Although I have not really got to talk to him I have seen the farm develop and it now has the appearance of a significant production and bottling unit inside the old farm buildings. Barney is very involved in Crediton Farmers Market, I met him at a dinner where they had won a prize. He is also very involved in the Food Tent at the Mid Devon Agricultural Show where I have had some cider off him for a few years. Even here he is very busy, as chief steward for two marquees and running his own large stand you would think that would be enough, but there is usually some other crisis. The stand may have run out of cider or last year he disappeared for most of the day as he had a problem with a keg withdrawal.

As far as I can gather from him his aim is to build up a significant cider business but remaining true to his love for genuine traditional cider, whilst at the same time embracing the modern possibilities and potential of the market. With his drive it is certainly happening. He had a huge fillip when he won the CAMRA Champion Cider at the Reading Beer festival. This is probably the highest profile award of the year, although some people would question how the competition is run. The entries are supposedly decided by CAMRA members but are largely dependent on what the wholesalers provide for the festival. The judging is carried out by the beer drinkers who attend the festival and at some CAMRA festivals they include products that most of us would scarcely accept as being cider. However I tasted some of Barney's the next week at the Devon County Show and his was definitely a good cider.

He has used the award as a springboard for growth and in 2011 supplied the Wetherspoons Pub Chain's October Cider event with a reported 1,800, 20 litre bag in boxes of cider. That is a lot of cider! His range of bottled ciders has grown to almost bewildering proportions including the likes of Devon Red, Devon Scrumpy, Shakey Bridge, Old Kirton, Redvers Buller, each with a nice story attached. These ciders range from very full flavoured traditional Devon ciders to lighter, lower alcohol ciders. Going with fashion there is also a Fanny Bramble, made with blackberries and celebrating Devon hedgerows and also a Bumble Berry. He also produces a significant quantity of apple juice.

At the Devon Country Show in 2011 I tasted his Devon Mist for the first time. This is his keg product made to appeal to the pub market. Very light and about 4.5% ABV it had all the hallmarks of a commercial keg cider.

The farm is open for bulk and bottle sales at reasonable times - though whether you catch Barney himself is open to question! Do check his website for directions, it is down a long track and is not obvious. Last time I visited I got held up for 20 minutes. where for some reason there was filming going on at a breakers yard. They held up traffic whilst they blocked the lane whilst they moved wrecked cars around before smashing them to pieces. Barney was of course not there when I did get through!

Anyway Barney, Marie and their staff are well worth the effort of meeting and I will continue to try to have my chat with him.

Sunnybrook Cider

Ivor Banks, Sunnybrook Cider, Cadeleigh, Tiverton 01884 855411 sunnybrookecider@yahoo.co.uk

Ivor and Gayle Banks and children live in marvellous old cottage in an idyllic valley just off the Tiverton to Credition Road. Ivor is a decorator by trade and has spent a huge amount of effort over the past decade doing the cottage up from a semi ruinous state when he bought it to the gem it is today. On one side of the lane is a farm with a flock of pedigree Hampshire Down sheep whilst on the other is a deer farm; I think this is the only cider maker I have visited with a view of red deer.

And I nearly finding missed them altogether. Towards the end of my investigations I was in Exeter at lunch time and managed to persuade the designer who was taking me to a business lunch not to go to the Bistros and Tapas Bars he seemed to have an inclination for but to take me to the Fire House - pub culture is far more my scene! The Fire House is one of the best cider pubs in the west. Serving good pub food and with plenty of real ale it always has at least four or five draught ciders and it was here that I spotted a five gallon barrel on the bar of Sunnybrook Cider. The pub was very pleased to furnish me with a phone number and a week later I searched Ivor out.

Ivor started making cider after he moved into the cottage. There are a few old trees in their two acre garden and the first year he was horrified to see the apples just left to rot on the ground so the next year he decided to make some cider. He has been making now for eight years and has reached the 7,000 litre threshold. As it is just him on his own he is currently reluctant to push beyond that. As when you produce your 7001st litres you owe for duty on every litre already made - somewhere around £3,000 - you need to make a lot more cider to make the same level of profit. He is however having a shift around of his mill and press hoping to utilise a natural drop in the ground to use gravity to take out some of the strain of lifting apples.

He now has about 40 cider apple trees of his own but also buys some from a commercial orchard at Cheriton Fitzpaine. More apples are bought to him by friends and he supplies them with some cider back in return. His first cider was made with an old oak screw press but he found this very slow and built a bigger one. He now has a Voran P2 hydraulic press which he was very lucky to pick up reasonably cheap. A friend of his dad was talking to a chap in a pub about Ivor's cider and this put him onto a chap who was giving up making cider to try a brewery instead. Nowadays with the revival of interest in craft ciders these always seem to fetch silly money. He is dubious about belt presses, not only because of the high price tag but because he feels contact of the pomace with the air and the bacteria and yeasts on the racks and cloths is an important part of building the character of the cider.

He ferments in 1,500 litre rotaplast tanks and then matures in 100 gallon oak barrels. As he goes through one barrel at a time the taste of his cider will vary from one batch to the next - one of the great defining features of craft cider. He tends to sell all his cider as a medium, draught in bag in boxes or 2 litre PET bottles.

He largely sells through pubs and as well as the Fire House regulars include the Thorverton Arms, The Royal Oak at Nadderwater and Jazzy's in Tiverton. Other outlets include the Cheese Café in Crediton, Thorn's Farm Shop and his wife Debbie has a stall on Tiverton Market each Friday. The cider also makes its way to many functions.

They do also have a licence to sell from the cottage though they have not done anything to advertise the fact. He is discussing with one of his neighbouring farmers about putting a sign up on the main road and is also about to start work on a website. At the moment he would rather callers came in the evening - though it is probably better to ring first to check there is someone around.

I am very glad that I have searched out Sunnybrook Cider and look forward to tasting it again.

Ye Olde Cider Bar

East Street, Newton Abbot, TQ12 2LD

I had heard about The Cider Bar in Newton Abbot for many years - well before cider became fashionable. However, it was not until recently, just after it had been awarded the CAMRA Cider Pub of the year 2011 accolade that I managed to squeeze in a visit whilst searching out the local cider makers. It is on a busy road just away from the town centre in Newton Abbot and is one of very few genuine cider houses left in the country. Cider houses used to have a different form of licence and sold cider, no beer or lager - wonderful.

It is a very basic traditional pub with no frills or fancy pretensions. I loved the cheese and onion roll I grabbed for my lunch so much that I had to have a ham roll as well. Both excellent - who needs more? I thought at first I was going to be disappointed with the choice of ciders, there seemed to be too much emphasis on the ciders of non Devon commercial giants Thatchers (under various guises) and Westons. Fine though their ciders are it reminded me of Bristol where there is also a big producer dominance in the cider orientated pubs.

However ,when I started looking at the notices above the bar and barrels around I discovered that they do indeed now stock a number of good traditional Devon ciders, Sam's from Winkleigh, Reddaways, Wiscombe Suicider and Brimblecombe amongst them - and Sheppy's from just over the border into Somerset.

The pub has been run by legendary landlord Richard Knibbs who has been in charge for 41 years and apparently it has been in his family for 80. Unfortunately he was not there when I visited but I must comment on how impressed I was with the bar staff - a friendly girl called Holly. She said she had been there a year and it was the best job she had ever had. Obviously used to dealing with people who are not really sure of what they want she led me through a simple question and answer

process to identify my choice of cider.

Still or sparkling? - still
Cloudy or clear? - cloudy
Dry, medium or sweet? - dry

Winscombe Suicider or Weston's Old Rosie? - Suicider please.
As it was what I had already chosen suggest that the system works.

Mind you she nearly blotted her copybook by suggesting I might prefer it as a ginger beer shandy. Not that I mind a cider ginger beer shandy but that was not what wanted.

Maybe it is not really a pub to take the family to, but I am sure I will drop in again when I am down that way.

Venton's Devon Cyder

Mark Venton,   Clyst St Lawrence, Exeter EX15 2NL 07811 963385
www.ventons.co.uk

Mark Venton has been cider making for seven years but in that time he has developed an amazing practical knowledge. He is a carpenter, joiner and builder by trade

*Mark Venton,
sticking to the
traditional*

who when he came to live at a smallholding in the village was distressed to find a large quantity of apples going to waste in his small 'cottage' orchard of around 60 old standard trees comprising a mix of cooker's, eater's and traditional varieties of Devon cider apples. After two year's of making small quantities with a small borrowed basket type press, he decided to use them to make some cider on a bigger scale and being a carpenter built his own press with green oak from a neighbour's tree which had just been felled. A most impressive press it is too. He got hold of a pair of Victorian iron screws and built a traditional frame and bed for them to work in to form a large twin screw press with a bed about five foot square. Mark also has the metalwork for an even larger and more elaborate Victorian twin screw press which is waiting to be built.

He looked into getting the wood to make racks and the cost of rack cloths but when he found this would set him back £1,500 he did not have he decided to use straw. This has now become a permanent feature of his cider and as it costs him around £20 a season it would take a long time to cover the cost of racks. During the cider making season, with the help of family and friends, he presses on Sunday afternoons and it takes four to six days to squeeze all the juice out of each cheese including cutting back the sides to be re-pressed. He reckons that the time taken allows the natural yeasts and enzymes to start working at nature's pace and gets the best of the flavour out of the apples. He then puts the juice into wooden barrels for fermenting and storage with each barrel being racked at least twice. Mark currently produces up to 1500 gallons a year and reckons his average yield per cheese is 150 gallons although it can vary from 110 to 225 gallons based on around 55 to 65 sacks of apples per cheese.

Readers may be aware that from experience of many cider makers I have often found straw and wood a potential recipe for disaster and can lead to the worst kind of cider. Much of the undesirable cider I have tasted is made in precisely this manner. However Marks cider is certainly fine - what does he do differently?

For a start I think he has understood the traditional process and what it is trying to achieve - something missed by some producers who just repeat what has been done for generations. He always uses fresh clean barley straw for every cheese. He is then scrupulous about cleaning his wooden barrels. Here he uses a steam cleaner and the age old tradition of a sulphur candle to sterilise the barrel which may perhaps rather negate his statement of not using sulphites actually in the cider but that is being picky. He then regularly racks the cider from one barrel into another and he keeps barrels topped up and with a modern airlock to prevent air getting in to spoil it. Although there is no "organic" ticket, everything is made from unsprayed crops. Mark has also grafted 250 new trees from over 100 cider apple varieties over the last two winters and is intending to create a new orchard at home. Beehives have also been set up and this has significantly increased pollination and fruit set.

The effect of the racking is to attempt to slow the fermentation and reflects the advice of the makers in the !7th century 'golden age' of cider making. By slowing fermentation he hopes to leave a residual sweetness in the cider which would naturally ferment out to full dryness. Without filtering, Mark's approach is to rack the cider to clarity. He has nothing against cloudy cider but has the view with his own, that if it is still cloudy it is not ready. Because he uses trees from mature orchards the apples are reasonably low in nutrients a natural keeving sometimes take place which

further enhances the retained sweetness. In fact he has just rung me to say that even in this warm autumn where all fermentations have gone off like a   rocket he has still managed a natural keeve with the last two presses. Another effect of this prolonged slow fermentation is that it helps to exclude the air. Generally cider does not spoil whilst fermentation is taking place and bubbles are still rising - thus he has few problems with the dreaded 'film' yeasts forming on the surface and relies on natural processes rather than sulphites.

As well as the apple varieties from his own small but productive orchard, Mark gets apples from some of the local orchards which originally provided apples or juice for the former Whiteway's factory in Whimple, only a couple miles away down the lanes. These are all mature cider orchards which in their blend of apples tend to have a more limited choice of varieties selected for commercial production. These are probably not quite as good for the rich blend he is trying to achieve though this year with the bumper crop of apples and the increasing offers of apples from other cottage orchard owners, he has been able to be selective and choose only those he wants.

Mark had almost immediate success and fame when in only his first year of pressing on the newly built oak press he entered the Devon County Show and won first prize for his dry in 2009. In 2010 he repeated it with another first in the dry class plus third and fourth in the sweet class. He couldn't quite make it a hat trick in 2011 but a second, two thirds and a fourth across the classes, plus a 'Taste of the West' silver award continued his prize-winning success. He mainly sells through a few local festivals and pubs including the Firehouse and JDW Imperial in Exeter and the wholesalers are keen to take it to the many festivals and pubs further afield. John Hallam, Merrylegs, The Real Beer Company and The National Cider Collection in Sussex regularly pick up considerable quantities. J D Wetherspoon have also recently started to take good quantities which Mark sees as a clear and encouraging sign of the increasing popularity of real "cyder" with younger people who had only previously known commercial cider.

He poured a good sample of his year old cider for me to try. It was an excellent clear dry traditional cider without a hint of acetic acid. One or two of the barrels had a hint of residual sweetness about them as well as a good fruit taste and most importantly absolutely no 'off' tastes. As a general rule natural cider always tastes it's best in the cellar straight from the barrel but the gallon I brought home with me seemed to travel well. Mark is persistent in his efforts to serve his cider in it's natural draught form direct from the oak to avoid filtering, sulphiting and pasteurisation which he believes can all take something away from a good traditionally made natural cider.

His dry he has branded Skippy's Scrumpy. When he first started making cider he had suffered a torn knee ligament and walked with a pronounced limp, or skip, for a period and the nickname has stuck. His medium he calls Apple Vice and his sweet is Sweet Maid in Devon. He has experimented with a few bottles, is aware of the increasing demand for bottles and bottles to order for customers such as Green Valley Cider at Darts Farm but is fundamentally interested in producing traditional draught with the bulk of the cider going out in either 5, 10 or 20 litre bag in box or 5 gallon polypins.

He is proud of Devon's prestigious cider or "cyder" history and is committed to doing his bit to revive it's former reputation and standing but feels that Devon is still suffering from the idea of low quality 'scrumpy' and that over the past 50 years too much poor quality cider has been produced, particularly for the tourist trade. He is still trying to produce a traditional cider but to get it right. In these days of increasing sophistication and scientific tampering with products to produce 'what the public want' it is a very brave stance to take - but on the evidence of what he is producing it is a very worthwhile stance and his efforts have to be applauded - I really think many of the new artisan enthusiasts should listen to how he is going about things. Using wild yeasts, oak barrels and natural processes, Mark's ethos is to produce a consistent quality rather than a consistent flavour. Every barrel is a unique creation.

Although it appears very much a one man operation Mark comments that none of his efforts would lead to anything if it were not for the support and help of his wife Sharon along with assorted family and friends - which is very much the cider making tradition on smallholdings and small farms throughout the cider making counties.

West Lake Cider

George Travis and Linda Davis, West Lake , Beaworthy Devon EX21 5XF 01409 221991 www.west-lale.co.uk *SWECA*

"There isn't a high local population so we have had to find other places to sell our produce' says George Travis. I found West Lake Cider in the heart of rural Devon up the lanes from Halwill Junction - a small village I had never heard of before but the first settlement of any note I had been through since Okehampton about a dozen miles to the south east.. As its name suggests Halwill Junction once had railways but, other than some photographs in the only pub, it is only a distant memory.

The area is marketed as Ruby Country, named after the local Devon Ruby Cattle, with the disused railway line gaining a second life as a footpath, cycle route and bridleway now known as The Ruby Way - a tourist attraction.

George and his partner Linda came to this part of the country from the Wigan and Leigh areas in Lancashire a few years ago. They had both been school teachers and were looking to do something different. Something with an educational, environmental, tourism feel. Somehow this led to them drifting into cider and juice making on their 13 acre small holding with production in the former farm dairy. There were existing old apple trees and in their first year they borrowed some equipment and pressed some apple juice which sold well at local farmers markets. This encouraged them to buy their own equipment and do more the next year. They have since planted out some more apple trees including 30 heritage varieties

They have followed a philosophy of doing what their customers have asked them for. As a Chartered Marketer I find it fascinating how many businesses miss out on this essential aspect of marketing. So many small businesses make what they want to make and expect people to buy it. Catering to known customer needs is often a more sensible route. They started making cider when customers suggested it and following the cider revival in recent years it now makes up nearly 50% of their production - bag in boxes have allowed them to expand this side of the business faster.

They have a twin bedded Voran rack press and specialise in doing small runs, single variety juices and ciders. They also do a lot of small batches of production for other people and organisations. Like the chap with holiday cottages who supplies apples for juicing which is turned into an own brand to place in the cottages as a greeting for the guests. They have the apples from RHS Rosemoor and give then juice back to sell. They also have a mobile mill and press which they hire out to individuals who want to try it themselves.

One product their customers asked for was cider vinegar and demand for this has grown so much that they are now pressing some apple juice specifically for vinegar. I seemed surprised that there was such a demand for cider vinegar but George listed the common uses for it: hair rinses, treatment for athletes foot, arthritis, feeding to horses, chickens, lambs and as a salad dressing. Obviously where I was going wrong was assuming that all vinegar is for chips! They are also beekeepers who produce and sell honey.

They find their policy of providing what customers want has meant that they have had to do little marketing - demand just seems to steadily grow. Their juice and cider goes to a lot of shops including Chris Coles' Green Valley Cider shop at Darts Farm. West Lake are privileged to be invited by CAMRA to help supply the annual Devon County Show's Ales of Devon Tent. Another important Chris is 'Chris the real ale man' who comes every Wednesday, has a van and distributes real ale from the smaller breweries to the North Devon and Exmoor pubs; cider makes a good addition to his range.

The West Lake range has continued to grow through customer requests. Some people wanted a sweeter cider so they sweeten with cane sugar and then pasteurise the bottles. Some requested a sparkling cider so they bought a small two head carbonator and do their own gentle carbonation. Currently they are experimenting with upmarket bottle conditioned ciders using the traditional champagne method.

West Lake has developed into a nice lifestyle business - with the addition of a barn conversion as a holiday cottage. I hope it has ticked some of the things they were looking for when they moved south to this depopulated area of the country. They obviously still have time for some other interests as an innovative alpine garden constructed on the roof of one of their buildings shows.

Winkleigh Cider

David Bridgman, Winkleigh Cider, Western Barn, Hatherleigh Road, Winkleigh, Devon EX19 8AP. Telephone 01837 83560

Winkleigh Cider Company is in many ways the ghost of Devon cider past. It is the reincarnation of Inch's Cider and celebrates that fact in everything it does.

Sam Inch was a young local farm worker during the Great War who according to legend was given apples in lieu of pay and used them to make a renowned Devon cider. His business grew and after the Second World War was one of a number of commercial scale cider makers in the county though dwarfed by Whiteway's. The manufacturing site expanded from a farmyard setting to a cider factory employing up to 90 people at its peak. Sam Inch was succeeded by his son Derek who after his father died in 1986 sold the business to a partnership in 1989. The partnership went in for a large scale expansion and boosted production up to a million gallons a year and it became a national brand. However, in 1996 the partnership sold out to the UK number one, Bulmer's for £22 million who, despite assurances, only continued producing at the plant until 1998 when production was moved to Hereford and the site was put on the market.

That would probably have been the end of the story but for one man, David Bridgman and his family. David came to work for Sam Inch as a 16 year old straight from school. He initially came for a month to help with the pressing season, but ended up working with Sam for 20 years until he Sam's death and then stayed with the company. He has now been working on the site making cider for over 40 years. When Bulmer's put the site on the market David, with support from his wife, brother and sister in law Margaret made an offer for part of it which was accepted and the Winkleigh Cider Company came into being.

David is an unassuming man with a friendly smile and a love of talking about cider. He hopes to get involved in SWECA but finds that he is so busy with the business that he doesn't get time. I quickly discovered in my attempts to make an appointment to see him that Tuesdays and Fridays are out as he does his delivery rounds. However, don't hesitate to visit on those days as they have an excellent shop, where tasting is essential, unusually manned by the helpful Margaret. When I did eventually get to see David I had not allowed time for the journey getting down from the

north of Devon and only had an hour with him - something I intend to rectify as soon as I get a chance. His knowledge of the Devon cider scene is excellent and there were many more things I want to ask him - including a look around the factory.

When they started business in 1999 they did so on a wave of public sympathy for the way Bulmer's had treated the company - commonly seen as a disgrace. In particular they were able to pick up trade with a lot of the pubs in the area and that still forms the bulk of their trade both in draught and kegged ciders. They obviously could not use the Inch's name - but wisely chose the name 'Sam's' which in Devon was synonymous with Sam Inch. Ye Olde Cider Bar in Newton Abbot, the 2011 CAMRA cider pub of the year, is a good outlet for their cider.

They buy their apples from local orchards within a 30 mile radius of Crediton - usually the same orchards that supplied Inch's for many years. They now produce around 60,000 gallons a year and do just about everything in house. Apart from the family shareholders they only employ one full-time worker and a part-time office administrator.

They look to make a drinkable light tasting cider to appeal to public pub drinking taste. Their ciders are not quite as heavily tannic as I am used to in Somerset but are ideal ciders to drink on a warm summer day and quench the thirst. The main range of 'Sam's' draught ciders are a dry, medium and sweet made to 6% alcohol. They also make 'Autumn Scrumpy' at a slightly stronger 7.5% as a medium sweet and medium dry. Their keg range goes by the name of 'Poundhouse' and includes 6% medium and sweets and also a 4% 'Poundhouse Crisp' which is now proving very popular. Most of their bottled ciders are produced in the plastic 2 litre PET bottles - Sam's Poundhouse Traditional, a sparkling product again in Dry Medium and Sweet.

Winkleigh cider is very much like David, a straightforward and pleasant product without pretensions. They do what you would expect of them. It is a survival of a commercial, industrial, cider making heritage that was taken for granted through from the inter war period until the 1970s and 80s when the large producers swallowed up nearly all these local cider factories - or squeezed them out through competition. Nationally we reached the position where Bulmers and Gaymers dominated the market in a very unhealthy way. It is only now that new producers are coming through on a big enough scale to take their place and to provide the general public with a genuine choice.

Do go and visit the shop at Winkleigh Cider, or look out for it in pubs around the county.

Wiscombe Suicider

Tim Chichester, Whitmore Farm, Nr Colyton Devon. 07976 585465

There is in this country, well at least the West Country, a curiously undefined cultural sub-class which I will refer to as 'Folk Rustics'. It is not gypsies, nor is it travellers or hippies, it is not the rural poor but perhaps its members at times get mistaken for one or more of these.

It has to do with rural life, woodcraft - though not necessarily. It is very much associated with folk music - though not necessarily. It may have quite a bit to do with horses and dogs - though not necessarily. There is an element of old farm equipment and rural nostalgia - though not necessarily. You can recognise its members by a prevalence of tattered donkey jackets and worn out jumpers - though not necessarily. There can be an element of rural pursuits and farming - though not necessarily. There appears to be a laid back attitude to work and money - though not necessarily. In speech they may have the broadest of rural rustic accents - or maybe public school. You may find them at steam fairs, woodcraft fairs, farm auctions, shows, festivals - or you may not. They could well be into cider - though not necessarily

It is a sub-class where I am interested in a lot of the same things as them and have a considerable empathy - but even though I have occasionally donned a coloured neck scarf I am not a part of it. However, Tim Chichester definitely is. I identified him as a real character the moment he walked into the cider event organised by Matthew Bryant at Hinton St George last September carrying a barrel of cider. He immediately became a focus of attention and livened up the room.

Tim occupies around 600 acres of mixed land in the hills south of Honiton. Much of the land is woodland, he has a saw bench and this is a big part of his work. Some of the land is bog and some of it is pasture. He appears to run a flock of about 150 sheep, 40 horses, some guinea fowl, turkeys and breeds a few raccoons - yes raccoons. As a divorcee he lives alone in an old tumbledown cottage that would drive any woman spare, though he seems to have a succession of girlfriends. Around the house is an extensive yard of sheds and cages, tractors and landrovers, horse drawn equipment, dogs, cats, and an amazing selection of old bits of farm machinery and of course a lot of old cider making equipment and barrels.

His pride and joy is a unique - he thinks - mobile crusher and press with horse gear to work it. He takes this out to some of the fairs and shows where it is a bit attraction, especially as he usually has a donkey to work it and a raccoon with him. He also has a circular stone horse-powered apple crusher made out of some heavy looking blocks of granite. This one was interesting as he says it comes from Somerset. I had not picked up a tradition of these crushers in Somerset, more in Devon and Gloucestershire. He has a big traditional wooden vat which I would estimate holds at least 600 gallons. It has a manufacturer's plate on it proclaiming it was made in Frome by a vat maker I was totally unaware of and now will have to investigate. There are a number of presses but the main one is a huge single screw press next to another mill driven by an old Lister engine. The eye is also caught by a huge portable steam engine - looking like an ancient Puffing Billy it is an industrial piece of kit from a brewery in Herefordshire which he uses to heat water to steam clean his barrels. And of course there would be the remains of a crashed WWII Meschesmidt fighter plane in the field above the yard, part genuine and part fabrication.

It is a fascinating place where the actual cider almost falls into insignificance. However, Wiscombe Suicider is a quite well known product. He has some apples of his own and collects others elsewhere locally. He produces it on the vintage equipment so it is not surprising that it is reputed to be of variable quality - and strong. I had a pint back in the autumn in the Cider Bar Newton Abbot - the CAMRA National Cider pub of the year and it was excellent. He also sells to some more local pubs including the Hare and Hounds on the Honiton to Sidmouth Road. The English Cider Centre in Sussex frequently collects some although as John Reakes of the wholesaler Merrylegs has moved up to Hereford or somewhere he is seeing less of him - this is something a number of South West Cider producers have commented on and is a mite concerning. Hopefully another wholesaler will emerge.

In the autumn Tim holds a big party/cider shindig with around 200 guests. Unfortunately I couldn't make it last autumn but I certainly hope to be invited next.

Tim's son Jack is now another young cider maker. He has registered with the HMRC as a separate entity - he lives on a separate unit in the woods somewhere further down the valley. HMRC were happy it was a separate business until they were listed at the Nottingham CAMRA festival as Wiscombe Suicider and **Wiscombe Apple Jack**. I think they may need to sort this out - and even if I am just about okay with the humorous Suicider I am not sure Trading Standards will live with the name Apple Jack, which, of course, is an illegal and dangerous product made by increasing the strength of cider by freezing it. Unfortunately this rather concentrates some of the toxins with disastrous effect. I am also not sure it quite matches the product that Jack is trying to produce. He has his own set of equipment which is rather more modern and he is looking to produce a more clear modern cider using largely the variety Dabinett. Last year he got his apples from Mark Rogers, another young rural heritage enthusiast who is featured in the Dorset section of this book. I certainly wish him luck.

Meanwhile I will certainly look forward to meeting both him and Tim again - the world is a better place for having people like them, and the whole folk rustic sub-culture, around.

Yarde Real Cider

Paul Gadd and Rebecca Jacks, Yarde Farm, Stoke Gabriel, TQ9 6SJ

I must admit I was thankful to be able to ask Richard Hunt for directions to find Yarde Real Drinks. I had printed off the Google Map but it just looked like a maze of lanes, but clear instructions to turn left at the crossroads at the top of the rise as you enter the village of Stoke Gabriel, take the second right and it is down the lane just about got me there.

Yarde Real Drinks was not quite what I expected. The wonderful branding and bottle labels and the 'foodie' appearance had led me to think that I was going to something that was a bit more corporate. In fact it turned out to be a very pleasant lifestyle business. Paul and his wife Rebecca came down from London about 15 years ago to raise a family. Paul does the manufacturing whilst Rebecca looks after the marketing and business side - plus from the evidence of my two visits seems to be responsible for running the two teenage daughters around.

They are renovating a pleasantly situated bungalow and production happens in a large storage shed and self-constructed lean-to on the edge of a semi derelict nursery a hundred yards or so back up the lane where I found Paul dressed in heavy waterproofs working through a shower of rain at his Voran mill and press. He makes up to the 7,000 litre threshold of cider but they also make far more apple juice, elderberry cordial and other quality drinks. They like experimenting and he gave me a bottle of beetroot and apple juice to try. Very nice, refreshing and pleasant though it may not find its way onto my weekly shopping list!

The valleys around where they live have many cider orchards which used to provide apples to the Whiteway's factories. Green Valley took on some of them when Whiteway's shut, but when one year they didn't take them and the apples were going to waste Paul decided to have a go and for the past 10 years has been making commercially. All their apples come from a 5 mile radius and as Paul says the local farmers are a bit on the traditional side and have just left the orchards alone so there is a good blend of apples. For their apple juice they choose the less tannic of the cider apples and add local Bramley apples which although quite sharp can provide a very sweet juice. Although they do not usually pasteurise the cider they of course have to for the apple and fruit juices and Paul has devised a large home-made

pasteuriser modelled on some of the very expensive commercial ones.

It was nice to see an innovative cider maker. They have a shed which is absolutely packed to the gunnels with both filled bottles and empty pallets of bottles waiting to be filled. Quite how anything can be found and got out I am not sure, though Paul does comment that his small forklift is a godsend. Paul spent some time climbing around the shed to identify things for me to taste. One stack of bottles were apparently an attempt at keeving which had not quite worked while another was a go at bottle conditioned cider - which certainly tasted fine! At the back of one side of the shed was the cage of their Bonded Store. They 'make' Devon's only cider brandy, though Paul expresses irritation with the press who often report that he has a distillery. It is their cider but it was taken to Julian Temperley at the Somerset Cider Brandy for distillation then brought back to mature in their store. It is only in a small way but is certainly an innovative move. Most of their cider and juice production is bottled into the 500ml bottles though they also do 1 and 2 litre plastics and 3 litre wine boxes as well as some smaller bottles for some of the cordials.

They sell their entire production locally between Exeter and Plymouth. A certain amount from the farm gate as a blackboard in the hedge in the lane mentions. Most is sold through farm shops, village shops and restaurants or the odd pub where 20 litre bag in boxes are proving popular. A major outlet are the local National Trust shops and tearooms and of course Dart's Farm which is a significant outlet for just about every Devon producer. They also sell through their own stand at a number of local shows, markets and food festivals; the Totnes Agricultural Show and 'Fishstock' in Brixham both come to mind.

I was delighted to meet Paul and Rebecca. They have a really nice little business but continue to look for ways to develop. Having already commented on their wonderful bottle label, way ahead of the branding of most smaller cider companies, I was surprised to hear that they think it is time to come up with a new one. Well if they can improve on what they have got I am certainly looking forward to seeing it.

Other Devon producers

Devon has been particularly problematic in identifying who is and isn't producing cider. When I sat down with Chris Cole, with his lists and others I had come across from the internet and UKcider in particular I had about 40 names. I have discovered a few new ones since then as well but have ended up with a list of little over 30. There seems to have been a rash of people who start up with enthusiasm but there were a number where when I phoned their wives informed me that they were not making any this season. There also seem to have been a number of cider clubs and non commercial producers included in some lists.

I hope I have found all the important makers and that this section may fill in some of the gaps. Though I make no claims to it being 100%!

Aston Manor Cider

The massive producer Aston Manor from near Birmingham who produce most of the supermarket own brands as well as a number of their own brands, which we do not come across much in the South West, apparently have a bottling operation in Tiverton.

Aston Manor are quite possibly the third biggest cider maker in the country but few people have heard of them unless they are fond of looking at the small print on labels. They also produce some of the strong ciders sold at much less than 40p a unit, such as Frosty Jack which my local Tesco's is currently selling for £3.75 for two litres whilst if I worked out the price at 40p per unit it should be a minimum of £6.00. This is the type of product which most of the industry was trying to remove but companies without a strong rural cider tradition still seem to want to produce and risk damaging the well-being of traditional producers who rely on farm gate sales.

I understand Aston Manor bottle on the site of a former brewery in Tiverton that had for a time been used by Devon Cider before it collapsed.

Sunnyhayes Cider

Alan Smith, Woodbury EX5 1EZ 01395 232223

Sunnyhayes are mainly an apple juice manufacturer who also do a range of pleasant light tasting ciders. I met their cider maker Adrian Sutter their at the Source, Taste of the West Trade Show in April 2011. He was a very friendly and enthusiastic fellow and urged me to go in and see him.

As it is not far off my route to Exeter where I go virtually every month I thought a suitable time would easily come along. I phoned him in Mid December and he was most apologetic that he had to make a delivery to Bristol on the day I wanted to call. Since then I have phoned on a number of occasions and left messages on the answer phone to no avail so unfortunately I have not a lot more to say on them at the moment.

Not to be confused with Sunnybrook Cider!

Fowlers Scrumpy Company

Keith Fowler, Fowler's Scrumpy Company EX3 0PE 01822 617333

Cripple Cock is a well know if somewhat embarrassing brand that is seen in a lot of tourist areas. It is not the image that the cider industry is trying to portray of itself at the moment and seems to be beyond the advertising guidelines issued by the NACM which suggest labels etc should not feature drunkenness.

However, that has nothing to do with the reasons I have not followed this one up with more urgency. That is more to do with the fact that a reliable source suggested to me that they do not actually make any cider and that this is another own branding of someone elses cider.

Luscombe Drinks

Luscombe Drinks, Dean Court, Lower Dean, Buckfastleigh, Devon TQ11 0LT, 01364 634036 www.luscombe.co.uk

Luscombe Drinks definitely exist and they do make a very pleasant light cider in very small bottles. Their web site explains that it is made to the highest quality standards and includes apples from old Devon varieties. Having had a bottle to drink on a few occasions I can confirm that it is very pleasant and drinkable.

However, the company is very much more involved with a much wider range of soft drinks and juices. Of 17 products on their web site only one is cider and having talked to them on a number of exhibitions I definitely get the impression that although they like cider they do not really want to be identified as a cider producer.

Their quality products are available widely and many of the soft drinks are very well worth while trying as well as the cider.

Thompstones Cider

Andy Thompstone, Ashburton Devon TQ13 7QZ. 07812 50008 www.thompstonescider.co.uk

I have a feeling this is the prime cider I should have made a bit more effort searching for. It has an excellent website which says all the right things and I should really have made a bit more effort to get to Dartmoor. Still it leaves both you and me something more to be searching out

Sauls Farm Cider

Nigel Kemp, Sauls Farm Cider, Chumleigh, Devon, 01769 580750 **SWECA**

Although listed as a SWECA member producer doesn't seem to have a website of his own and I have yet to meet him. He is listed by quite a few of the Devon websites. He supplies cider, apple juice and honey and his shop is open Monday to Saturday 10.00am - 5.00pm. Apparently they also sell Taw Valley Wines and orchard and vineyard tours are available. I apologise for not having searched him out yet.

Kennford Cider
Kennford Cider, Kennford EX6 7TS 01392 832298

According to a CAMRA site I found, this is apparently a long established cider maker just to the south of Exeter I am afraid I know little more than that. That particular CAMRA site seems to list quite a number of makers who I can confirm don't exist but this one may well.

Summary
There are probably quite a few more makers in Devon. If websites were kept more up to date it would be a lot easier to track them down. However, I really have had great fun searching for cider in Devon and am really delighted about much of what I have found. The prospect of there being more out there is encouraging.

Section 3

Dorset

Young members of the Strong family in the Orchard at Devon Nectar

In search of Dorset Cider

Dorset is a fascinating county, smaller than the others featured in this study, without a motorway and a history of impoverished agricultural labourers. Yet it is the county of Thomas Hardy and much of our picture of a rural past for England is built with the images he created.

In terms of cider Dorset appeared to be totally lost. When I first started searching for cider in the 1980s I think there was only one producer listed in the early guides. That was Tay's Farmhouse Cider on the Crewkerne to Lyme Regis B road. Sitting right on the border with Devon, Tay's farm was on the Dorset side of the road. I called for cider a couple of times and wished I hadn't. It was not well kept. Some people like acetic sour cider but it is not to my taste. I gave it a second chance but it had not improved so I did not really mourn its passing when I noticed it had closed nearly a decade ago now.

However, when I came to look closer I soon became aware of the remnants of a deeper heritage that I am delighted to say is now reawakening in a big way.

The area of Dorset I know best is the western part of the county and in particular the Marshwood Vale. I had spent many hours driving up and down the narrow lanes, into the small villages and hamlets, looking at churches and chapels as I helped my wife research her family history - yes in those days it was an activity not a piece of internet research. I then visited many of the farms when I was a salesman for Dalgety Agriculture. I was aware of an odd reputed place or two selling cider in Whitchurch Canonicorum and orchards around Melplash, Stoke Abbot, Netherbury and further down towards Bridport. Early programmes by Hugh Fearnley Whitingstall in his River Cottage Series featured the local, co-operative 'Cider Clubs' from Chideock and Monkton Wylde or Symondsbury, I think, it was, as a living tradition, the sort TV producers love.

In the north of the county along either side of the A30 there appears to have been a cider tradition. Here the county boundaries of Somerset and Dorset intertwine in a quite anarchic way and you can never be sure which you are in. Nigel Stewart of Bridge Farm Cider at East Chinnock is a fine Somerset cider maker, though he was bought up just the other side of Yeovil at his parents farm at Sandford Orcas, just over the border into Dorset where he still has an orchard. He also sources as many of his apples as he can from the many small traditional orchards in that area on either side of the border. Last autumn, just a few miles further along and down into Dorset, I gave a talk and cider tasting in the village hall at Stourton Caundle, the home of Blue Vinney Cheese. Afterwards I sat in a group of people and found myself talking to Larry Skeats, legendary shepherd, former publican and agricultural collector, author of the book 'A Shepherds Delight.' It was obvious that he and his friends felt that cider was very much part of their rural heritage.

The Isle of Purbeck also has claims to a good cider heritage and further along the coast out into the New Forest in Hampshire there was and is a strong pocket of cider making, as featured so evocatively by the late Jack Hargreaves in his 'Out of Town' TV series, and a tradition carried on today by Barry Topp of New Forest Cider and others.

The heart of the current revival has been in West Dorset. Driving down to Bridport as you pass the Netherbury and Melplash area you are aware of extensive commercial cider orchards. These were mainly planted from the 1970s onwards for contracts with Taunton Cider and the growers were members of the Norton Growers group, named after Norton Fitzwarren where the Taunton Cider factory was located. However, there is no smoke without fire. One of the growers is the inimitable Rupert Best who as part of a busy life runs the superb cider section at the Bath and West Show. Talking to Rupert you discover that his grandfather was the first of the family to harvest and plant cider apples at Hicknowle Farm, Melplash. He too was for many years a cider steward at the Bath and West Show but was also a farmer and cider maker. In the 1950s he teamed up with some of the other small cider makers in the nearby villages of Netherbury and Stoke Abbot and they jointly marketed their cider under the brand of 'Linden Lea' evocatively named after the famous poem by Dorset poet William Barnes. A number of small cider makers carried on in these villages until very recently when old age to them giving up.

However, a local builder, Nick Poole, stumbled into the scene and in ways he could never have imagined has transformed Dorset cider. In 2000 he had rented an old orchard to graze a horse for his wife. The apples were so thick on the ground that he had to pick them up and he looked around for some friends to join him in making cider. Thus was formed the West Milton Cider Club who were lucky enough to obtain use of a shed and with a press made from scaffolding poles and powered by a bottle jack started producing cider.

In 2001 Nick was chairman of the village hall committee in the next door village of Powerstock. He came up with the idea of raising funds by having a cider event. They were given 30 gallons of cider from 7 local makers, mainly from the Chideock Cider Club and with the welcome support of Bridge Farm's Nigel Stewart. Much to their surprise nearly 200 people turned up and £500 had been raised. Under Nick's organisation the Powerstock Cider Festival has continued to grow and now its problem is that it is too popular. They have to restrict it to 30 producers and it is an all ticket event which sells out in advance every year. It has become the hub for Dorset producers. Nick kindly invited me to be a guest in 2011 and I had a marvellous evening meeting a wide variety of producers both local and from further afield. Skreach Cider from Cornwall and Cider Workshop's Ray Blockley from Nottingham amongst them. The standard of cider was mixed and included two of the most acetic, rough ciders I have come across. However, there was a lot that was excellent and in a year when fermentations had been slow over the cold winter there were some beautiful examples with good residual sweetness.

In 2011 the ever resourceful Nick started a competition at the Melplash Agricultural Show. Although local in origin the show has been held a few miles down the road in West Bay, Bridport for very many years. I was honoured along with writer and poet James Crowden, to be asked to judge this inaugural competition. There must have been over 20 producers each entering a dry medium and sweet and James and I spent a most enjoyable morning tasting and comparing. The standard was on the whole high and we were delighted at the end of the blind tasting to discover that the majority of the winners were Dorset producers.

Nick's energies took another direction when he teamed up with former Long Ashton scientist and pomology adviser to the National Cider Makers Association, Liz Copas who lives near Crewkerne. Nick had become interested in the varieties of apples he found in the local orchards and realised that many were different from the usual selection. Together with Liz they got funding from the Chalk and Cheese project and for 3 years ran the DATA project investigating the 'lost' Dorset varieties. I can remember both at Melplash Show and the Bath and West looking with fascination at the reprints of early large scale Ordnance Survey maps of the area from the last quarter of the 19th Century on which they had marked all the local orchards, to many people this was an eye opener in itself.

However, the project has produced much more tangible results. On a very fine Saturday morning in March 2011 I joined a small group of enthusiasts in the field behind Melplash Village Hall for an event orchestrated by Rupert Best and Nick Poole. The highly respected propagator John Worle was down from his Hereford nursery to help plant out a new heritage orchard of Dorset varieties. He had bought with him a big supply of around 200 trees which local people had pre-ordered at a subsidised price to plant out at their own homes and farms to distribute these varieties through out the county. John gave a demonstration on how to plant trees, there were a few short speeches from local dignitaries and we retired to an exhibition and tastings in the village hall. This was followed by an excellent lunch for many of us in the Half Moon public house opposite. The varieties that have been rediscovered and propagated include such evocative names as Golden Ball, King's Favourite and Buttery Door. An excellent booklet on the project has just been produced by Liz Copas in April 2012.

This project has led to the question being asked as to what a Dorset cider would have tasted like. From his studies in local orchards Nick feels that there was once a wider mix of apples than that which remains today. Many of the good bittersweet varieties that could only be used for cider making would have almost certainly been grubbed up in favour of dual purpose cookers and eaters, when land was put into more intensive agricultural use. These general purpose apples tend to produce a thinner more acidic cider which arguably may have been the popular local taste. However there is enough evidence of good bittersweet varieties, to suggest that Dorset cider makers were once looking for that fuller tannined flavour of Somerset. This was especially so in remote unchanged orchards in the west of the county, where the land was of no agricultural use. Here there are still trees from the early part of the 20th century, where obvious moves had been made to introduce new bittersweet varieties like Bulmers Norman, Yarlington Mill and Dabinetts.

Historically cider in Dorset would have probably been predominantly sharper and less tannined, and distinctive from Somerset cider until the introduction of the improved bittersweet varieties.

This same picture of mixed apples for the distinctive features of a county's cider has come across in Cornwall, Devon and now Dorset. Reading old histories it is obvious that a wider choice of apples always had been used and even if we look at the results of early competitions of the Bath and West it is obvious that even in Somerset a lot of the prize winning ciders were made with Kingston Black, a bittersharp.

Could it be that mixed apple cider is the norm, and that the heavy reliance on, and almost monoculture of, bittersweets for commercial ciders that is found across the West Country and especially in Herefordshire, is not what many traditional ciders tasted like. I will have to go back to Liz Copas's Somerset Pomona to investigate more of what can be found in Somerset to see if there was a tradition of more mixed ciders there.

Anyway Dorset cider is now alive and kicking. One of the problems with this search for Dorset cider is that there are now so many new small producers who have only just got underway that I have to second guess which are going to make it. I will feature in the coming pages a few of those I met but, in Dorset in particular, I have a feeling the 'other producers' section will throw up some people worthy of a visit.

Notes from Liz:

I took some more budwood this last year from a second batch of Dorset finds for John Worle to propagate. I don't think that we will have a Rupert launch again, although I am sure that he will fill the gaps in his Linden Lea with the new. We are still finding more, helped by a few enthusiasts who know where to look. Charlie Newman [Square & Compass, Purbeck] has found a couple, as has Russell from Kingcombe who travels the county for work as you used to do.

Up in north Dorset the picture is rather different, many more bittersweets and quite a few bittersharps. Just rereading Hardy's Woodlanders I have come cross several references to 'bittersweets' as opposed to 'John Apples' which I presume to be dual purpose apples, so I am convinced that in Hardy Country, Blackmore Vale, Dorset cider had a more tannic pungency to it, more like the taste of cider over the border in south east Somerset. Well the borders do wander a bit in that part of the world. Cadbury, Sutton Montis, Yarlington, even Wincanton are some of the best bits of ciderland from where many a prize winning batch of fruit came to the Cider Institute in the early 1900s.

This last season, autumn 2011, I took Nick off to meet an apple enthusiast from Shaftesbury, one of those who spends every journey looking over hedges for trees. David took us down the lanes around the town, Stour Row [Bo Rutter's cider territory] and up to the north of Gillingham. Just the remnants of orchards were left but amongst them, a few well know vintage varieties; Fillbarrel, Cadbury, Cap of Liberty, Lambrook Pippin.
Marnhull proved to be a rich area, many I couldn't put a name to, but plenty of tannin.
I have found Cadburys in several central areas from the Vale down to Maiden Newton, an excellent, seemingly long-lived variety.

I am busy putting together our finds in a little booklet, don't know what to title it yet. But here are the varieties, old, new and newly named.
Sharp Apples
Buttery Dore, Stubbard, **Moens Farm Tangy,** *Golden Ball, Sour Cadbury, Ironsides, Moonsshines,* **Dashayes Crab** *and* **Marnhull Mill** *[The ones in bold are unidentified and have been given new names], Kings Favourite, Fair Maid of Devon, Tom Putt, and Blenheim Orange.*

Sweets
Sweet Blenheim, Woodbine, Slack-ma-Girdle, Northwood, Tom Legg, Bell, **Hains Late Sweet**, *Sweet Coppin and Sweet Alford*

Bittersharps
Warrior, Cap of Liberty, Lambrook Pippin, **Marnhull Bitters**, *Dorset Long Stem,*

Bittersweets,
Winter Stubbard, Golden Bittersweet, **Marlpits Late**, **Meadow Cottage, Golly**

Knapp, Loders, Charlie's Seedling, *Fillbarrel, Dashayes Red [tannin 0.97g/l!] and Cadbury*

This all took some detective work! But as you can see, there are plenty of bitter-sweets. This all leads me to think that West Dorset taste was once much like that of Devon, more acidic, and further east into the county, the taste was more like that favoured in Somerset, restrained bittersweet.

A commercial Dorset orchard

Rupert Best, Hincknowle, Melplash **SWECA**

I wanted to find out how a real professional cider apple grower ran a cider orchard so I got in touch with Rupert Best who not only organises the excellent Cider Tent at the Bath and West Show but also has commercial orchards at Hincknowle near Melplash in Dorset. I went to visit him on the 8th of November 2010 - his second last day of collecting for the season when after an open season the winds and rains had arrived with a vengeance leaving everything feeling muddy and autumnal.

Finding him was the first task. I suspected as much when multimap had its little red marker in the middle of a considerable white patch with no lanes marked anywhere.

I decided to look for the nearest lane slightly to the south. First time I missed the turning off the Beaminster - Bridport road but found it when I doubled back. I drove along this narrow winding lane for a considerable distance - most of the time looking for somewhere to turn around as I realised I had gone too far. I found a farm track which appeared to take me in the right direction which went up the side of an orchard - promising. But after another field and the track deteriorating I thought I had gone far enough so I turned around. I discovered later I was within about 100 yards of my target and there was a way through.

My luck now changed as back in the lane I had to pull into a gateway to let a small tractor pulling a sort of trailer with apples in the back. I asked directions. I had to go back to the Melplash and turn right opposite the pub and right into the farm after 100 yards. Great. I am not sure that my interpretation of 100 yards would quite agree with Peter's, as I later discovered the tractor drivers name was, nor could I find a farm. However, I eventually located an unlabeled driveway heading in the right direction and halfway down discovered a lorry blocking my way.

The lorry was backed under an ingenious gantry and there, just making sure he could totally fill the lorry from above with apples was Rupert, wearing shorts as befits his former nautical status.

The Bests have been at Hincknowle since the 1930s and cider apples have always been grown on the farm. However, it was in the early 1970s when Rupert's father started to make it one of the key commercial crops when, encouraged by Taunton Cider, they planted their first early bush orchard. They now produce around 900 tonnes of cider apples a year from 45 acres of bush orchard and there is another 10 acres of traditional standard orchard. That is enough apples for well over half a million litres of cider.

The two main bush orchards were planted in 1972 and in the 1990s. It was thought that bush orchards only had a short life however the 1970s orchard is going still going strong. More attention to agronomy over the past few years and better use of fertilisers has pushed the yield back up to 15 tonnes an acre whilst the 1990s orchard is producing an amazing 25 tonnes an acre.

The varieties are all familiar cider varieties. In the early bush orchard there are four varieties planted in alternate rows, Dabinett, Yarlington Mill, Michelin and Chisel Jersey. Rupert suggest the Jersey is slightly too late, but this is what they are harvesting now at the end. In the 1990s orchard half the trees are Dabinet and the rest are slightly earlier varieties Fiona and Major. They have another smaller orchard with Kingston Black along with some other varieties and have recently planted more Kingston Black as they can get a considerable premium for these apples.

Rupert Best and Chris Vye at the end of the harvest

The harvesting season lasts for eight or nine weeks, though this year they had a week or so in the middle between the early and later varieties being ready. They send away around 130 tonnes each week. Most of Rupert's workforce is seasonal apart from Chris Vye who is manager and really runs the show. He has been working for the family for many years. There is also Ben, who is just about to retire, well, he is well into his 80s but seemed to be enjoying himself raking up apples in the orchard. At this late stage of the season two of the casuals have finished but there is a Polish lady in her 60s helping Ben with the raking. As mentioned earlier Peter, a local farmer, fits in work driving a tractor in season.

Compared to my back-breaking efforts to pick up apples there is an impressive selection of machinery being utilized. Rupert has worked closely with Somerset Fruit Machinery of Martock and much of his kit is their early prototype models. Still it seems to do its job very well.

They have the right kit to shake the trees properly. A tractor comes along with a grab on the side which clamps on the tree and mechanically shakes it. I still find it hard to believe that they can do four trees a minute and do it so there is hardly an apple left on the tree.

After that a tractor with a big blower comes down and blows the apples in to a row and the team comes along to rake any apples that have missed into the row. Then another machine picks up the apples and lifts them into trailers which are then driven off to the loading bay were they can be dropped into lorries waiting below.

When I think of the effort we had to put into picking up our two tonnes it nearly wants to make me cry. Although the process may sound industrial it doesn't feel it. Like most agriculture it is dealing with natural product outside in the countryside largely dependent on the weather and the vagaries of nature. I can think of a lot worse ways of making a living.

Rupert's apples go to some of the leading cider manufacturers in the region. 50% is still under contract to Gaymers. He also sells to Thatchers and Sheppys whilst Burrow Hill buys most of his Kingston Black, other producers such as Cornish Orchards, have an odd load and this year a load even went to a vineyard / cidermaker in Wiltshire once he had found the right size lorry to fit under the gantry.

The price of cider apples has slowly risen to the nearly acceptable. In 1983 they were getting £123 per tonne before it crashed down to £78 and remained at around the low £80s for most of the 1990s. His usual price is now approaching the £110 mark as long as they are clean and without stones. Dabinet fetches a 10% premium as it is probably the most popular apple for general cider making whilst the considerable premium for Kingston Black has to be set against the fact that it is a relatively low yielding variety.

Rupert's 10 acres of standard orchard are a bit of a financial non-entity. He makes a bit of cider himself from a thick juiced variety called Reinette de Brue but he is not currently making commercialy. Rupert's father used to make some cider commercially, Rupert can remember when there were 12 traditional farm cider makers locally and in the adjoining parish of Netherbury. The last of these died last year. They used to do some joint marketing under the name of Linden Lea Cider; a name taken from a popular poem by the Dorset poet William Barnes.

He did try to turn his standard orchard into organic but found that there was a negative premium for the apples! Plus the soil association, never easy to work with, started to raise questions about the feed used in the pheasant pens.

Orchards large and small are a wonderful part of our landscape and heritage in the South West. However, it is vital to recognise that they are very mortal. Even standard orchards are unlikely to last much longer that the life of a man - and without constant care that time is likely to be much shorter. Many of the older traditional orchards we see today were planted in the 1950s and the oldest probably in the 1930s. If we want traditional orchards to be a continuing part of our lives we have to ensure we look after those we have and encourage planting for the future. It is good that there are a number of initiatives under way.

Dorset Nectar

Oliver and Penny Strong, Strong Orchard, Pineapple Lane, Waytown, Bridport DT6 5HZ 07515 806546

I first tasted Dorset Nectar at the Powerstock Cider Festival in 2011 and I immediately though that it was aptly named. It was an excellent fruity cider with a good level of residual sweetness. Later in the summer when I, along with James Crowden, was judging the ciders at the Melplash Show we gave it a couple of firsts in blind tasting. This is a serious, quality cider and I was very much looking forward to my visit.

I found it down some very narrow lanes at the southern end of the Marshwood Vale.

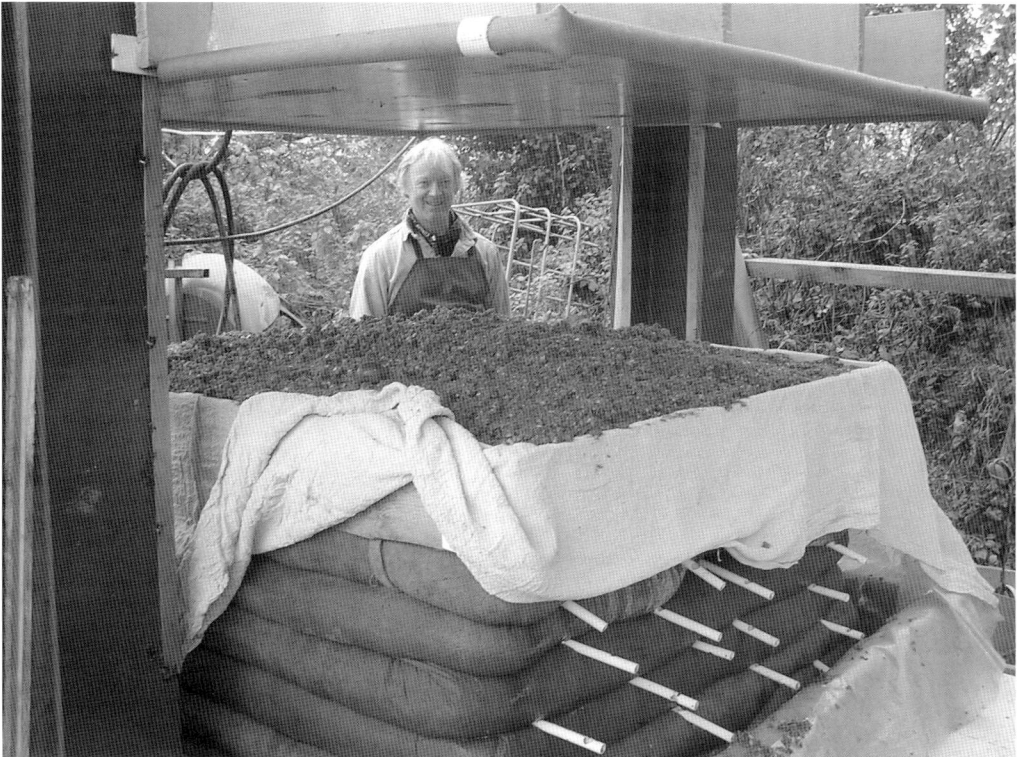

Oliver Strong ready to press on their massive home-made beast - Thunderbird

107

I was just despairing when I came across a colourfully painted gate behind which was a fantastic looking mature bush cider orchard. I could not at first see their temporary bungalow, tucked away in the top corner, though I could see the buildings where cider was being made surrounded by the winter of 2012 sea of mud.

Oliver and Penny although of English descent still have South African accents which they have not lost in 25 years of globetrotting. Much of that time was spent in America where they were into topiary and growing plant sculptures through aluminium structures made by Oliver. However seven years ago they moved to Dorset to their orchard paradise. They have five children aged between 7 and 21 and eldest son Dante is very much an essential part of their development as cider makers. He won a 'Golden Spanner' award and a 'Welder of the Year' award from college for his welding skills which he used to build their most impressive beast of a press with two 50 tonne hydraulic jacks. Being practical engineers is a trait I have spotted in many cider makers.

The 14 acre orchard was originally under contract to supply Gaymers and has sophisticated equipment for loading lorries. However when they wanted to start some cider making of their own they enquired as to whether they could split the apples between themselves and Gaymers but Gaymers wanted all or nothing. This provides rather more apples than they can currently cope with and they have sold some to other cider makers like Rose Grant. I am sure it is the blend of apples in the orchard that contributes to the quality of the cider; it seems to contain a richer variety and better seasonal spread than many commercial orchards I have come across. It includes Taylors, Tremletts Bitter and Nehou as earlies; Harry Masters Jersey, Sweet Coppin, Yarlington Mill, Browns and Coates Jersey as mid seasons and Dabinet, Chesel Jersey and Porters Perfection as late season. I note a number of sweets and sharps in the selection. They have also started to plant out some new trees mixing some desert apples, for juice, and some traditional Dorset varieties.

They have had a relatively steep learning curve in cider making, equipping themselves gradually as they go. They say that Andrew Lea's book on cider making has been a major inspiration and that they have picked up other skills from producers such as Rose Grant. They know they have made some mistakes along the way but are learning from them. I particularly liked their 'green' approach. The orchard has now achieved an organic certification though their current cider is not covered by this. I asked how they intended to feed the ground and they are starting to paddock graze both some Kune Kune pigs - which allegedly live off grass - and poultry giving them eggs as another product to sell. They are looking to bring in more bees both to help pollination and give them honey products - their logo is a bee, linking back to the Dorset Nectar name. An interesting extra is that they are currently following a policy of allowing all apples to naturally drop off the trees before harvesting - on the very logical reasoning that this is when the apples are ripe and the starches have been turned to sugars.

In 2010 they made 19,000 litres and this past winter reckon to have made around 36,000 litres which is quite impressive and currently well outstrips their sales. Penny comments that they are finding the marketing side of their cider quite hard work in a market place where there are plenty of competitors. They sell through a mixture of stalls at farmers markets, restaurants, deli's and a couple of pubs most sales coming in the summer. Where it is being sold in bulk they have switched from 5 gallon plastic barrels to bag in boxes to ensure air doesn't get in to spoil their cider. They also supply some food festivals, notably a seafood festival in Weymouth. They seem to be still mainly bottling and labelling by hand which is an area they may need to sort out to get into the 500ml bottled market in a larger way - the cider would well justify this.

Their range includes a dry, medium and sweet and a Dabinet single variety which is very good. They try to only sweeten the sweet as they are usually able to find medium with some residual sweetness depending on the time of the season. Their son Dante has also been experimenting with an elderberry 'cider'. In a separate shed they are developing live enzyme vinegars and are also looking at different flavoured vinegars. And of course they make apple juice so there is something for all on their market stalls.

I liked the Strongs and the ideas and ideals behind their cider. I loved their orchard and their ciders. I certainly hope that they can manage to identify more markets to sell into - it is a cider that deserves a bigger audience.

Kingcombe Valley Cider

Russell Croker, Kingcombe Valley Farm, Dorset. 01300 321079

I first met Russell's brother Paul a number of years ago when I was working for Dalgety Agriculture at Chard. They farm in that wild and largely deserted tract of country in the hills off the Crewkerne to Dorchester road. Given the huge tourist influence only a few miles to the south, it is amazing when you come inland what a forgotten part of the country Dorset is with its hills and vales. It is full of narrow lanes on which you can drive for miles meeting nothing but tractors.

I met Russell at a SWECA meeting and then met with both him and Paul down at the Powerstock Cider Festival last year which is very local for them. Russell makes about 1,000 gallons of a straightforward bittersweet cider and they have also tried a few single varieties including Morgan Sweet. At the moment most of their apples come from a former Taunton Cider orchard at Rimpton near Yeovil but Russell has now planted out 80 trees of their own which he reckons will thrive in their south facing valley. An old farmer next door used to make a considerable amount of cider so there is a heritage in the area. Some more apples come from a relative of his wife at Shave Cross down in the Marshwood Vale, another very rural but different Dorset landscape. His new orchard includes many of the standard bittersweets and 12 of the varieties from the project to revive Dorset apples. The only problem is he does not seem to have written down which varieties he received and planted out!

Russell built a press around a pair of twin screws he had heard about. They salvaged them from a former cider barn which burnt down 50 years ago in the nearby hamlet of Loscombe. Apparently they had to dig them out of a bank. They combined these with a large beam of oak and built a concrete base. After pressing they ferment their juice in plastic and then mature in former red wine barrels.

Kingcombe Valley Cider is only sold wholesale, Russell works full time for a company supplying agricultural buildings so the cider is very much a hobby and farm gate sales are not possible. It is available in local pubs, food festivals, and events such as 'Maiden Newton at War' a big World War II reconstruction gathering. It is currently only available draught. Producers like Russell are perhaps as close as you come to a true revival of the traditional farm house cider makers who were relatively numerous in the country until about 30 or 40 years ago.

Lulworth Skipper (Dorset Cider)

Martin Inwood, Lulworth Skipper (Dorset Cider), Culeaze, Wareham Dorset, BH20 7NR. 01929 471853 www.lulworth-skipper.com

This morning I made a really stupid decision. I had taken the week off work to try to finish writing this book. After 12 months I had to take the decision to do a telephone interview with some of the producers who I already knew reasonably well but I had not managed to visit - a relatively small number. Martin made me feel very guilty as he said how much he would have liked me to visit to sample some of his ciders which he is very pleased with. My mouth was watering and I almost put the phone down and said I was on my way even though it is probably over a 100 mile round trip. Instead I have been stuck either on this computer or on the phone thinking non-stop about those samples I could have been tasting. It has been a hot sunny day and my mouth has been getting drier and drier - we all make some stupid decisions in life and this would seem to have been one of them.

The thing is Martin really is a good cider maker. I blind judged the ciders at the Melplash Show with James Crowden last year and we gave his dry cider a first. I

The rusty screws...

have also bought a few bottles of his Lulworth Skipper cider over the past year or so and it really is rather good. He is a nice chap as well and I have met him at a couple of SWECA meetings and out and about - even if he is an Independent Financial Adviser it hasn't stopped him developing some good cider making skills! I really will have to make an effort to visit him sometime over the summer. I think he must enjoy giving cider to appreciative audiences as he was telling me that he has a landlord coming around for a sampling - an excellent way of gaining another outlet I should think!

Although now very much a Dorset cider maker Martin originally comes from Mary Tavy, South Devon. His first experiences of cider were the classic helping with the haymaking and he can remember helping to build the cheeses on a big old press belonging to a nearby farmer. In fact even when he started cider making about 6 years ago he was still taking the apples back down to Devon to press. He had been making cider on an amateur basis for many years, along with beer and wine - anything you can drink. When he moved to Dorset there was a big orchard just down the drive from his cottage. He thought he would make some cider. It was okay but nothing special despite being matured in oak. He met up with Rose Grant, his nearest cider making neighbour, and she has been a great help to him with advice and making sure he has trod the right road. The first advice was to find some proper cider apples - the original orchard was mainly dessert apples. He now sources apples from a cider orchard not far up the road which had been planted in 1965 and another orchard at Sturminster Newton.

...and the press he made with them

He makes around 7,000 litres a year to stay within the threshold and although he is considering going beyond has reservations. He does everything himself whilst keeping the day job going as well. Fortunately his work is based from home and so he is able to strike a balance by rising early to load the press, leaving it to run whilst he attends to his office.

He built his impressive press himself around a pair of old twin screws he had bought. There is an excellent photo sequence of this on his website. He calls his cider Lulworth Skipper after the very rare butterfly which is found in the county. He wanted to combine his love for nature with something which was iconic to Dorset. It makes a very attractive label for his 75cl wine bottles. He finds this size works best for him as it is the right shape and price for the many tourists to the area to take home with them as gifts. He also supplies bag in box to various local pubs. Martin believes in a totally natural cider so it is all dry to medium. He will only very reluctantly add a touch of sweetener if someone is specifically asking for a differentiated medium from dry. The cider of his I have drunk is naturally on that cusp between medium and dry. I remember at Melplash I had to check with a hydrometer to ensure that his dry was genuinely a dry. His cider is 100% juice, fermented in plastic IBC's and then matured in oak. He does all the bottling himself. An engineering neighbour has helped him build a double head vacuum bottler from readily available parts at a fraction of the cost of bought equipment.

Definitely a cider to look out for.

Mill House Cider Museum

Penny Whatmoor, Mill House Cider Museum, Overmoigne, Dorchester 01305 852220 www.millhousecider.com

This is one of very few actual tourist attractions for cider in the region, let alone Dorset. Penny's father built up this wonderful collection of old cider presses and equipment when no one else was interested in it. For a very moderate entry fee you can go and browse around and watch a video on cider making done on some of the museums equipment. There are 50 odd largely timber presses of all shapes and sizes. It is a shame that so much of the timber gets exposed to elements and is in danger of decay.

In the autum they sometimes run cider making demonstrations and make a small amount of their own cider - though I suggest ringing to find out details, the website does not look fully up to date.

There is also a separate small museum of clocks and the main part of the business is obviously the nursery. When I visited in spring it was full of bedding plants and I bought some sweet pea plants to grow on. Penny was working in one of the green-

houses of the nursery - cheerful and smiling as ever - with a robin perched beside her. Later that evening she came to the Powerstock Cider Festival on back of her fiancés moterbike with some of the cider made during the demonstrations last autumn. Unfortunately I forgot to taste it!

There is an attractive little shop selling interesting range of bottled ciders and also some from further afield. Penny says she wants to give people a variety of tastes - not just local. The draught cider was Julian Temperley's from Burrow Hill in Somerset.

Marshwood Vale Cider

Tim Beer, Marshwood Vale Cider, Telephone Cottage, Mutton Street near Marshwood, Dorset DT6 6HP www.marshwoodvalecider.co.uk **SWECA tbc**

It was on the Cider Workshop online forum that I first came across Tim. I was starting to put together my searches for Dorset Cider and was intrigued to come across a reference to Marshwood Vale, a part of the country I know well. Online Tim comes across very much as the traditionalist with a slight scepticism of bureaucracy and as someone only willing to go so far in adopting modern practices. This was exactly what I found - an embodiment of the rustic ethos.

Tim was exactly right for this part. In his 50s, shortish, rustic hat and jacket, beard, glasses and a rich rural accent. He said he had been making cider on and off for nearly 30 years - very similar to me in fact - but had really got back into it in the last few years. I never really got to the bottom of what he did for his main job - the noble profession of a 'bitofthisandthat' to earn a crust. But he was certainly full of enthusiasm for his cider.

I first met Tim at the Andy Jarvis's yard in Stockland, Devon whom who I have not yet had the pleasure of meeting. From the equipment strewn around and the press cuttings on the walls Andy is obviously a vintage rural machinery enthusiast with a leaning towards woodcraft, saw-benches - and cider. Tim started the generator and took me into the back of the barn where there was a delightful cider shed. Wooden barrels along two walls, a belt driven scratter and a large traditional wooden press. Possibly the nicest traditional farm cider set up I have seen in all my travels. A cat or two were wandering around which Tim pointed out as the only efficient way of rodent control they had come up with. Andy and his mates make their cider in the traditional way. I understand nine of them made or had made for them cider last winter, a gang from 4 or 5 to a dozen get together of an evening and it takes an hour

and a quarter to build a cheese using straw to tie in the layers. They leave it overnight and press it the next evening. The juice goes straight into the wooden barrels - filled to overflowing - and is left to ferment. Even when I visited in January 2011 there was still plenty of froth coming out of a bunghole. The cider shed tradition is one that is alive and well in Dorset, Somerset and here in Devon. When I wrote my book on Somerset producers I was accused of not knowing what I was on about as I had left out some major producers. I had to point out that as it was a guide to cider that you can buy I could hardly identify unregistered cider makers. In fact, as it was I ended up inadvertently featuring a couple of these.

Tim has plenty of tales about the old cider sheds all over Somerset. During the late 1970s he worked on Somerset County Council road mending gangs. The whole gang drank copious amounts of cider, including the foreman and they visited he says 'literally 100's of cider sheds'. When the weather rained off work they would sit in the caravan playing cards and drinking cider, on occasion even having to send the lorry back to the depot to collect more.

That winter Tim had had his apples crushed at Andy Jarvis's yard at Stockland, Devon and then last winter he had Hecks crush his apples in Street, Somerset. He takes the juice back to his small cottage in Mutton Street, nr Marshwood, Dorset where it is fermented out. I visited Tim there during the late winter of 2012 when he was recovering from a particularly nasty spell of gout which has afflicted him on and off all his life. He is hoping to rearrange his small garden so he can erect enough sheds so he can move the whole process into the sheds and he is looking to set up a number of vintage presses which he has in bits in his garden.

Tim says his apples come from Dorset, Somerset and Devon, he gets them where he can. Tim is currently having a go at grafting some cider apple trees so he can raise some interesting varieties for his own use and possible sale. He has come across two previously unnamed varieties of which he has high hopes.

Tim has had huge help in learning his cider making from the Heck's brothers in Street. His first efforts were with juice he bought from them and he says that the only reason his cider is any good is because of the advice they have freely given. This is a sentiment I can honestly endorse, they are an exceptional cider making family.

Over the past year or so I have had a number of Tim's ciders to drink, they are always full bodied tannin rich traditional ciders. As he makes a point of, every barrel is different and he is always experimenting with single varieties and different provenance barrels. When I visited he showed me a 100 year old Scottish whisky barrel. Tim has also taken great efforts to find outlets for his ciders in the local pubs and farm shops. He has found himself often held back by the places wanting to stock something sweeter or weaker which is rather against his cider philosophy. However, as he needs to earn his crust he is trying to see what he can do whilst upholding his own principles which has led to some heated exchanges in the online cider forums where he feels justly annoyed with criticism from people who don't really understand his philosophy.

Tim hopes to be out and about selling at some at local events around the three counties borders (Devon, Somerset and Dorset) in the summer. He also has a good website to check out for the latest news. I sincerely wish him luck. Keeping the rustic ethos alive has to be a crucial part of our celebration of the cider heritage.

Purbeck Cider Company

Joe Hartle, The Purbeck Cider Company, Lower Scoles Farm, Kingston, Wareham, Dorset, BH205LG www.purbeckcidercompany.co.uk
Tel/Fax 01929 480090 **SWECA tbc**

Joe Hartle is an enthusiastic young chap. He grew up on a Dorset dairy farm which decided that dairying was not the way forward. His parents diversified into Ice

Cream and founded the well-known Purbeck Ice Cream Company which makes some delicious and innovative flavoured ice creams and sorbets. Joe returned from travels in New Zealand and decided that cider was the way forward for him. He still farms a flock of 300 sheep but now two fields have been planted out as cider orchards whilst he shares some of the farm buildings with Purbeck Ice Cream.

He started in 2006 with some of the initial run being made into a delicious cider sorbet by Purbeck Ice Cream. It is interesting that none of the ice cream makers I know really seem to have managed to use the cider flavour to any great commercial extent, even though I know a few who have experimented - even with cider brandy. I used to love cider flavoured ice lollies as a child - perhaps it was that that started my cider interests.

Joe started cider making with apples from Somerset orchards near Yeovil and Castle Cary however, he is now keen on making sure he uses Dorset sourced apples. The first orchard he planted was with traditional Dorset varieties from the Symondsbury project. His own orchards are slowly providing fruit though as he increases his output, he is still buying in most of his apples.

His main cider is a dry variety he calls 'Joe's Cider' and sells both draught and bottled. He also produces a sweet version and a single variety Dabinet. This year he is looking to increase his production as he has very high hopes for a new mildly sparkling product, 'Dorset Draft', which again will be bottled as well as draught. He has investigated the name as there was concern about using 'draught' for a bottled product but according to the dictionary there is a usage of the word 'draft' which just means a 'serving of a beverage' so he should be covered.

Although I had previously sampled his product I only met Joe a couple of weeks ago at a South West England Cider Makers Association meeting, the first he has attended. I have not had time to visit Purbeck yet but wanted to make sure I included him in the book. He has a Voran hydraulic press and mill which you can see a clip of in cartoon form on his website www.purbeckcidercompany.co.uk I must admit that this is a bit different to most of the cider websites you come across but original and effective. He says it needs a lot of updating but I certainly hope it doesn't lose its quirky originality.

Joe also makes a range of 'Jurassic Juice' - and didn't quite seem to understand the joke when I asked if this was crushed rocks. It is of course his brand for Dorset apple juice and he usually tries to get a Cox and Bramley blend of apples. Joe mainly does his own bottling of juice and cider but is at the stage where he really needs to consider moving forward and perhaps investing in some less labour intensive systems.

Just a word of warning - be careful not to muddle Joe's Cider with 'Old Joe's Country Cider' which you sometimes see around at shows etc. Although this appears an authentic craft operation it is an outfit selling rather industrially produced cider from a cider making factory.

Joe sells most of his Purbeck ciders locally where there is a strong market from tourists in the summer or in pubs and shops around Dorset just stretching into the west of Hampshire in the Southampton area and up into south Wiltshire.

Roger's Cider / Twinways Cider Company

Mark Rogers, Melplash, Dorset 01308 488367

I went to visit Mark on the 17th February. When I phoned he had said that it would be a very convenient time as he was certain to be around as they had recently had a baby. I had not realised quite how recently until I saw Freya, his wife, nursing their Valentine's Day born daughter!

I had first met Mark and Freya, about a year previously at the Powerstock Cider Festival and I had met them again at the Dorset Show and one or two other odd places since then. They both have engaging smiles which ensures a friendly welcome. Mark with his mop of fair hair and wild sideburns an interesting match with slim red haired Freya.

They had had a hectic year with Mark reorganising his business away from his father's farm near to Dorchester to the delightful thatched cottage they are renting on a farm in Melplash where the owners are restoring the farm to traditional standards. It was obvious talking to Mark that he has a deep understanding of agricultural history which he says comes from a passion for vernacular architecture. He is currently doing some hedge laying for his landlord.

100 yards across the road is the five acre Twinway's orchard which Mark has been renting from a different landlord for the past few years. This is a gem. Almost adjoining Rupert Best's Hinknowle Orchards and just down the road from the Strong's these are some of the best commercial orchards I have seen. Well maintained mature bush orchards originally planted by Taunton Cider they are said to be on the same soil strata as some of the best South Somerset orchards and the fruit produces some wonderful cider. The apple varieties may be a bit predictable; Dabinet, Michelin, Chesil Jersey, Yarlington Mill and fortunately Brown's Apple a sharp to mix with the standard bittersweets. His five acres two years ago produced nearly 100 tonnes of apples. Last year was a biennial off year but he still harvested

nearly 60 tonnes. As well as making his own cider he also juices about 4,000 litres and sells a fair few apples to other cider makers as well. Last year they went as far afield as Leicestershire and Wales.

He started making cider almost by accident. He was working picking up apples and a silage trailer full of apples got delayed for some reason so he decided he might as well make cider with them - about 5,500 litres of it! A year of so later during a very muddy autumn he was helping tow stands into the Dorset Show. One of the stands he towed in was Piddle Brewery. He got talking to them and found they were thinking of making some cider themselves - he suggested they try some of his and took some in for them to taste - he is still supplying them now. He established a similar link with Dorset Brewing Company and along with one beer wholesaler the three customers take the majority of his production. He is now up to the threshold limit of 7,000 litres per annum and expects to take the big step of breaking through that in the next couple of years.

When he sells directly himself for local events, festivals and bars he calls it 'Roger's Cider', basically as he was too busy to think up another name. Last winter he moved his press and production to former stables on the edge of his orchard. He is hoping to get planning permission to extend this and incorporate a Cider Shed into it which could be open for events and education. His large traditional twin screw press is certainly quite impressive and holds a big cheese. He makes three basic ciders; a sweet, 'Farmers Reward', a medium 'Furze Cutters Distraction', and a dry 'Hedge Layer'.

All three taste clean and fruity as befits the quality of the fruit going into them and each has a distinctively different blend of apples. Interestingly he sweetens by blending back in the apple juice which he pasteurises after pressing. He tries to match the blend of juice with the blend of apples in the cider. He is also experimenting with a bottle conditioned cider made by a hybrid method of his own which he describes as 'fanglais'. It all certainly seemed to taste very pleasant.

Cider is one third of his business as he has two other strings to his bow. The second is honey and he manages a large number of hives producing some specialist varieties of honey as long as he can find the right locations to place the hives. The third string to his bow is 'Filberts' who sell beeswax products, candles, cosmetics etc. I came across him on this side of his business on a trade stand at a tourist business orientated trade show near Exeter in January. If you add to this that he does three farmers markets a week in Dorchester, Swanage and seasonally in Wareham selling cheese for a local cheese maker you can see that Mark is an incredibly busy person.

Hopefully 2012 will not have quite as much turmoil and change as 2011 and Mark can continue to develop his cider business in harmony with his new family!

Cider by Rosie

Rose Grant, Winterbourne Houghton, nr Blandford Forum DT11 0PE 01258 880543 www.ciderbyrosie.com www.ciderbyrosie.co.uk *SWECA*

I think it is fair to say that Rose Grant is not one of your run of the mill cider makers. For a start she wins a lot more competitions than most - from my tastings her cider always seems good and is often excellent. When I was honoured to judge the farmhouse cider classes at the Bath and West with John Perry, a blind tasting, we were delighted to find we had selected hers as the winner - for the second year running. It is unusual for a cider maker to be a greyhaired lady in their 70s with a grip of steel handshake.

I had met her before on a number of occasions at shows and at SWECA meetings but this was the first time I had sought her out at her attractive cottage home in the delightful Winterbourne Houghton right in the geographical heart of Dorset. She had spent the first half of her career in the RAF where she rose through the ranks as an electronic engineer.

In her late 30s she left the service and moved to Dorset and after a few years pooled resources with her sister in law and family to buy her cottage, now 30 years ago, whilst carrying on her career as an engineer for a manufacturer of optoelectronic devices in Dorchester.

She also had a bit of a hankering after 'good life' style hobby farming and bought two acres where she had pigs and a jersey cow and planted her first half a dozen apple trees. Ten years ago for the Queen's Golden Jubillee she was looking to organise a fund raising village event and as someone else had bagged the open garden idea - gardening and semi-tropical plants is another of her interests - so she organised a cider and cheese event instead, with some of the cider she had made. Such was the positive response to her cider that she was encouraged to make a lot more. She went to her favourite pub, the amazing Square and Compass at Worth Matravers, and the landlord Charlie wanted to stock her cider and so the business grew.

She has a very well set-up cider house adjacent to her cottage with a large French hydraulic press which dates from the 1920s. It had previously been used by Vernon Bland, a well known former Gloucestershire cider maker. It wasn't quite what she had been looking for but she quickly realised how lucky she had been to get it. She has a set of three stainless steel tanks each holding about a pressing of 400 litres at a time. She then ferments in 1,000 litre IBCs and when fermentation is finished blends all her cider into a big plastic agricultural storage tank which holds 6,000 litres, the blending of the whole season being important to get the properties of both the early and later apples together. She only makes a straight dry but will reluctantly add some sucralose where commercial needs must.

Most of her cider is sold into pubs, especially the Square and Compass, but of course the margin on this wholesale trade is not very great. To try to add value to her produce she has started bottling in 500ml bottles and these seem to be going well. However, it is all extra work as she is carrying out the entire operation herself.

She also makes a keeved champagne style cider which tasted very nice and she can see herself trying to specialise in this as age forces her to take it slightly easier!

Being slightly out of condition myself I struggled to keep up as she led me up the public right of way across two fields which conveniently directly connect her cottage with her orchard. She found that with the presence of badgers it became impossible to practically keep livestock and over the years has gradually planted out the full two acres as orchard. She now gets a couple of tonnes of apples a year from this orchard and also buys some from the orchards of Oliver Strong. There is a rich variety of apples, pears and walnuts in her orchard. Mainly cider varieties but also some cookers and desserts with an emphasis on older varieties. One of her favourite apples is Ashmeads Kernel and she makes juice with this and has even tried a single variety cider. In the bottom of the orchard is a nursery bed where she has temporarily planted the Dorset Heritage varieties she got last year as part of the Nick Poole / Liz Copas project. She is hoping to plant these out as part of a community orchard in the village - after all she says, she can't guarantee she will be around in 10 years. I know what she means but as she strides ahead of me I can't help thinking that she probably will be.

Rose has also been a huge help and example to many fledgling cider makers. Locally in Dorset she has been a big practical help and advisor to many of the new cider makers who have been starting up in recent years. She has also become famous nationally and internationally for her blog, first on UKcider and then on Cider Workshop which still remains a valuable source of information for aspiring cider makers. She says that with bottling and travel etc she has found it difficult to keep the blog up over the past couple of years - and that also she has said all that she can say. Not sure about that - good common sense is often a valuable asset in online communities!

Anyway it is well worth searching out Rose's cider in either the local pubs or those on the Isle of Purbeck where she seems to sell most. She is one of the characters of the cider scene, her energy is an example to us all and she makes a quality Dorset cider.

Twisted Cider

Ben Weller, Sherborne, Dorset 07841 841289 www.twistedcider.com **SWECA**

Young Ben Weller was nearly missed from this guide as I didn't realise he was making his own cider. His colourful apple peel logo is quite a common sight in the internet and on his sign-painted van. He is mainly known as a 'modern' wholesaler, sourcing innovative cider products from around the country and even internationally from Thistly Cross in Scotland and selling them mainly into the Bath and London markets.

Although I quite like the modern and innovative ciders he is looking to source, there is no doubt that some of the terminology on his website is enough to make a cider enthusiast like myself seriously blanch. The phrases 'Apple Cider' - a tautology, and 'Perry Cider', an absolute nonsense, are not likely to cut ice with me. But the fact that he is willing to look at innovative fruit ciders is good as long as they are genuine high quality high juice products made with traditional ingredients in the traditional way. If there is a market out there for this sort of product I feel it is slightly silly for cider purists to ignore it - they should be putting their effort into ensuring traditional craft standards are maintained.

Talking to him it seems that the business is not growing as fast as he would like at the moment. The naturally squeezed margins as a wholesaler make returns slow and he is now looking to considerably expand his own cider making activities. He has been making cider for around five seasons now but only for the past two in commercial quantities. He is based in Dorset near Sherborne and there is a small orchard on his home farm and he is sourcing other apples from local Dorset orchards. Last year he made around 3,000 litres on his home-made press.

He is looking to make a considerable expansion for the 2012 season and is actively trying to source about 50 tonne of cider apples. Currently his own cider is   usually only available at occasional events but that is something he is looking to change.

The Square and Compass

Worth Matravers, Swanage, BH19 3LF. www.squareandcompasspub.co.uk

Let alone being one of the CAMRA's best cider pubs in the country this is just one of the best pubs full stop. Its location sets it apart for a start. Up narrow lanes on the 'Isle' of Purbeck you park in the public car park and walk down into the little hamlet. Right in the centre with panoramic views out over the sea you will find the Square and Compass. If the weather is at all reasonable the stone hewn patio with numerous rough benches will already be full. Patio is perhaps not quite the word to describe this area of uneven hard standing which seems to have grown out of the local rock. The pub has been run by the succeeding generations of the Newman family for over 100 years. One suspects it has changed considerably in that time but it gives you the feeling of timeless permanence.

I am told that there is excellent walking from here. I would not know; in a number of visits I have not felt the urge to leave the pub. You will probably go in through the front door and join a queue in the narrow hallway. Two or three staff will be serving as fast as they can through a narrow hatchway which does not in any way warrant a description as a bar. The queue sometimes moves incredibly slowly as bar staff have to get the correct selection of J2O's, 'somethings and tonic' and other odd drinks - even including halves of lager shandy which take an age to serve. Why people want these when a wonderful choice of real ale and good ciders is set out before them on a couple of blackboards I have no idea. This pub serves one of the best selections of that I know of anywhere. In visits over recent years they have usually had excellent ciders by the Dorset treasure Rose Grant and from my Somerset favourite Hecks'.

Plus, holy of holies, they have their own cider. Charlie Newman has stepped back from running the pub himself and concentrated on making ciders out the back. I am not sure I can think of another pub that makes its own ciders on the premises. I finally managed to meet Charlie at the 2012 Powerstock Cider Festival where in a beret and stripy jumper he was excuding a very French persona. He is now making about 18,000 litres of cider a year all of which he sells through the pub. I think he is the envy of many for having such a captive audience. Speaking to him he experiments with a number of single variety ciders and has an interest in different apples varieties. I tasted an American Mother single variety, a dessert variety which made a reasonable cider. For the pub his three main brands are 'Kiss Me Kate', Eve's Idea, and the superbly named 'Sat down be cider.'

If you remain inside the pub after being served and turn to the right you will find the seating area. During the day this is often a quiet haven; an unspoilt interior with many of the benches and tables being of an indeterminate age. Why so many of the customers seem to want to sit outside rather than in this authentic setting I can never quite fathom - but I like to sit down in the cool. Fortunately it is a pub that has not succumbed to the temptations of becoming a restaurant but a simple range of excellent pies is available, ready heated to hand to you.

Rather surprisingly it seems as if nearly half the interior area of the pub is dedicated to a museum of local fossils. This may or may not appeal to you but it certainly adds to the quirkiness. On one visit on a weekend afternoon I found a stall out the front selling Westcombe Cheddar Cheese from just down the road from me in Somerset. I subsequently spoke to Tom Carver who is the cheese maker, and is also known to make a drop of cider. He says a chap just turns up some weekends and buys a lot of cheese and carries on down to the coast to sell it. Well worthwhile though, one of the only three Cheddars in the country still produced with natural rennet and unpasturised milk.

For me the Square and Compass is just too far away for a comfortable afternoon's drive. I have to find other reasons to be in the locality. However, it is always worth the effort.

West Milton Cider

Nick Poole, 1 Pear Tree Cottages, West Milton, Bridport, Dorset DT6 3SHW 01308 485235 nspooleltd@btconnect.com *SWECA*

Nick Poole has been mentioned, just a few times, in the introduction to this section on the search for cider in Dorset. But it is now time to focus on him as an innovative cider maker in his own right.

His cider making started more or less by accident in 2000 and in the early years was carried out as part of the West Milton Cider Club. However, the urge to make more controlled experiments of his own was too strong. This was fuelled when he met a French cider maker who was over in Dorset looking for a lost variety of apple. The two became friends and Nick went back to France to see what was done over there. He was intrigued with the differences in the way the French made their cider, and in particular the keeving process.

This has led to Nick chasing the Holy Grail for cider makers; a natural cider with residual sugars. Traditional producers in England have tended not to go down this

Nick Poole and James Crowden, poet and cider writer, at the planting of the Linden Lea orchard in Melplash

route since the 17th century when there was a spell of innovation in cider making that has probably not been repeated until the past decade. In keeving the cider throws up a brown cap in the very early stages of fermentation - the so called 'Chapeaux Brune'. This contains a lot of nutrients and if the rest of the juice is siphoned from underneath it and then fermented the lack of remaining nutrients tend to result in the yeast running out of steam and leaving a cider that is slightly lower in alcohol but deliciously sweet tasting. If bottled there is often enough 'go' left to produce a natural, slight fizzyness.

This keeve can erratically occur naturally but the French use an enzyme to induce it. Even when using the enzyme there is a lot that can go wrong: the keeve doesn't happen, if the weather is too warm the fermentation may go too quickly, the fermentation may carry on until the cider is dry, no natural fizz may form in the bottles - just for starters. It is also quite a wasteful process as up to one third of the original cider can be lost. However, Nick persevered and eventually was absolutely delighted when he won a major cider making competition in France!

He eventually decided that he would see if he could sell his cider to the public and first tried in 2010. He did about 800 bottles in his first year and sold out, for 2011 he had 3,000 bottles to sell. This is a considerable proportion of the just over 1,000 gallons he made in total for the year. Much of it made with apples from the orchards of near neighbour over the hill Rupert Best. He sells his keeved cider as 'Lancombe Rising', Bottle Fermented Sparkling Cider with a 4.5% ABV. Having tried it a couple of times now I can confirm that it is delicious. The name 'Lancombe Rising' comes from the crossroads up the lane from his cottage in the village of West Milton where he has his buildings where he now makes his cider.

The rest of his production is a high quality draught cider with great attention being taken to detail. He then back sweetens with keeved cider which even in small proportions gives the cider a quality and richness of taste that makes it stand out from the crowd.

Sales are mainly local and a lot comes from farm shops and delicatessens, he mentions in particular the award winning Washingpool Farm Shop which has for two years running won the Taste of the West Award in the farm retail category. I can remember when it was just a few boxes of muddy vegetables! Fruits of the Earth in Bridport is another significant outlet. His draught cider can be found in a number of local pubs including the Cider Bar in the Bull Hotel in the centre of Bridport.

In 2011 Nick had a stand in the food tent at the Melplash Show for the first time. Judging from the fact that when I went to buy a couple of bottles he had run out and left his wife manning the stall while he went to get fresh supplies I would think he had a successful time. Oh, and of course, you can find his cider at his Powerstock Cider Festival!

I hope I haven't made Nick sound like some sort of superman. He is a really nice quietly spoken chap who just gets things done. He and his ciders are certainly worth searching out. I know I will be - repeatedly.

Other producers in Dorset

Dorset has a rapidly evolving cider scene and it just doesn't seem possible for someone like me to keep track of every producer as they emerge, especially assessing whether they are commercial or not. There are a number that I know of or suspect which I have either not got to or have left out. The following is a list of these.

Castle's Dorset Cider

Malcolm Castle, Crabs Bluntshay Farm Whitchurch Canoncorium, DT6 6RN 0127 48064
Mr Castle was famously described by James Crowden in his book Ciderland as 'his cider is as dry as his wit'. I met Mr Castle a few years ago when he had a stall at the Gillingham and Shaftesbury Show where he was selling his honey and cider, bottled in a selection of obviously recycled non matching bottles. I did not really have a chance to assess his wit, but his cider was certainly dry.

He makes it down in the Marshwood Vale on a very old press and prides himself on using very traditional methods which naturally lead to a very traditional taste. He can apparently be found at many local farmers markets.

Brindles Vintage Cider

Bo Rutter, Stour Row, nr Shaftesbury SP7 0QW 01747 852320
I met Bo Rutter and tried some of his cider at the Powerstock Cider Festival last year. He has been making about 100 gallons of cider a year since the mid 1990s. He should not really be in this book as he says he is not registered but his cider turns up at the occasional festival.

Dorset Cider Company

Jonathan Purssell 07710 804805 and Alistair Bowerman 07887 968408
I met Jonathan and Alistair at last years Gillingham and Shaftesbury Show where they had taken a quite impressive cider stand. They said it was very much of a first step and I tried both the ciders they had on offer - one of which I remember as being quite good.

I have spoken with them on the phone a couple of times since then trying to arrange an appointment to visit them, but I sensed that they did not seem quite ready. Googling them there obviously has been a website. The link mentions a small local company set up in 2010, but there is currently a block on all listings for Dorset Cider Company. That really seems to be all I can say at the moment. They seemed decent guys so I hope they manage to develop their cider making.

Talbot Harris Cider Co

Tom and Steve I think. cjtharris@hotmail.co.uk.
I met Steve at the Powerstock Cider festival 2012. They have just made 2,000 litres for the first time on a farm near Burton Bradstock - the cider I tasted was a straight-forward farm cider.

Cranborne Chase Cider

Bill Meaden. Blandford Forum 01725 553715 cranbornechasecider@gmail.com

I met Bill at the 2012 Powerstock Cider Festival. Run by Bill who is the brewer at Sixpenny Handley Brewery. I had some of their beer last summer at the local cricket club and it was excellent. He is now making cider on his own account which he hopes will be sold alongside the beer from the brewery. Cider tasted reasonable and he seemed a decent sort of chap so I hope to be seeing him again.

Presses at the Mill House Cider Museum

Section 4

Somerset

A lovely cider orchard at West Bradley belonging to Mr Edward Clifton Brown.

In search of Somerset

Somerset and cider are pretty synonymous. Surveys of people's perceptions of the county of Somerset clearly show that cider is one of the things most closely associated with it. Even with the relatively recent abominations from Ireland and Belgium if people were asked to give a location for cider it is likely it is Somerset they will mention. With the world's second largest cider mill in Shepton Mallet, now owned by C&C brands who own Magners and with the presence of Thatchers at Sandford - one of the national top five producers - and some of the larger 'small manufacturers' like the widely contrasting Sheppy's and The Original Cider company - it is certainly true that there is a lot of cider made in Somerset.

Somerset also has the biggest concentration anywhere in the country of traditional family farmhouse cider makers who have been producing for a number of generations. Although there are a few scattered around other counties and in particular in Devon, nowhere else can match a list of traditional families that includes, as well as Thatchers and Sheppy's, Hecks, Perrys, Rich's, Bennetts, Wilkins, Crossman, Naish, Harris and Willcox. There are also many other cider makers who have been established on farms for decades such as Julian Temperley at Burrow Hill and Nigel Stewart at Bridge Farm.

Although I am originally from Sussex I knew of Somerset as the cider county by the age of 11. Mainly through the exploits of the Somerset Cricket team in the Gillette Cup and pictures of the Somerset yokels taking cider and straw to Lords.

It is interesting to speculate on when this close association between Somerset and cider dates from. Somerset has always been one of the 'cider counties' but during the 17th and 18th centuries it would be fair to suggest that Devon along with Hereford had the 'intellectual' ownership of cider. They seem to have been more of the 'gentry' who promoted and developed cider in those counties. The orchard census figures quoted in the Cornish chapter show that at the end of the 19th century Somerset only had the third largest area of orchards - though was very close behind Hereford and Devon. When the growth of large cider companies began in the late 19th century Bulmers of Hereford probably set the pace, though Weston's of Hereford and Gaymers in Norfolk seem to have been founded earlier. Even Whiteway's in Devon with huge growth in the early years of the 20th century came before the emergence of large commercial producers in Somerset.

However, the 'intellectual' leadership of cider and the raising of standards of the product had already begun to shift to Somerset before the end of the 19th century. The Bath and West and Southern Counties Show travelled around the whole of the South of England at that time yet when the first cider class were held 8 of the 14 entrants were from Somerset. By then, under the patronage of Squire Robert Neville Grenville of Butleigh in the centre of Somerset, F W Lloyd was already carrying out scientific research on behalf of the Bath and West Society into the raising of quality standards for cider. This attracted support from most of the West's County Councils and it was at Long Ashton in the north of Somerset that the National Fruit and Cider Institute was set up at Long Ashton.

During the first half of the 20th century the number of commercial scale cider businesses grew in Somerset. The most significant was the Taunton Cider Company in Norton Fitzwarren, Like Bulmer's this grew from ecclesiastical origins with cider made by the Reverend Thomas Cornish in his Heathfield Rectory. It was his gardener who became head cider maker when the company was set up in the early 1920s. In the same decade Redvers Coates started his company in Nailsea. Both of the companies were very positive with their marketing, creating the appeal and aura around Somerset cider. There were many other commercial companies as well. The Quantock Vale Cider company in North Petherton, Clapp's in Baltonsborough and of course brewers and cider makers Showering in Shepton Mallet whose history stretches back well over 100 years before they invented Babycham. There were other farmers producing on a considerable scale and providing brewers with their cider for their owned pub estates.

Taunton Cider developed some strong brands during the 1960s and 70s including Blackthorn, Autumn Gold and Natch which gained such a market share that Taunton became the second largest producer to Bulmers. In the last quarter of the 20th century there was a consolidation around the then Showering led Allied Breweries which resulted successively in Coates, Whiteways, Gaymers and then in the late 1990s Taunton Cider all being swallowed up and gravitating to Shepton Mallet, the only significant alternative to the predominant Bulmers. By then however, the association of Somerset with cider had become very deep rooted into the national consciousness.

Another important factor that has helped further the association of Somerset with cider comes from The Wurzels. It was in the 1960s that Adge Cutler and his band combined folk music, country and western and a bit of German umpah band to come up with the style of music now known as 'Scrumpy and Western'. Many of their songs were drinking anthems to cider. Adge was unfortunately killed in a car crash a few years later but the band under Pete Budd and Tommy Banner went on to achieve international fame with songs like 'Combine Harvester' and are still out there performing regularly. The style of music spread and there are now something like 40 acts detailed on the Scrumpy and Western website maintained by Frank Blades of the excellent Mangled Wurzels. 'Drink up thy Cider' has become a standard for wherever music and cider appear together.

In general the number of farms that made cider nationally was steadily declining throughout the 20th century. As farming became more mechanised and each farm focused on a particular specialism there was less time for traditional mixed farming. In the West Country many farms focus on Dairying with the Milk Marketing Board guaranteeing them an outlet for as much milk as they could produce until quotas were introduced in the 1980s. The 1970s also saw the imposition of duties on cider production over 1,500 gallons a year and the complications of VAT. Most farmers decided that making a bit of cider was more trouble than it was worth. However it was in Somerset that the traditional lived on seeding the healthy number of cider makers we have today.

Is there something particular about Somerset cider that makes it stand out from the others? In cider circles the county is known for its heavy tannin ciders made in particular with the juice of bittersweet apples. This gives it the 'farmhouse' feel in the mouth and slightly chewy body. We have seen in earlier chapters that all three of the other counties covered in this book try to give themselves an identity for their cider, suggesting they do something slightly different to this with the inclusion of other apples including sharps and dual purpose apples.

This reliance on bittersweet apples in Somerset is certainly the conclusion of Liz Copas in her superb Somerset Pomona published in 2000. However, if you read the book and especially delve into part 3 at the back of the book some interesting variations appear. Of the Somerset Apples detailed in the book only 36 out of 88 are bittersweet - and it is quite noticeable that a greater proportion of the older apples identified were not bittersweet. A number of the bittersweet varieties mentioned were developed at Long Ashton but it would be very misleading to suggest that they were only interested in bittersweet varieties. Liz's book lists the 34 Vintage Cider varieties identified by Professor Barker at Long Ashton in 1947. Of these 34 only 18 were bittersweet. It would seem that traditionally a much wider variety of apples would have been used for cider making in Somerset. What is undoubtedly true however is that since the Second World War, and in particular since the 1970s the commercial plantings of cider orchards, especially those by the larger cider makers, have been very predominantly of a narrow range of around 10 bittersweet varieties. In fact Liz suggests that over 50% of the apples planted nationally have been of two varieties, Dabinett and Michelin, the latter of which does not make a particularly good quality cider. This is not just the case in Somerset. The commercial orchards of the last 40 years in Devon and Dorset are also of these varieties. If we go to the orcharding areas of Hereford and Worcester the same story arises perhaps to an even greater extreme and may be reflected in a slight 'sameiness' in many of the ciders of larger manufacturers north and west of Bristol and over the border into Wales.

Notes from Liz
I certainly agree that Somerset's traditional farm orchards probably carried a wide range of flavours at one time. Of the fruit sent to LA from Somerset in the early 20th century there were plenty of local varieties, many synonyms, many useless seedlings. But there were many bittersweets amongst them. Largely due to Prof Barker selecting his 'vintage' varieties, those worthy of fine blending, his broader selections include sharps and sweets with the aim of creating 'balanced' ciders and finding interesting flavours. Certainly 100% bittersweets would be excessive. Sweets extended and sharps added the all important malic acid to create that balance. Somewhere near 50% bittersweets would be more than enough. This is what we used to advise for new plantings for private owners. 50% bittersweets plus culls or a mixture of sharps and sweets. Commercial orchards were needing the tannin of course, able to dilute with culls or dare we mention it, use malic [expensive option these days]

This focus on few varieties has been driven by the requirements of the cider factories around the high yield levels and the ripening times to suit their production schedules. As orchards have a limited lifespan even most of the smaller traditional orchards have been replanted with these varieties. From this it can be seen that although there has always been a strong bittersweet content in a traditional Somerset cider it would also have contained a good number of other varieties. Julian Temperley in his excellent orchards at Burrow Hill boasts of having over 40 varieties as do Sheppy's. he owns some fine traditional varieties, not the most desirably behaved 'orchard' varieties, but flavoursome.

Even whilst identifying the bittersweet as the defining taste of Somerset ciders Liz Copas also mentioned that in the south of the county, spilling over into Devon and Dorset there was a tradition of using sharps. Sharps were also identified as being used in the north of the county whilst a strip between Shepton Mallet and Wincanton was well know for using sweets. Plus of course there is the Kingston Black phenomenon. This bittersharp apple is widely acknowledged by many as being the best apple for making a single variety cider. The trees are a cider orchard grower's nightmare, vigorous growing but often diseased and poor cropping. However, many still grow and plant the variety. It continues to be included in many prize-winning ciders and despite all its problems is fundamental to farmhouse cider in Somerset.

In conclusion I think that whilst accepting the idea that there is an emphasis on bittersweet high tannin ciders in Somerset it is probably only in the last 50 years or so that this has become quite such a defining feature. I am sure that if you go back before that period there would have been a lot more variety in our ciders - each farmer having a particular taste from their own unique orchards. With the current interest in the heritage of cider and in old apple varieties I feel that in particular our craft or artisan cider makers will be producing some excellent blends of cider in the future.

Another excellent aspect of searching for cider in Somerset is that there is so much to see. Although the county surprisingly lacks a major interpretation centre a number of the cider makers provide something for the 'tourist' to see as well as just sales of cider. Perry's, Sheppy's and Rich's all have small museums as well as cafés and shops selling much more than just cider. Burrow Hill and Hecks in Street are also attractive places to visit and a visit to Roger Wilkins at Mudgely has taken on legendary status. Nearly all producers are happy to supply tasting. In addition there are small interpretative displays about cider at the Rural Life museum and the National Trust Property at Barrington Court which is surrounded by cider orchards from which they make their own cider.

And cider making in Somerset is alive and vibrant. At least six of the producers profiled in this section are new makers who have set out on their adventure in the three years since I produced the 'Somerset Cider Handbook'. These are interesting days for cider.

A Saturday afternoon in October

It was a pleasant afternoon in mid October when I went to visit Keith and Pam Johnson at their small holding in Bleadney between Wells and Wedmore. Although it was feeling distinctly autumnal is was still jumper rather than coat weather. Turf was still firm underfoot and had not turned to the plashy mud of winter.

Keith and Pam are retired farmers from nearby Panborough, but like most farmers they never retire. In their case they have just downsized to a smaller holding. They have a small farmhouse on one side of the road and the few farm buildings on the other. They had first asked me to go along to see them putting up a cheese for pressing a couple of years before, but as I was taking part in an apple day at the National Trust's Barrington Court I could not make it. This year they had renewed the invitation and had even rung up to make sure I had the date right so I felt obliged to go, and was very glad I did.

It was a simple low-key event. A number of people from their extended family, some neighbours from the local villages which extend ribbon form along the local B road. There were some friends from the Pilton Local History Group where I have given a talk a couple of times and a few local cider enthusiasts including fencing contractor Michael York (Yorkie), who I know from the Mid Somerset Show and his wife and some friends. Ostensibly the event had a slight charity raising element, but it

was far more about a social occasion celebrating traditional cider making.

There was an old mill run from a spluttering portable engine - the sort of mill which operates with such violence that it would probably give a health and safety officer palpitations - but grinds the apple to a fine pomace. Keith was too frail to be actively involved himself but sat and watched and chatted whilst sipping cider. Pam helped build the cheese wearing a decorated straw hat, helped by a tall bald headed local farmer. Chatting to this farmer and his wife I discover they were about to emigrate to New Zealand. They have a similar set of traditional cider making equipment which they are hoping to take out with them, packed in a container of their farm equipment.

The cheese is built on a large square wooden bed on an old rack press. A good depth of about four inches to each layer with clean straw spread between. The heavenly smell of crushed apples fills the air. We place wooden forms on top of the cheese and lower the beam of the press. No real pressure is applied yet. Weight alone seems to be enough to start a steady stream of juice pouring off the cheese, off the bed and into the waiting wooden trough. It is still running without any more pressure an hour or so later. The children attending having all sampled the sweet apple juice straight from the press. (Not quite politically corrects as according to Environmental health rules it should be pasteurised first.)

We are stood around drinking Keith's cider from the previous year. I had drunk some before. Dark and rich with that slightly macerated flavour that I speculate may come from the slow pressing of the cheese over a number of days. It retains far more flavour and natural sweetness then many farmhouse ciders. A display has been made of the numerous varieties of cider they have in their orchards. Many of which I have no experience of andwhich presumably add to the richness of flavour.

I met Bill Coles, a local home cider maker who uses this press for a couple of cheeses a year. I was glad to sort out a slight misunderstanding with him. The previous season we had both collected some apples from the Orchard of the Pizzeys near Wookey. He thought I had taken some sacks he had picked up and was waiting to collect. No way would I take sacks someone else had collected - I know how hard a work it is! Some opportune thief must have taken them.

There is an excellent buffet spread out on a table including those vital ingredients, bread, cheese and apple cake. Being someone with a bit of knowledge of local cheese I am intrigued by Worthy Farm Cheddar and its connection with the farm where the famous Glastonbury Festival is held. I discovered it is supplied by a former wife of the festival organiser and she sells it at Bath Farmers Market. It was a bit young and creamy for my liking of hard cheddars, but still very palatable.

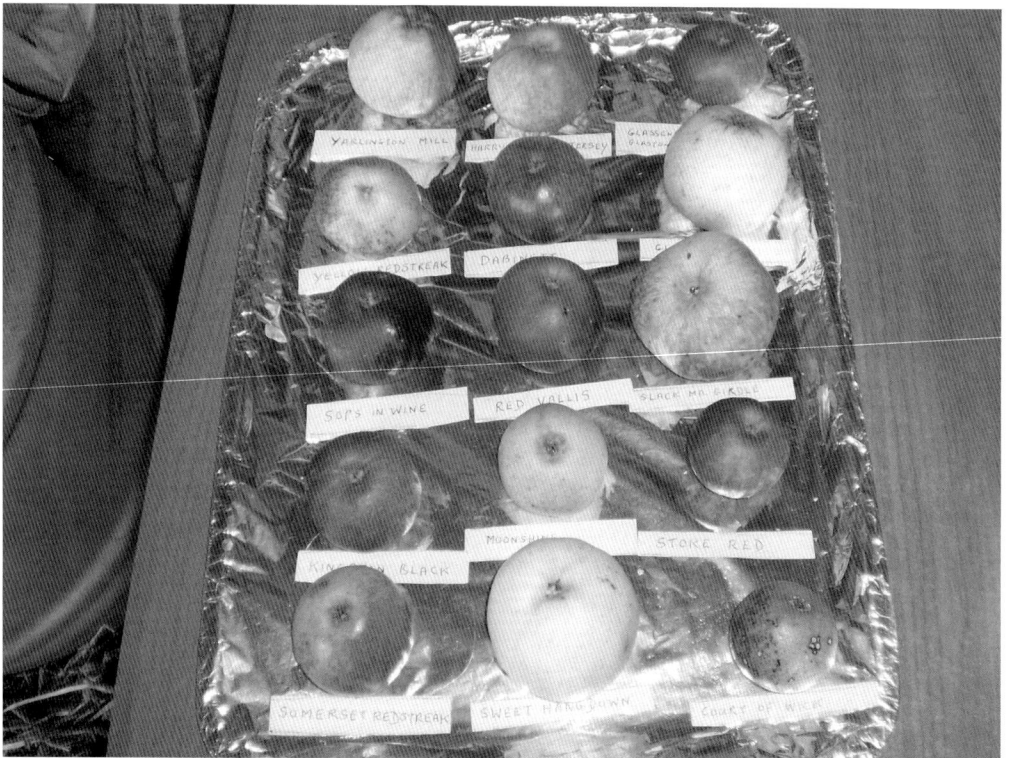

On the way to the event I had problems passing a cyclist on the winding road. I was delighted to find that this was Trevor Hoddinott. He is a farmer who I used to try to sell to up near Cranmore. He and his wife Pam have now passed the farm on to his son, something some farmers are tending to delay for too long these days, and they have semi-retired to a village just along the road from here. Trevor is a great enthusiast for old folk music and sure enough he is asked to 'sing for his supper' and unaccompanied he sings classic traditional songs. I seem to remember one from Devon about a dog which got drowned in a barrel of cider. The session finished with one or two songs where we could all join in the chorus.

It was a lovely afternoon, the mixture of social, traditional, cider and food in the Somerset countryside, just perfect.

Ashill Cider

Mrs Anne House and Mr Ian House, Ashill Farm, Ashill, Ilminster TA19 9NE 01823 480513

The most distinctive feature of Ashill Cider is the label they put on their containers - 'Cider with a Real Kick' - and the drawing of a high kicking dancing girl. It has a pleasantly dated look and in these days of political correctness some may wonder if it is totally appropriate. However, they once tried to go away from it with a modern apple based design and there was such an outcry from their customers that they soon changed back.

The cider business had been run for many years by Mrs House's husband until he died five or six years ago. Until that time she had not had a huge amount to do with the cider side of things apart from serving customers. However, she has carried on with the help of her son Ian and they have even increased and improved production. They make a very traditional Somerset bittersweet cider which they sell at the farm gate to local and tourist passers by.

Their own orchard has now just about come to the end of its life but they have been lucky to obtain supplies of apples from a local retired farmer, Mr Male who likes to pick up the apples and deliver them by trailer. The House's have upgraded to a Voran press from the old twin screw one which still sits in their shop. They sell a dry and a sweet in their simple and straight orward range and in a number of different sized containers.

When I called on a Saturday afternoon in March, Mrs House was about to go into hospital to have a hip replaced on the following Monday, she hopes it will relieve some of the pain she has had in recent years. I hope so too because she is someone I have enjoyed meeting, a good dry sense of humour and aware of far more than you would suppose. When you call at the farm to buy cider there is a please toot your horn sign for service and it always seems to work.

One lovely story about Ashill Cider, which although now dated I make no excuse for repeating, relates to the building of the Ashill bypass in the 1980s. The village of Ashill now has a rather quiet but wide road running through it as the bypass has taken the traffic and runs a field or so lower down. This obviously lost them a lot of passing trade so they decorated a wagon with some cider barrels, made it look really attractive and stood it in one of their fields above the bypass to let people know that cider was available. It looked so good that Somerset County Council made a postcard out of it to show off the county at its best - and then ordered its removal as it didn't have planning permission! Very typical of local government in this country.

Barrington Court

Rachel Brewer, National Trust, Barrington Court, Somerset 01460 243129

In recent years part of the build up to Christmas for our family has been a visit to the Mistletoe Fair in early December at the National Trust Barrington Court. Part of the reason for this is the interest in the history of this originally Tudor building and the involvement of William Strode who bought it the 1630s and considerably extended it. The Strode family came from Shepton Mallet and William Strode become a merchant trading between London and Spain and incredibly wealthy - almost a Richard Branson of his day and he and then his children were key players in the history of Somerset during the Civil War and the later Monmouth Rebellion. Both my sons, Richard and James, wrote essays and dissertations related to this as part of either their graduate or postgraduate studies and my wife Christine has transcribed many Strode wills.

The Mistletoe Fair gives an annual opportunity to get into the house without paying the NT entry fee. To get from the car park you have to walk through some of the orchards that surround the house, usually with some apples still left hanging on the trees or rotting on the ground - the National Trust believes in leaving some for wildlife. The house provides a marvellous setting for the fair in the numerous empty rooms. Crafts, food and drink predominate and the stallholders all dress up in Tudor garb. The regular attendance by Henry the Eighth may be a bit of a puzzle as I don't think the house was built until he had chopped of the head of the last of his wives but with a background of Tudor music and performances of mummers plays make

this is an atmospheric event to savour - especially when you add in the seasonal presence of mulled cider. The excellent Honeypot Cider are regular stallholders - see the section on them - as is the Barrington Court's own cider.

A few years ago, when I first called at Barrington about cider, it was the responsibility of Helen MacDonald who is the catering manager here and two other local Trust properties. Helen is still involved and drives the making of a range of both chutneys and fruit wines. However, by the time I contributed to an Apple Day in late 2009 the ebullient Rachel Brewer had taken over as 'Pommellier'. I believe this suggests 'everything to do with apples', presumably of French origin as so many pretentious food and drink terms are. The National Trust had decided to take its orchard and cider heritage seriously and there are also orchards at a number of other local properties.

The first ciders they made were very very dry, usually a blend and a Kingston Black in 75cl wine bottles. However their ciders have moved on and in the past couple of years they have been very palatable. Indeed they won a class at the Bath and West in 2011 - much to Rachel' delight! A friend who was visiting the show spotted her certificate and she had to drop everything to dash up to the show straight away to see it! They also won some classes at the South West Winter Fair. As well as at the Mistletoe fair I tasted some of their cider in draught at a cider evening in Hinton St George where it was one of the best on offer. As well as their blend and Kingston Black they also do a Yarlington Mill single variety.

Barrington Court also has a display room for cider in one of the outbuildings. Some old equipment is exhibited and some explanatory boards including one with a recipe for a very strong cider that was traditionally made on the estate. This includes molasses amongst the ingredients - I confess to having tried using molasses to increase the sugars in a cider and all I will say is that it may not be to everyone's taste. However Barrington Court Ciders themselves are well worth looking out for.

Bennett's Cider

Viv Bennett, Chestnut Farm, Edithmead, Burnham on Sea, TA9 4BH 01278 785376

'Bennett's Cider. Made at Chestnut farm in the heart of Somerset. A family business for five generations.'

So proclaims the attractive new label which now adorns the container you buy your cider in when you visit the Bennett's. This new label is a sign that something is stirring down at Chestnut Farm.

In recent years Bennett's has been possibly one of the most rustic, traditional cider makers in Somerset after Naish at West Pennard. In the days of Viv's father it had been a considerable cider business providing the pubs of Holts Brewery's plus many local working men's clubs. When they had sold out of their own they had to source cider from the like of Rich's and Roger Wilkins' grandfather in the days when they were a bigger supplier than either of these stalwarts of Somerset farmhouse cider. In the 1970s and 1980s they used to win awards in all the major cider competitions across the country. However, once Holts Brewery was sold, and the new road from the M5 into Burnham cut through the farm, the business seemed to lose momentum.

Viv still makes a steady 3,500 gallons a year. Most is sold from the farm gate to a mixture of diehard regulars and the many tourists who flock to the caravan parks on this part of the Somerset coast. He produces what could be termed as an 'authentic' cider. Dryer and more sharp than most people's tastes these days but that seems to be what the tourists want. If a pint of 'scrumpy' doesn't make them wince on the first mouthful then they seem to feel it is not the real stuff. The cider industry has to be aware that different people are looking for different things - it is the public who decide whether to buy or not.

Viv has continued to win a steady trickle of awards, for his cider. His cider shed has them pinned to the beams, gathering a thick layer of dust and mildew. I borrowed some of them for a display at the Mid Somerset Show a couple of years ago and it was only when I went back on a recent Saturday afternoon tour around that I eventually managed to return them to him. I am not sure if he had noticed they were missing!

Apart from farm gate the Bennett's also attend a few shows and events to sell their cider. Their stand is a rustic as the rest of their image. They put a couple of barrels and the containers in the back of a cattle trailer which they park up and let down the ramp. You stand on the ramp, at a rather uncomfortable angle to taste the cider and make your purchase. I am not sure how this arrangement performs in terms of gaining sales compared to the slightly more sophisticated bars of most of their competitors.

In recent years Viv has largely made the cider with the help of his daughter whilst neither of his sons, now in their late 20's had paid a lot of attention to it. However in the past year I had seen one of his sons manning the stand at shows. On my recent visit Viv confirmed that his youngest son, Duncan, is now taking a bit more interest. They have been tidying up broken branches in their orchards and they have bought a dozen or so new trees to plant in some gaps which occur inevitably over the years. Duncan is talking about next spring in getting a friend of his who is an arborist to give the orchards a proper tidy up. It is good to see that the business looks like it will continue.

Meanwhile Viv is well worth going to see. He is a genuine old fashioned Somerset farmer with a wrinkled and weather-beaten face and a strong accent. He is not a ready raconteur in the way of a Roger Wilkins but when you do get him talking he has a wonderful memory for the past and a host of tales about cider in days gone by. You won't find modern sophisticated cider here and it is strictly plastic container only - however for the student of cider heritage this is definitely one to search out.

Blackmore Vale Cider

Alan Berry, Lily Lane, Templecombe 01963 370716 *SWECA*

Alan Berry has named his cider after the loose geographical area which straddles the Dorset and Somerset borders. He is, however a Somerset man from a few miles up the road near Bruton and Templecombe where he has lived for many years is just in Somerset.

Alan, in his early 60s, has now retired from a career that saw him start as a carpenter, qualify as a Chartered Surveyor and spend a lot of years as a local government buildings control officer. His cider heritage dates from helping with the haymaking on is grandfather's and neighbour's farms where a drop of cider was very much part

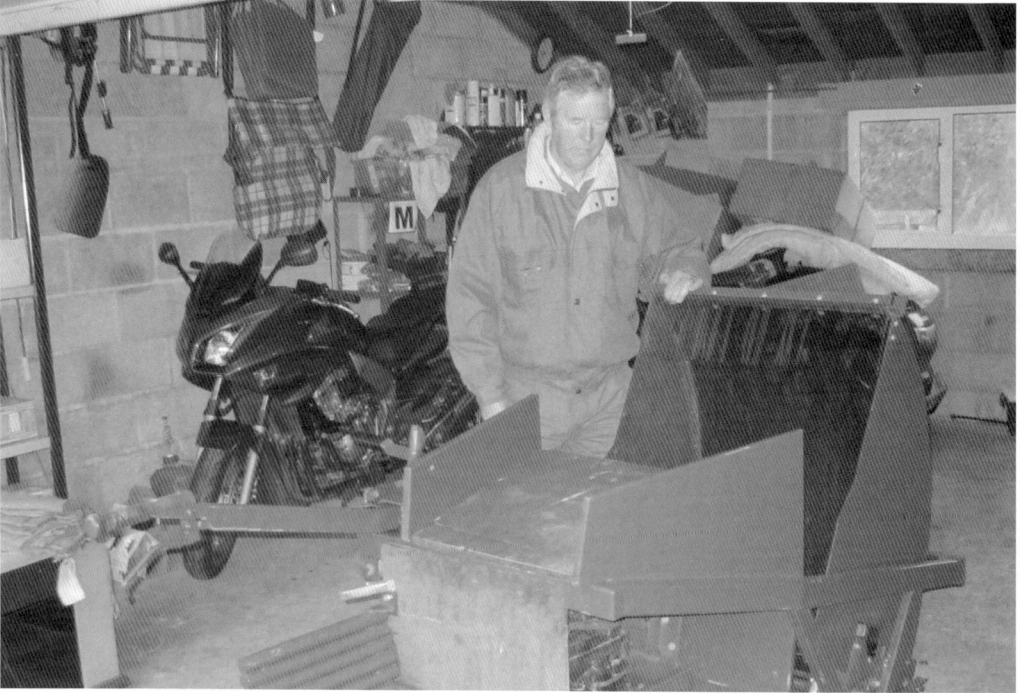

of the occasion. He came back to cider following a wedding at Hornsbury Mill about 10 years ago where he was drinking cider and thinking how nice it was and it dawned on him that he could make it himself. At first it was very much just a hobby but over the past four years he has increased the scale and now makes just short of the 1,500 gallon threshold each year and also bottles some natural apple juice which is very nice. A lot of help and advice has come from the Gaymers cider maker Bob Chaplin whose parents live just down the road.

He sources his apples from a friend near Galhampton, one of those orchards that Gaymers a few years ago decided that they didn't need the apples from. The owner pulled some trees out but has left an orchard that provides more than enough apples for Alan. He also has planted a good number of apple trees in this two acre garden with his sheds to produce in at the bottom of the orchard. I have drunk his cider a number of times of the past few years, always finding it particularly rich and fruity and often with some good residual natural sweetness - though he does sometimes sweeten with cane sugar to meet customers tastes. He was delighted to win the best cider at the Mid Somerset Show in 2010. Although Alan uses only unsprayed apples, natural yeasts and avoids sulphites he is not able to call it organic, our over-protective regulations in the UK..

One of the fascinating things about Alan's production is the amount and variety of largely homemade equipment he uses. Much of this has been made for him by his aerospace engineer son Mark. Homemade mills and presses I have come across a number of times - but a first was the homemade apple harvesting machine. Modelled on commercial equipment it uses the wheels and frame of an old ride on mower and took Mark nearly a year to make. As someone who still breaks his back every year to pick up apples I must admit to being very envious. To go out and buy a piece of equipment like this new would cost approaching £5,000. He ferments his cider mainly in plastic barrels and has devised an interesting way involving car tyre valves to top feed carbondioxide to ensure air stays out as barrels empty and spoilage is avoided.

Alan sells his cider in bag in boxes, 3 litres, 5 litres, 10 litres and 20 litres. He does produce a few 500ml bottles but finds this hard work especially as he also bottles and pasteurises his apple juice in 75cl wine bottles. Most of his sales come through farm shops, a pub and Dikes Supermarket in Stalbridge - plus the odd local festival. His sister also sells some for him on a market stall she has on market days in Wells.

Alan takes the quality of his cider seriously. He is a nice chap who like many of us likes to chat about cider and cider making to fellow enthusiasts. His is a cider worth finding.

Bridge Farm Cider

Nigel Stewart, East Chinnock, Yeovil BA22 9EA 0135 862387 www.bridgefarm-cider.co.uk **SWECA**

Nigel is probably one of the cider makers you have to search least hard for. He is out and about with his cider bar at so many agricultural shows, historic farming events and festivals that, with his large moustache, he is a very familiar face to many. Mind you he slightly confused me by recently sporting a full beard; however I was assured this was only temporary. In fact he has stands at so many shows, sometimes different shows on the same day that it may not be him manning the stand. Quite often it is Richard Macey who works for him, or sometimes Nigel's wife or daughter or other assorted friends.

Although very much a producer from South Somerset he also has claims to dual county status. At Dorchester Show on the first weekend September he appears as Sandford Cider the name of his parent's farm in Sandford Orcus in North Dorset where he gets some of his apples from. Though Nigel himself was not at the Dorset Show last year as he was running his stand at the Great Dorset Steam Fair. The next weekend he had a similar clash with Frome Cheese Show and the Sturminster Cheese Show.

I also saw him at North Somerset, Bath & West, Gillingham & Shaftesbury and Melplash shows. Along with Devon producer Chucklehead he is one of the show regulars and I have already mentioned in this book what a great job the two businesses do by selling excellent ciders to the public. By implication you can tell that there are other ciders sometimes being sold to the public that are not quite as good.

Nigel is one of the select group of my favourite producers. Over the years I do not think I have ever had a bad glass from him although I have had quite a few elsewhere. He started making cider about 20 years ago, largely as it felt the right thing for him to be doing given his interest in old farm machinery, farms, orchards and old apple varieties. His farm and shop is at East Chinnock and is very easy to find on the Yeovil to Crewkerne Road. He makes his cider in a totally traditional way, washes, mills and presses the apples on a large old hydraulic press and ferments in a mixture of oak, steel and plastic. He has his own orchard by the farm which I have watched grow from a few spindly twigs twenty years ago into the mature orchard it is now. He has another orchard at his parent's farm at Sandford Orcas and he makes a point of gathering apples from many old orchards in the Yeovil and north Dorset area which he worried were falling into neglect because no-one was using the fruit.

Nigel makes a fine range of ciders based on his traditional dry, medium and sweet. He sells his ciders draught or bag in the box and bottled, both 75cl and 500ml. He also now makes a high quality bottle conditioned cider, and is experimenting with a bottle conditioned pear cider. He does not lose any sleep over the debate as to whether it should be called pear cider or perry. It does include juice from perry pears though he still calls it Pear Cider - indeed he even makes a joke on his label as to it not mattering what it is called but what it tastes like. He also makes a range of Single Variety Ciders, usually Browns, Kingston Black, Brown Snout and Dabinett. He has just presented the queen, during her visit to Crewkerne, a special 'Cider' a Diamond Jubilee blend named after one of her Dorgies - called Cider.

For his show stands an important part of his offering is his apple juices and he makes an excellent juice from Brown's Apple - as a sharp it has a far better level of acidity for juicing than most other cider varieties.

He is also getting some of his cider turned into cider brandy by Julian Temperley at the Somerset Cider Brandy Company. He is here on very select ground and I think is the only cider maker who Julian is currently supplying. Nigel has a five year old which I am looking forward to a taste of and promise to save up and buy a bottle - he says it is very smooth.

Although Nigel may be away manning his stand there is usually someone around the farmyard to sell cider or juice to callers. If you are not going to be bumping into him at a show or event make sure you visit him at the conveniently situated farm soon.

Burrow Hill Cider and Somerset Brandy Limited

Julian Temperley, Pass Vale Farm, Burrow Hill, Kingsbury Episcopi, Martock TA12 5BY. 01460 240782 www.ciderbrandy.co.uk *SWECA*

Julian Temperley is one of the most influential and important people in the craft cider industry and has been now for well over 30 years. He has led campaigns and pushed the boundaries of the industry further than anyone else, championed the product and helped many individual producers. The craft or artisan cider market would not be anything like it is today without his influence.

I knew all this and said so when I wrote my first cider book three years ago but I have learnt a great deal since then, nearly all of which has reinforced my impression. I was very much looking forward to seeing him again and getting his views on a few issues where I wanted clarity. I was fortunate enough that even though I arrived unannounced he spent an hour and a half talking to me as we wandered around the cider mill whilst he did odd jobs and spoke to others. You don't so much 'interview' Julian as ask the odd questions and listen and realise that he has not only answered that but a dozen other questions you would have asked if you had thought of them - or managed to get them in.

There was a big matter to talk about on this visit. He is obviously very concerned about government's announcement that it is working towards putting a minimum price of 40p per unit on sales of alcohol. This was a subject that I had already written about and I was delighted to find that my analysis as far as it went was exactly the same as his - though his went so much further. In essence we both agree that the danger is to direct sales from the farm gate, that there is such a groundswell of opinion in favour of stopping binge drinking that campaigning against the 40p price would not be constructive, that natural farmhouse cider bought from farms is not a cause of binge drinking and that the best way forward is to seek some sort of limited exemption for those affected.

Julian's analysis went a lot further. He is disappointed that he can't see getting much support from the larger producers - or indeed from some of the larger farmhouse producers who having moved into bottles and higher value products will only have a small proportion of their sales affected. Julian sees it as a threat to the core tradition of farmhouse cider. Going into a farm and buying direct from the barrel is the essential link with the agricultural past and perpetuating the complete heritage of cider into the future. A customer has come into the shop and bought a gallon of cider, a young chap and his wife and a young child. Julian observes that it would do immense injury to the industry if they could not do that - it is one of the seeds that keeps cider going.

We go down to his bond store and see the barrels of his superb Cider Brandy lined up and Julian stresses the importance of the wooden barrel as an image of cider, another thing he sees as essential to retain. The 'matured in oak' tag is more than about the quality and taste of cider but is about it's tradition and provenance. He used the time to roll a barrel fresh back from the cooper into the store; he views them as valuable assets and feels the industry should be encouraging coopering.

Back in the shop two young families had arrived from Scotland, he quickly works out that they were doing a cider tour and in fact made a bit of cider of their own in Scotland. I am not quite sure what he made of that but he spoke very politely and encouragingly to them and poured them a taste of his cider brandy.

Somerset Cider Brandy is a revival of an old 17th century tradition which is entirely down to Julian with help from his fellow director Tim Edwards. Julian may not have taken on the world but he had to take on the licensing authorities in this country, overcome total apathy almost amounting to obstruction from British authorities and succeed in overturning EU rulings where the French were protecting their own interests. I think most people would have thought this was totally impossible. They have now been making Somerset Cider Brandy for over 20 years and it is an excellent drink at the connoisseurs' edge of the cider spectrum. I am not usually a spirits

person but must admit to a great admiration of this product - especially the more mature 10, 15 or 20 year old versions where it has obtained a mellow smoothness which only the best spirits do. It is currently so successful that he is running short of the more mature years.

The other area I wanted to talk to Julian about was apple varieties. He is passionate about his orchards, at 150 acres he is one of the biggest private orchard owners in the country let alone county. He grows 40 varieties and reckons there is another 40 varieties of which he has odd trees. The land around him at South Petherton is one of the recognised prime cider apple growing places in the country along with patches around Baltonsbourgh and Wedmore. All Julian's ciders are blends and he is not at all in favour of the current fashion for single variety ciders. He does not think that many of the single varieties available could have the taste and stability without chemical intervention and 'terroir', the linking between the soil, aspect and habitat that the trees are grown in and the taste and quality of the cider.

I particularly wanted to ask him about the information I had been gathering around a wider variety of apples being used in the past rather than the reliance on bitter-sweets. He seemed to think this quite probable but commented that he tends to make ciders with a reasonable amount of tannin in them. He was very proud of his new season bottled Burrow Hill straw pressed Somerset cider which had just arrived, and quite rightly so. Made with a blend of at least 11 varieties of vintage cider apples it is a truly excellent cider as it is in most years. Three years ago it was the favourite cider of experts like SWECA secretary Bob Chaplin when I wrote my first book. Two years ago it won the Bath and West Show masquerading under a Glastonbury Abbey label. This season's is slightly drier than last and if I could afford to be drinking bottled cider this really would be one of my first choices.

Whilst walking with Julian around the yard I discovered that there were now two cider buses. The cider bus is an iconic part of the Glastonbury Festival and I visit it every time I go, on a number of occasions. However apparently last year they inadvertently found themselves contracted for the bus to attend two events on the same weekend. The world can not be a worse place for having two!

Somerset Cider Brandy is available widely, indeed many other cider makers sell it. Burrow Hill cider is also available in many pubs and other outlets, well worth drinking. However I think the best place to go to get it is at Pass Vale Farm itself, to taste and buy farm gate and whilst there have a wander around his orchard trail. After all people have been going to the farm to buy cider for at least the past 150 years. As Julian says, farm gate sales are an essential part of the living tradition of cider and crucial for the long term sustainability of the product.

Crossman's Prime Farmhouse Ciders

Ben Crossman, Mayfield Farm, Hewish, BS24 6RQ **SWECA**

'Prime Farmhouse, Traditional Somersetshire Cider, Made By Ben Crossman Cider Maker,' reads the very attractive label which Ben sticks on your container when you buy his cider. The label is based on the label that his grandfather used 50 years ago and reinforces the tradition of cider making.

I have deliberately tried to rewrite each of the articles on Somerset cider producers to make sure I am not just repeating my book of three years ago. However, in the case of Ben Crossman I make no excuse for repeating the paragraph above. I bumped into Ben at a recent SWECA meeting and said I would have to come and see him to update my report. He looked momentarily puzzled before telling me that there was nothing to update. Of course there isn't - that is the whole point of Crossman's cider. It is just what if says, traditional Somerset cider as it has been for generations.

Ben's grandfather was a Naish who farmed at Stonehouse Farm on Kenn Moor not far from Weston-Super-Mare and it was there that Ben started his cider making with his grandfather's equipment. He later moved it to his father's Mayfield Farm at Hewish between Congresbury and Weston-Super-Mare where he then purchased his own equipment including a Beare hydraulic press from the former commercial cider maker Hill's at Staverton in Devon.

Ben has two orchards. His pride is his bush orchard across the road from the farm which he planted in 1987. It contains all bittersweets recommended by Long Ashton Research Station: Improved Dove, Harry Masters Jersey, Tremletts Bitter, Sweet Coppin and, where he has needed to replace trees, Dabinett. He also has a standard orchard including Somerset Redstreak, Michelin, Dabinett, Chisil Jersey, Brown Snout, Bulmers Norman, Yarlington Mill and Vilbre. He also harvests apples from a few other traditional local orchards where they would otherwise rot. He is an orchard enthusiast and in the autumn he contract harvests for quite a number of commercial orchards picking up between 500 and 600 tonnes of apples a year. At the SWECA meeting both Martin and John Thatcher were among the people he was talking to.

Given his autumn harvesting commitment he carries on pressing apples late, well into January. Part of this is because of the variety Ashtons Brown Jersey which is a very late apple from a former Coates orchard at Abbotsleigh near Bristol. Most of the apples in the orchard are destined for Thatchers but this variety ripens too late for their production schedule, indeed the apples are often still hanging on the trees at the beginning of January.

Ben is one of the closest producers to Bristol and Weston Super Mare so both residents and tourists make the trip out to pick up cider for parties from his small farm shop where you can also purchase eggs and cheese. His cider is sold straight from the wooden barrels which stand along one side of the shop. He produces around 10,000 gallons a year of traditional 100% juice cider. He makes a 6% dry, medium and sweet from which his medium is the best selling, a good fruity flavoured cider. He also makes a couple of specials at the slightly stronger 7%. At the time of my visit he had available a draught single variety, Tremletts Bitter, and a medium dry Home Orchard Special which tasted very nice. Each year he tries a number of single varieties but if he doesn't think they are anything special he will put them back into the general blends.

With the growth of interest in cider Ben has been trying to get his cider out to more outlets. Festivals and the English Cider Centre are frequent purchasers along with putting his cider into some local farm shops and even limited sales via the internet. However I make no excuse finishing this piece with the same paragraph I did last time.

'Ben Crossman is a good example of what many people like to see - a traditional family farm operation selling traditional cider. As his label says 'Prime Farmhouse'. It may be a phrase that is more usually used with livestock but it certainly also fits the traditions of cider making here.'

Dick Willows

Richard Hudson, Broadlands Cider Company, Box Road, Bathford, BA1 7LR.
01225 85780 www.dickwillows.com

I had slipped out of a business exhibition in Bath for an hour or so to catch up with Richard. I arrived just as he was starting one of his cider tours and joined in at the back. He explained, in his own ageing hippy laid-back style, about his role as a craft cider maker - about planting his orchard many years ago and how you get the juice from apples and ferment it. He is very much a 'natural' cider maker, using traditional varieties, 100% juice and no additives at all other than little bit of sugar if sweetening is required to meet people's taste. He has a very nice set up with a new Voran press and mill and is producing about 11,000 litres a year nearly all of which is sold through his interesting shop. The tour finished with some cider tasting and a bit of bread and cheese, the cider was an excellent traditional Somerset cider.

It is a business that has come a long way in the three years since I first met Richard in March 2009. He was then just about to take over the Broadlands Fruit Farm shop. He had previously had access to make cider the previous winter but the shop was in a bit of a rundown state with much of the space out the back seemingly being used for junk storage. The shop sold no cider made on the premises and largely provided a selection of commercial ciders from other manufacturers masquerading as traditional.

Richard was then making his cider along with Denis France and they were coming at it from slightly different directions, Richard very much the traditionalist whilst Denis with the enquiring mind of someone with a home wine making background. After a couple of years they each went their own way and Denis can now be read about under Hand Made Cider.

Now the shop is a hive of activity with a lot of interesting and quirky outlets using the space out the back. The shop itself has been upgraded to make a very nice farm shop-come-deli with a good selection of cheese and other local foods as well as the cider. The shop now majors on their own cider but there is also an excellent selection from the likes of Heck's and Janet's Jungle Juice from Westcroft. However there is still a fair bit of the silly name commercial product available with Black Rat from Thatchers via Moles Brewery and a number of products from Original Cider Company including the infamous Moonshine. I asked Richard how selling products like these fitted in with his own traditional cider making ethos. He commented that he believed in allowing the customer choice but wants to make sure they know what they are buying. He says that you can explain the difference to some customers but they will still go for the Moonshine. I think his approach is right, there is a wide variety of ciders available and there is no clear right and wrong - but I personally do get a little irritated by industrial products with low levels of juice from concentrate, mixed with water, glucose and additives pretending to be traditional local cider.

Tasting is encouraged and most cider is sold in two litre 'milk bottle containers'. There is also a range of interesting bottled ciders and cider brandy etc and even some beer available draught.

Dick Willows is definitely a location worth visiting, especially if you are in the north of the county where there is not a lot else - it is only just inside the border from Wiltshire.

Fosseway Cider

Phil Briggs, East Pennard, Shepton Mallet 01749 600400 www.fosseway-cider.co.uk *SWECA*

The old Roman Fosse Way carves across the country from somewhere near Hull to somewhere near Exeter. South of Shepton Mallet there are some very straight fast sections where traffic thunders along and cars doing 60mph are likely to be causing a hold up.

The road weaves imperceptibly between houses built alongside the road in very narrow strips. These probably date from days before the discipline of tarmac when seasonal mud would have made the roads much wider as horses and carts tried to find a dry route. Possibly around the time of enclosure squatters would have claimed some of this wider road area and built houses. The long narrow plots are a distinctive feature today. On one of these plots a mile or so south of Wraxall you can come across the appropriately names Travellers Rest, one of those pubs in the middle of nowhere which somehow survives. Its current survival is largely down to Ian and his wife who make excellent landlords serving good food along with keeping it a proper pub. One night last year I was there for a skittles match, Ian was also the question master for a pub quiz and there were drinkers watching sport on a big screen. One of the pumps on the bar is for an excellent pint of Doom Bar, the other for a local cider - Somerset Glory from Fosseway Cider.

On a Sunday afternoon, if you are lucky, there may be a large gentleman sat on a stool by the bar along with some of the other locals. This may be Phil Briggs who only 150 yards back up the road makes Somerset Glory and his other product the bottled Fosseway. He will probably be drinking Guinness. I have challenged him about this, because Phil is a chap who really likes his pint of cider, but he reveals that he just can't bring himself to pay for his own product when he has plenty just down the road - he has a point, though actually the cost is very reasonable. Somerset Glory is an excellent drinkable draught cider - uncarbonated, slightly sweetened to a medium and consistently refreshing. You can find it in a few other pubs, the Red Lion along the Fosse at Babcary or the excellent Plough in Taunton are good bets. There are others in south Dorset during the summer and a couple of pubs near Euston in London.

Phil makes his cider at his bungalow where he has a 40 tree apple orchard in the paddock behind and obtains the rest of his apples in nearby Hornblotton or in Ditcheat. He has been making cider for four or five years now spreading from initial sales at Castle Cary Rugby Club. He planted his own orchard five years ago and it is just beginning to bear. Varieties include Browns, Ellis Bitter, Harry Masters Jersey, Yarlington Mill and a Devon variety Tan Harvey which I have not heard of before. He is looking forward to doing his own 'Orchard Blend' as soon as there are enough apples.

The season before last Phil with the help of friends, pressed an ambitious 16,000 litres of juice and had enough stock left to cover this season as well. It was hard work pressing this much through a Voran pack press and I get the impression that this coming season Phil may well outsource the pressing a few miles down the road and bring the juice back home to ferment. His current interest is converting his double garage into a bottling plant. There is good logic in this as bottles seem to be the largest potential market for artisan cider makers. There are very few who are not trying bottles in one way or another. Phil has already built up a good trade with shops for both the bottled version of his Somerset Glory in 500ml bottles, and for the 75cl bottles of his excellent premium Fosseway Cider. Unfortunately outsourcing bottling is an expensive option which takes out most of the potential margin whilst bottling yourself on anything other than a very small sink top scale takes a lot of expensive equipment.

Phil has been gathering second-hand equipment for over a year. In his garage he now has two large pasteurisers, a filter, two different carbonators, bottle fillers, cappers and assorted other items. When I saw him in early March he was awaiting delivery the following week of a 250 litre old milk chilling tank so he can bring the cider down to temperature. It will be interesting to see this in operation - especially if he can offer a service to other small-scale cider makers!

Fosseway also sell through a good website www.fosseway-cider.co.uk. It is a cider well worth hunting out and I am quite frequently tempted to stop in The Travellers Rest for a pint as I drive up the Fosse on my way back from Yeovil.

Glastonbury Cider Company Ltd

Dan Brooke, Nic Crowley and Damon Brook Honeysuckle Farm, Cinnamon Lane, Glastonbury BA6 8BN 01458 831354

It is sometimes quite surprising to discover something that has suddenly sprung up almost on your own doorstep - especially when it is something quite exciting. The first I heard about Glastonbury Cider was from a long time acquaintance, cello maker Kai Roth Thomas, who I bumped into in Shepton Mallet Market Place just before last Christmas. Knowing my interest in cider he said that his brother in law and a couple of friends had just finished pressing 22,000 litres. I was totally bemused - 22,000 litres is a considerable amount for first timers.

A few emails followed and one Saturday morning I made a visit to meet up with a chap called Dan Brooke. Dan is a cheerful entrepreneur I would guess somewhere around 40. He showed me over his holding, Honeysuckle Farm in Cinnamon Lane, where he has three eco holiday cottages in a wonderful setting at the bottom of Glastonbury Tor overlooking the moors. There is a legend that Jesus's trader uncle Joseph of Arimathea sailed to Glastonbury when boats could get right up to the town. Some even suggest they sailed as far as Pilton and up to the medieval age, though a recent history of the village thinks that this is because a reference mistakenly muddles Pilton / Pylle with Pylle on the River Avon on the way up to the Avon Gorge to Bristol. Local supposition is that Cinnamon Lane is named after the spice some of the traders bought with them. That is as may be but what is certain is that it is a great spot. It is located on the bottom 'step' of the Tor which towers above on the northern skyline. Cinnamon Lane has a considerable cider heritage. Dan pointed out a shack with a blue door which used to hold a cider maker whose press is now in the Rural Life Museum. Further up the lane as it swings around towards Edgarley School is a smallholding farmed by 83 year old Marcus Govier who Dan says has a 300 year old press and still makes a drop - but only for his own consumption.

Dan also runs a couple of licensed cafes with a business partner on Glastonbury High Street. He has lived in the area all his life and was originally an agricultural engineer - a common theme in cider makers. He makes up the central third of Glastonbury Cider. It all started rather casually when another third, Nic Crowley a piano tuner from the talented Glastonbury musical family, and Kai's brother in law, found that a lady friend in West Pennard had rather a lot of cider apples available. He got together with Dan and Dan's brother Damon. Damon currently runs The Barton Inn in the nearby village of Barton St David but is probably better known for his Festival Bars and Festival Catering. They have had a long-term presence at the Glastonbury Festival including running the bar in the Avalon Field and attend festivals all over the country.

Anyway the three brought a Voran pack press off of E Bay - which turned out to be the old press from Darren Wilcock of Wilcock's Cider who was upgrading to a belt press. They got hold of a second-hand apple harvester and they just started crushing cider apples. They built a timber shed over the press and put the juice into numerous 1,000 litre IBCs. They still haven't had time to concrete the floor. Once they had used all the apples from Pennard they looked for more and picked up in places such as the late fallers in Glastonbury Abbey and some Kingston Blacks from as far away as Taunton. When I visited in early March some of the IBC's were still fermenting away. Apparently first tastings have been quite encouraging and they are now thinking about what to do with it. This is a worry for some producers and I have come across a number who have made far more cider than they have been able to sell. I somehow don't think this is going to daunt Dan and his friends who although laid back seem to have a lot of entrepreneurial drive and the contacts to make things happen.

They are going to have some flash pasteurised into Bag in boxes by near neighbours Orchard Pig. This can be sold through pubs and perhaps festival bars - though probably not Glastonbury where the drinks franchises are tightly controlled. More exciting is their bottling. They have got in touch with Steve Brooksbanks from Pyle Vineyard. I last spoke to Steve three years ago when researching my Somerset Cider Handbook. He had in the not so distant past sold a very good strong cider but had decided not to do anymore with that and to focus on bottling wine both from his small vineyard but more from the grapes of others. According to Dan he is now going to bottle for them in both 75cl and 500ml bottles. An interesting feature is that he is going to use wine making expertise and equipment to fine filter the cider. The hope is that by removing the yeast they will get a stable product which retains natural sugars. Some purists will suggest that fine filtering strips out flavour but I am not sure that this is the case. The excellent premium bottled products that come out of the Shepton Cider Mill such as Stewley and Newton Vale certainly do not taste any worse for it and there are potential taste destroying problems with the alternative pasteurisation. I am very much looking forward to tasting this. Interestingly they are also for now going to leave the product still rather than carbonate.

There are other exciting things going on. Honeysuckle Farm now includes a 12 acre sloping field leading back up to the Glastonbury to Shepton Road. Already 40 apple trees have been planted including the locally named Camelot, Stoke Reds and a local variety Honey String which I have not previously come across but is highly rated by local orchardist John Dennis. There are plans to plant more trees as the field is reclaimed from 20 years of neglect. In the field there is also a convenient large flat platform a little distance above the farmhouse. On this, when needed, they can erect a temporary timber and canvas structure and they have a licence for holding weddings and other events. This can be rented along with the cottages to accommodate guests! The spot has extensive views out over the Somerset Moors which start abruptly only a small field away. They have imaginative ideas about other events and training schools which could be held here throughout the year.

They already have their own minute microbrewery and along with the very strong Glastonbury green eco ethos it is exciting to think what could happen here. I will watch with interest.

Gold Rush

Jim Lockyer, Bere Cider Company, The Shack, Woodpecker Lodge, Bere, Aller, TA10 0QX. 01458 250166, 07934 424797

Jim's son in law Chris Smoldon sent me an email to introduce Jim. It sounded interesting so on one of those dull, grey, damp days between Christmas and New Year my son Richie and I set off to investigate, and were very glad we did.

Jim is a semi-retired farmer down on the Moors not really that far off the A39 at the eastern end of Othery off the road to Langport. Look for a sign towards Eggs for Sale, that is not them but by then you can see the strategically positioned cider barrel. Jim took over the cider making for his in laws before him twenty odd years ago and it seems fitting that it is now his son in law Chris who is helping take it forward.

The main feature is The Shack. Apparently these former cow stalls has undergone a 'refurbishment'. A new weatherproof roof has been put on and there is an impressive selection of third hand chairs. When we arrived the operations chief taster (drinker), engineer and neighbour Chris Dyer was helping get a patio heater going. This had been in the possession of Chris Smoldon for seven years without ever being used until he had the brainwave of using it for this worthy cause. The engaging Jim is a great talker, to put it mildly. One feels the main purpose of the cider making is to provide people for him to talk to in The Shack and he claims to be available at most times - though a phone call may be advisable to ensure there is someone there.

The cider is a good clean standard Somerset dry cider, tastes beautiful straight out of the wooden barrels and Jim is keen to get you to taste it. As he says he is not sure how much cider he sells but he seems to give a fair amount away! He mentions one regular 'hippy' customer who comes in most weeks for two gallons but samples a fair amount in doing so. As long as you buy some - that is all that matters. The cider, philosophy and atmosphere remind you of the legendary Roger Wilkins at Mudgeley. However, here the 'sweet' is gently flavoured with a touch of sucralose rather than Roger's sometimes harsh use of saccharin.

Jim and Chris have increased production over the past three years to now near the threshold. Jim is quick to praise his son in law with raising the standards. Taster Chris Dyer confirms that previously it had often been virtually undrinkable but now with greater attention to detail, cleanliness of barrels and introducing a stainless steel bed onto their rack and screw press they are turning out a very nice drop. They are also beginning to experiment with marketing themselves a bit. They have had a stand at a few local food fairs and have come up with the 'Gold Rush' name. This originated with some Morgan Sweet single variety they made that was particularly 'golden' but it is an apt enough name for all their cider. Farm gate sales remain their major outlet though.

Chief taster Chris is also a good supplier of customers. He has a couple of holiday cottages and makes sure he brings all the holidaymakers over for a taste of the cider and to experience the atmosphere of The Shack. For many this turns into the high-light of their holiday.

Richie and I really enjoyed sitting, chatting and 'tasting' until all to quickly two hours had passed in convivial company. Discovering mutual people we know, discussing the cider making scene, ribbing Chris Smoldon on being an insurance salesman - "What's wrong with that, at least I am not an Estate Agent!"

This is what cider should be about - a social as well as drinking experience. As it is on route to Taunton I expect I will be visiting again before too long - and I hope many of you reading this will also make the trip.

Handmade Cider

Denis France - Handmade Cider, Slaughterford Mill, Near Chippenham, Wilts. SN14 8RJ, 07590 265804 www.handmadecider.co.uk

Denis is one of the most enthusiastic cider makers I know and is sure to end up making an excellent cider. He started making home-made wine alongside his moth-er and allegedly progressed into cider when he couldn't afford the sugar for his apple wine. I previously knew him from Broadland Fruit Farm near Box where he made the cider, but he and Richard Hudson have separated their working relationship and Handmade Cider was set up in the summer of 2010.

In November 2010 I had a circular email from Denis asking people to attend his 'last pressing of the season and to look at his refurbished Beare Press. Hence on an absolutely freezing cold late November Saturday my son Richard and I ventured out into the wilds of Wiltshire on a voyage of exploration.

Firstly please note I offer my excuses for not covering Wiltshire as a separate coun-ty in this study. I have given a cider talk in Wiltshire and been asked about it at a book signing in Bath however unfortunately I have not been able to identify much Wiltshire specific heritage or that much of the cider revival that is going on through-out the county. As yet I have not found any clue as to a distinctive style of Wiltshire cider.

However although his cider premises are in Wiltshire, and he is now seeking to make some commercial gain from that fact, Denis deep down believes himself to be a Somerset cider producer because the majority of his apples are Somerset bitter sweets and bitter sharp - many of them from only a few miles away from me in Shepton Mallet.

Anyway to get back to our exploration. We skirted the west of Bath and got up onto the Bristol to Chippenham road before heading east. It was a very alien landscape for a Somerset cider drinker with the wide fields and large skies of the southern Cotswolds. It was then that I discovered that I had forgotten the map. I had looked at it and knew we drove along the road until we got to a place called Ford and then turned off for what looked like a very small attractively named settlement called Slaughterford. We were heading for Slaughterford Mill. I do not use a Sat Nav. I have this thing about them being an insult to my intelligence. I have maps and a sense of direction why do I need an electronic aid. I notice that the younger gener-ation have now become totally reliant on them. They arrive at a place and have no idea how they have got there and could not find there way there again. Anyway on this occasion I found my way myself. There was only one turning to the right in Ford and okay the road was extremely narrow - especially the almost hidden fork where I went the wrong way. However, my sense of direction told me I was going too far to the left so I took the next turning on the right. I then used the logic that a 'mill' was likely to be a former water powered mill and therefore at the bottom of the hill where the water runs. Sure enough before too long we ended up in front Slaugherford Mill, an old mill in rather ruinous state.

We drove in past a 17th century mill owners house on which there was at least some signs of restoration. Taking our life in our hands we explored a bit further and at the far end found a couple of cars and a bit further on again found some dumpy bags full of apples and inside a building which appeared to have some sort of roof we found Denis and friends wrestling with an obviously self fabricated sack hoist of industrial proportions.

The buildings turned out to be an old paper mill and the fast flowing stream was very evident. One of those relics of industrial archaeology which you find tucked away in remote deserted spots around the countryside when location was determine by natural sources of power. As Denis commented there was plenty of scope on the site and he already had his eye on another building for a potential bottling plant.

Denis France with his restored press

However, on this freezing cold morning that looked to be some way in the future.

It quickly became evident that this was not in fact Denis's last pressing of the season. He was well behind schedule because of the need to install his new press and the equipment to keep it supplied with apples. He and a team of friends and labour were starting work between roll-up cigarette breaks. The apples were in half tonne dumpy bags outside the open front of the building and these were tipped for washing and sorting. At first they looked totally unusable. Black ones, rotted and bruised ones and a profusion of dead leaves. Firstly they were roughly sorted by hand to remove the worst then dropped into a wash tank. From here they were scooped into a plastic crate and blasted with a pressure washer and eureka some wholesome apples emerged.

These were tipped into an alarmingly powerful belt driven scratter which produced well smashed pomace which was then transferred into a slowly rising cheese on the press.

Denis had been flitting in and out all morning. Mainly setting out directional signs so that people could find the place, but also getting the barbeque going for baked potatoes. There were three polypin of Denis's cider on offer for sampling. A 2008 vintage and a single variety Yarlington Mill were excellent and we kept returning to them during the morning as we indulged ourselves in discussing cider making techniques.

At last the cheese was ready for pressing and Denis focused his full attention on the job in hand. The press is his pride and joy and he had spent much of the summer and autumn restoring it since he found it in a scrapyard in Calne, Wiltshire. It is an old (probably over 80 years) Beare press made in Newton Abbot in Devon.

By now a reasonable number of spectators had gathered. Denis started the press with an impressive amount of noise and power. All morning the weight in the cheese had been pushing juice out under its own weight and over 100 litres had already been pumped across to the waiting 1,000 litre tank. Now, even with the pump running non-stop, it looked like it may be swamped by the surge of juice as around another 200 litres was squeezed out in about 10 minutes.

My next visit was as I was finishing writing this book on Good Friday 2012. Denis had opened his cider mill for the weekend so I went along for some tastings. Most of the ciders were those he made in late 2010. This time the day was sunny and compared to my previous visit an absolute heat wave - though in fact it was still quite chilly. Denis was selling an excellent selection of ciders. I was impressed with a bottled conditioned Yarlington Mill and Browns Apple blend which tasted excellent. Denis is quite into bittersharps like Browns Apples at the moment. Another bottle was a Yarlington Mill blended with a proportion of Crimson King to get the acid up a bit - Yarlington Mill tends to taste a bit thick on its own. He had a light Lambrook Pippin, again bottle conditioned which was his favourite. I preferred his Woodbine Blend, apples he collected from a Woodbine Farm. This was a keeved product and tasted like a good wine. There was also a bottle he had sent away for carbonation. It was really quite a good 'commercial' type cider but was not in the same class as the others. He was a touch annoyed with the bottlers, he had sent of 1,050 litres and got back 850 with no explanation at all as to where the other 200 litres had gone! He is looking forward to the 10,000 litres he made in the autumn of 2011 being ready as he is itching to get on with some more blending.

Denis proclaims that one of the things holding him back is his reluctance at marketing and sales. He has a good website and whilst I was there he had a publican come in to taste. He bought a 20 bag in box to put on his bar - hopefully a new pub to supply and I must admit with a selection of real ale and ciders The Three Crowns in Chippenham sounds like somewhere I should visit.

Denis is a really innovative cider maker who is really into his task - I really wish him well and am sure he should be able to sell more of his quality ciders.

Harry's Cider

Harry Fry, Little Field Farm, Long Sutton, Langport TA10 9NS 01458 241324
www.harryscidercompany.co.uk

I think I first came across Harry's cider at that amazing pub The Halfway House at Pitney and then at the Queen's Arms at Corton Denham Though I don't think either are currently stocking it. Richie and I thought it was an excellent Somerset cider. I met Harry himself with his son at the Powerstock Cider Festival and made a note that I really must get to see him. Actually it was quite late on in the writing of this book that I got around to making the visit.

Harry describes himself as an ex-dairy farmer - not the only one in the pages of this book. As a young man he went over to New Zealand for a few years. When he came back his father suggested he might try his hand at becoming an orchard contractor. This never really got off the ground though it did lead to him working for Sir John Paget near Taunton looking after his orchards for a number of years. These were orchards for Taunton Cider who came in once a year to do the pruning so Harry can claim to have worked alongside Harold Holly a real orcharding expert.

In 1982 Harry bought the farm he still lives at near Langport and set up a 70 cow dairy herd which he milked for the next 20 years. He then went in to milking goats but found very little support from the agricultural agencies and his mind switched to other things. Since 2005 he has been farming a few cattle, a bit of arable, some orchard pruning and experimenting with cider. He currently has an excellent small brewery as tenants in one of his farm buildings but there he also has a good former cattle shed for his cider operations which he is still only starting to utilise.

One of his problems at really getting going with cider is in getting a regular suffi-cient supply of good apples. This is a bit ironic as his father lives locally and has an excellent 18 acre orchard planted for Taunton Cider. However, this is under con-tract to The Shepton Cider Mill / Gaymers and Harry is only able to have a few of the late season left behinds. There are plenty of apples grown nearby but paying top commercial rates gives a big cost.

Harry is keen to come up with a good commercial product that people want to drink. He has his own Voran press and reckons with a bit of hard work he can crush 1,000 litres a day, however that is only part of the operations and he seems keen to use commercial type facilities to produce his quality finished product. Most of his product to date has been sold in bag in boxes which he gets another local producer to fill and flash pasteurise to ensure lasting quality - another cost.

Then just before last Christmas his girlfriend, Ali, persuaded him to try a batch of bottled cider. He gave me a bottle of a good Somerset medium sparkling cider to try. He had warned me that he thought it had been slightly over carbonated, too much fizz, but it was a lot better than many I have tried. I can see what he is aiming at and think it will be a very good product - it is already enjoying considerable success in some local pubs etc. However, of course, the bottling operation is also outsourced so adding to the cost.

He is at the stage of thinking that he needs to bring some more of the process back onto the farm, possibly a small bottling line of some sort. He is looking at the possibility some of the rural business grants which have now become available. He is also experimenting with some keeved Normandy style cider. He used a blend of apples containing equal parts of bittersweet, dessert and sharps for this which sounds good, though he suspects he will be drinking the results of this years batch himself.

If you come across Harry's cider - bottled or draft - it is well worth trying.

Hecks Cider

Andrew and Chris Hecks, 9 - 11 Middle Leigh, Street, BA15 0LB 01458 442367
www.hecksfarmhousecider.co.uk

It is hardly much of a search for me to find Hecks. About 10 miles away in Street I have been a constant visitor for a number of years. When anyone asks me who my favourite cider makers are I inevitably reply Hecks. That is not that I necessarily reckon they make the best cider - but it is the combination of several factors. They make some very good ciders, an interesting range which changes during the year as new season ciders are ready or have matured. They are a nice friendly family too. Mother and father, John and Mary, are still around but the business is basically now run by brothers Chris and Andrew, or Andrew and Chris - it genuinely doesn't seem to matter which way around you go. Although you usually only see one at a time they are both fully involved. When you go out to shows you are also likely to come across their wives helping out - or even the in laws. Their children also now help out as well and Andrew's daughter Lizzie has even won competitions.

The family have been making cider in Street for around 100 years though their cider making heritage goes back further than that and can be traced to Chard in the 1840s. They have a great little cider mill and shop in a Street backroad. Street being an interesting place where the orchards and farms are still totally muddled up with the town which only grew less than 200 years ago when the Clark's shoemaking business expanded. They have both orchards of their own and source apples from many more old orchards around the area - including from the prime cider apple growing area around Baltonsbourgh. In their shop you can not only buy ciders but a range of fruit and vegetables and other local beers, souvenirs and of course their own range of Torside Apple Juice which offers a large number of varieties - and they were the biggest seller of my first cider book.

You can also see quite a lot of old cider making equipment and presses around the yard - though it is not really an organised museum as some other producers have. However, it is well worth a visit for the atmosphere and to taste some of their wide range of ciders.

I thought I had better go out and update myself to ensure that this entry was bang up to date for the book and search out some new information. I was quite surprised to find some. Back in the autumn they installed a new upsized belt press which after early teething troubles proved a great success. Andrew, whose day it was, now tells me that they are going to be installing a new bottling line, hopefully over the summer. It has been quite noticeable that they have at times struggled to keep up with supplies of their bottled ciders and juice, basically doing everything pretty much by

hand. Not that they are afraid of hard work. I arrived one Sunday morning and Andrew had just finished getting 36 five gallon barrels ready as a rush order for a wholesaler to take straight up to Wales somewhere for a festival where people were going mad for cider. Thirty six five gallon barrels takes a lot of lifting.

Anyway they are going to be demolishing one of their old storage sheds out the back and building a new more space efficient building to allow them to install the bottling line. Sounds like a good idea to me.

One of the great thing's about Hecks is that as well as their standard dry medium and sweet ciders, all very good, they also do a wide range of single variety ciders. Their award winning Kingston Black is famed far and wide and has won multiple awards. They also usually have Port Wine of Glastonbury available. Cider made from the apple Harry Masters Jersey, known locally as Port Wine in the Street and Glastonbury area, they store it in red wine casks and it makes a very nice mellow cider.

Then there is a whole series of other single varieties, some made in relatively small quantities, a choice of which may be available when you visit. One of my favourites is Dunkerton Late Sweet, an apple originally from Baltonsbourgh just down the road. Their website lists 18 possible varieties they may have. On my visit today they had my all time favourite, Browns Apple. Although this is theoretically a sharp apple it makes a wonderful single variety which is often slightly sweet. In blind judging at Melplash show last year I selected it as the winner of the sweet class - although it was only just into the sweet specific gravity permitted scale. Today they also had a cider at the other end of the scale, a two year old Porters Perfection, a very dry cider but with a really nice perfumed flavour to the front of it.

It is this not knowing quite what you are going to find on any day that makes visiting Hecks such a pleasure, plus of course talking to them about cider and cider producers. They are well known for the help and support they give aspiring competitors to themselves, but are quite understandably disappointed when people they have helped go and try to take their outlets off them.

Another tip is that during the summer they are quite likely to have seasonal fruit, especially plums when they get around to picking it from their orchards, as in the autumn they will have a good range of English apples.

And lastly I seem to have neglected to mention that they are one of the few Somerset cider makers who have really succeeded at also making perrys. They list six different single varieties. Most peoples' favourite is Blakeney Red. A really sweet and fruity drink that slips down a treat - though watch the stomach if you are having more than a couple of pints. The sweetness comes from the natural sorbitol in the fruit which is not fermentable. Sorbitol is also a well known laxative.

I sense that my enthusiasm for visiting Hecks may have come across quite strongly and I make no excuses for that.

Henry's Farmhouse Cider

Mr Pring, Tanpits Farm, Dyers Lane, Bathpool, Taunton TA2 8BZ. 01823 270663

In 2009 I spoke to Mr Pring and he suggested that they probably would not be making any more cider. His wife had died in a tragic accident a couple of years before and she had been the main force behind the cider business which had before then been on a reasonable scale. He was now concentrating on developing a touring caravan park in their orchards.

However, during the investigations for this book it became clear that they were still selling some cider so I thought I have better investigate it. On a Saturday afternoon run around I called at Tanpits Farm. There is a wonderful old farmyard with a collection of old agricultural equipment and chickens scratching around. There are still brown tourist signs to the Cider Farm. However, once I had pulled up in the yard there was little to indicate that they were selling cider.

A girl in her early 20's, I guess, got out of a van she had just pulled up in and myself and another gent who had just arrived asked her who was selling cider. She looked around and said she guessed it was her as there was no-one else around. She was one of the daughters of the family was actually very friendly and helpful considering she had just got in from a day's work and was in a hurry to get off out again. She said she thought the others had been to an auction.

She confirmed that they still did make a bit of cider each September. The yard still has an impressive array of rotoplast tanks for cider storage and she confirmed they still used a giant Bucher press - bigger than anything used by any cider makers other than the big commercial concerns of the county. The cider tasted fine - a traditional Somerset bittersweet cider with high tannins, the orchards are relatively modern commercial orchards, I understand Thatcher's now take many of the apples.

It could be worth your while to search out Henry's Cider and the farm is conveniently situated on the outskirts of Taunton. However, having talked to a few people apparently finding someone around to serve you can be a bit hit or miss, which is understandable as it is not their main business. I know of a number of cider businesses which have either shut or do not sell farm gate due to the problems of keeping someone around the farm yard all day for a small number of visitors.

Honey and Daughter

Bob Honey and Juliet Coles, Midford nr Bath, 07774 284499 www.honeyand-daughter.co.uk

Honey and Daughter, Midford Cider, was a real find. I was put on to them by my long standing friend and former customer Gordon Tucker. Gordon is a small-scale farmer and former lecturer in farm machinery who I have known for nearly 30 years since I first sold him chicken feed at his farm up the narrow lanes of Midford, near Bath. At the Bath and West Show he asked me if I knew cider maker Bob Honey who lives up another narrow lane at Midford. There followed a conversation on the phone where he persuaded Bob to buy a copy of my cider book and a promise that I would go and visit when I got a chance.

The visit took place in late October when I arrived to find Bob and his daughter Juliet milling and pressing a trailer load of cider apples, both wearing very fetching heavy green aprons. Bob is probably in his late 50s but looks considerably younger and has a very friendly greeting. His daughter Juliet who he introduces as Jules is his partner in the business and appears to take a full role in cider making. Bob was washing and milling the apples whilst Juliet was building the cheese. Bob has been a small farmer all his life but also ran a precast concrete products business which he sold in 2008 prior to setting up Honey and Daughter. He says he first started making cider about nine years ago when he planted his first small orchard. They decided to go commercial four seasons ago and have been making up to the 7,000 litre threshold. This season they have decided to really go for it and are targeting 15,000 litres. As Bob says "once you have gone over the 7,000 litre limit you have to double it before it becomes an economic proposition again."

They have set themselves up for production in a converted farm building on their small farm. They have a yellow funnelled Speidel mill and a double bedded Voran press which is ideal for the smaller producer. They are also fortunate in having plenty of space and have fitted out a section behind doors where they have a production and packing room which would be the envy of many who wrestle with the environmental health officers. The farm produces Aberdeen Angus beef cattle who graze in the orchards and enjoy feeding on the apple pomace in the autumn.

Unlike some newer producers I have come across they are not out for speed in production. It is more of a lifestyle business. Juliet says that they produce about 1,200 litres a day and Bob adds that it may not be a very long day! Juliet, who joined up with her father in 2008, fits working in the business around married life and bringing up two children. She had been a full-time mother since 2002 and before that had worked mainly in marketing and advertising - always useful skills for cider makers -

and selling specialist cheeses, another area with good synergies for cider! On the whole combining cider making with family fits very well though I had called during the autumn half term and she had had to 'farm' her children out as it was pressing season.

They currently have about 89 standard cider trees of their own. This is topped up by some very friendly neighbours from the village who provide plenty of windfalls and Bob is happy to use up to 30% of this assortment in his blend. They are currently investigating the possibility of planting out another five acres and are wondering whether bush or standard trees would provide the best option. They are also paying close consideration to what varieties they would plant. They currently have Harry Masters Jersey, Yarlington Mill, Brown Snout, Stembridge Cluster, Dunkerton Late Sweet, Slack Ma Girdle, Ten Commandments and Crimson King one of the more interesting blends I have come across.

The trees they are most pleased with in terms of productivity are the Dunkerton Late Sweets - a very local variety - and I wonder if this apple is what gives a distinctive fruity flavour to the sample of cider I tried. I once tried a single variety cider of it made by Hecks and that was certainly excellent.

They currently only make one cider. They ferment the juice out in 1,000 litre white plastic IBCs. They rack it into another IBC and let it mature. As it ferments out dry they find they have to add a touch of sucralose to get it to their clients taste, basically a medium dry. On sampling I immediately thought it was a filtered product as it was so clear but this is totally natural. All they do is strain it through a piece of muslin to get any bits out. They mainly sell to four or five local pubs and one 'export' client, a pub in Pembrokeshire called The Old Point House and a fair description of it is a good coastal village pub with a booming summer trade of regulars, holiday-makers and surfers.

One of the reasons for their success in pubs is down to a variant of the barrels on the bar. Some of the pubs take their cider in some smart small wooden barrels which as they are stood upright do not take up too much room. Inside these barrels they have a plastic bag of the bag in box variety and this keeps the cider fresh even if it takes a month to sell - a major advantage compared to the conventional five gallon plastic barrels which let in air and the cider can go off very quickly. However many pubs without bar space take the more conventional 20 litre bag in boxes.

They also bottle some of this cider in 2 litre plastic PET bottles and these are sold through the excellent Whiterow Farm Shop run by Steven and Heather Tucker at Beckington near Frome. And basically this is as complex as it gets. In previous years they have had problems running out of their cider by March and this year have made an effort to eke it out - although they were down to the last two IBCs when I visited. They are considering doing some 500ml bottles with a touch of sugar added to provide a bottle conditioned fizz. This is something they have seen successfully done by Dorset producer Rose Grant who has been a great help to them as she has been to many other new producers. Now they are doubling their level of production it will be interesting to see if they can keep their simple marketing philosophy. Unfortunately they can not do any direct sales to the public as it would not be feasible to man the buildings throughout the year but do look out for it in local pubs or visit the Whiterow Farm Shop.

Having taken up more of their time than I intended I left them to carry on with their pressing as another heavy autumn downpour swept over the hills. Very nice people, very nice set up (you can probably detect the note of envy) and most importantly, very nice cider. I hope to be seeing them again.

Honey Pot Cider

Colin and Julie Comben, South Petherton 01460 242539

For their shop at the smallholding which is open on Fridays only, heading west on A303 turn left at the South Petherton roundabout on the A303 and then after a few hundred yards take a lane to the left and it is along there on the left. It is open 11 - 6pm in the summer and 11 - 4pm in the winter.

The most recent time I met up with Colin and Julie of Honey Pot Cider was at the Mistletoe Fair at the National Trust's Barrington Court last December. They were dressed in Elizabethan garb, as befits the setting and selling some excellent mulled cider on their attractive stall.

Colin and Julie run a classic and environmentally sustainable life tyle business. They have a smallholding near South Petherton which is split into paddocks in which they graze their sheep for meat. Around the edge of each paddock they have planted apple trees and a small orchard of mixed dessert and cider apples in one corner of the holding. They keep bees to pollinate the trees and make honey. They harvest the apples and make cider and apple juice whilst the pomace is fed back to the sheep.

They sell produce at a lot of local markets, fairs and festivals. Cider is only a part of their offering which includes honey, beeswax products, relishes and preserves. I have now drunk the cider on quite a number of occasions. It is a light and fruity cider and is probably influenced by a reasonable proportion of dessert fruit in the blend. Very pleasantly drinkable.

They are very much after my own heart in experimenting with different styles and flavours. At the Mistletoe Fair they had some bottle conditioned cider where a bit of sugar is added to the still live cider when it is bottled to give an extra fermentation and a natural sparkle. Very nice it tasted too. My son Richie tells me that the bubble formed by this type of sparkling are a lot smaller than the bubbles forced in via carbonation so you therefore get a lot softer taste to the drink.

They have also in the past couple of years had a ginger cider and I believe an elder-flower version for us to taste.

Since I last wrote about them they have received the permission to open a small farm shop in their amazing multi purpose shed at their smallholding. I don't know if they also sell some of their lamb from there. It is only open on Fridays, I suspect they are too busy attending markets and fairs on most other days. Please do try to visit them, they come across as really genuine people who are trying to live the dream. I really like to support people like this. I hope my instructions are accurate enough to help you find their shop.

Lawrence's Cider

John Lawrence, Corton Denham, Sherborne, DT 4LS. 01963 220650 **SWECA**

Despite its address this cider maker is just in Somerset - down the lanes from Cadbury Castle. To me John is one of the more interesting characters in cider. I first came across him through a report in a local paper that he was delivering his cider in a Porsche. That didn't last long as a business stance - but the Porsche, or rather its successor, was an ingredient of a visit to John's double garage until the morning before my latest visit in March 2012. Apparently he had sold it to someone in Cornwall who had been up to collect it that morning. John needs the space in his garage for a major redevelopment he is just about to start.

However I need to go back a step first. The double garage is the hub of John's cider business. It is amazing how space efficiently it is set out with wooden racking containing neat rows of 200 litre plastic fermenting tanks. A Voran Press, a Speidel Mill and a bottling area with two small pasteurisers. John now makes around 5,000 litres a year, having grown from an experimental couple of gallons about 10 years ago before the bug really got going. Since my last visit John has really got into fermenting in oak and there must have been about ten 200 litre former wine barrels. Only a couple of these were in the racking - the rest were on two storey purpose-built wooden racks which he had the foresight to build on wheels so they could be moved around. Being a freelance aerospace designer by trade is obviously a big advantage when it comes to designing garage interior layouts.

John makes a good quality cider with mainly bittersweet apples from local orchards. In the past he was selling out far too quickly and for a long time I don't think I had tasted a mature cider from him. However, on this visit he poured samples from the wood for myself and both my son's, Richard and James - James being present as we were actually on a pilgrimage to the Queens Arms just along the road with an excellent choice of real ale - and Hecks cider. This cider was nicely mature, quite dry and had picked up a distinct smoky taste from the oak. His 18 month old 'vintage' was particularly pleasant.

Another distinct feature of John is his imaginative marketing. When I wrote my previous book he was pioneering placing polished wooden barrels on pub bars. Now he has gone a step further and for his best outlets is actually providing a beer engine and supplying the cider in some nine gallon moulded plastic casks he has got hold of from somewhere. This certainly should work well as long as the pub has a quick enough turn over of cider.

John has always focused on pubs for his outlets and they are still his main route to market. He also bottles cider for a well known local hotel / restaurant where his is the only cider on offer. He is always looking for more pubs to supply but The Camelot in South Cadbury would seem to be as likely a choice as any to find it. He also supplies a pub called the Natterjack near Evercreech where as far as I can see they don't sell it in the pub but fill 5 litre containers to sell as off trade.

Anyway - on to the exciting news. The reason John has sold his Porsche is to make room for his plans to extend his double garage. By the time this book is published if all goes well a two metre deep extension across the back of the garage will have been built with a loft above to enable him to bring his bottle storage back home rather than storing on a local farm. Another purpose is that he is investigating purchasing a belt press. We all have to accept passing years and he thinks a belt press will enable him to go on producing for many years, though I would imagine it will have to last a good many before it gives any sort of commercial payback!.

John is a really nice chap - always ready to have a good chat and share his cider making experience with others - we all learn off each other. He has a sign outside his bungalow and says if the pick up truck is parked in the drive he is quite happy for people to drop in on him - though phoning first would be advisable. He is a cider maker paying real attention and care to the detail in his cider making and on the evidence of this latest visit his cider is certainly worth tasting.

Lilley's Cider Barn

Chris or Marc Lilley, 01761 432847 www.lilleysciderbarn.com

Lilley's Cider Barn may sound a very nice place to go and visit - but unfortunately it is just an illusion. Lilley's is in fact a cider wholesaler who have some own brand products made for them.

Son Mark runs the wholesale side whilst father Chris is more into organising events. He runs both the Bristol and Bath Cider Festivals and these are quite a good bit of fun. I have visited the Bath Cider festival a couple of times. It is a very student orientated event held in the large Bath Pavilion behind the rugby ground. Something over 100 assorted 'cider's' and 'perry's' of various origins are available to drink. There are simple ploughman's or pork rolls to provide stomach filling and a Scrumpy and Western Band to provide the music.

Often the band are my friends the Mangled Wurzels, a tribute band who have gone one better by introducing a lot of their own material. Many would now rate them as preferable to the original Wurzel's who, although still fun, have tended to become parodys of themselves, just 'Wurzalising' others artists numbers; well they are knocking on a bit. However at these festivals when you get a 1,000 people singing along to the Mangled Wurzels own 'Tractor' song the atmosphere can be amazing.

As far as I am aware the Lilley's own brand drinks are I understand all made for them in the Original Cider companies very industrial factory at Clutton Hill. They are very much products of the 'silly name school' of various strengths: Crazy Goat, Pig Swill, Bee Sting, Star Gazer and Fire Dancer. I must admit a soft spot for their 'Apples and Pears Cider' a 5.2% keg which you sometimes find in pubs, an unchallenging fruity sort of a drink.

As wholesalers they also distribute the Welsh Gwynt Y Ddraig, a producer who has grown very fast and does produce some excellent ciders alongside some which to my taste seem rather bland. The range is also boosted by two of Rich's farmhouse ciders, some ciders from the usually excellent Weston's ciders, though I have been very disappointed by what they have seemingly provided to the festivals and the range from the Original Cider Company itself. I know last year Richie and I went along to a Cider festival in a pub in Gurney Slade which boasted of having over 30 ciders - I admit to being a bit disappointed on arriving to find that it basically consisted of just the Lilley's own and their wholesale range. There was nothing from the half a dozen producers within 10 miles of the pub.

These festivals do raise an interesting question; how many ciders do you need to make a festival? With the 'drinkaware' campaign, all cider makers are meant to be encouraging sensible drinking. Last year for one of their Bath Cider Festivals I took both Richie and my younger son James. Between us we averaged three pints each - James was the driver, he is more of a real ale and even lager man, and only had one of these. Buying cider in halves meant that between us, sipping from each others glasses we tasted 18 ciders each. This is probably far more than most people who would be taking a less dedicated role to tasting. Looking at my tasting sheet 18 ciders hardly made a dent on the list of 115 on offer. My favourite on the night was a Gwynt Y Ddaig Dabinet single variety. Elm Farm Scrumpy scored a 0 and I have no intention of finding out where it came from, whilst a concoction from the ubiquitous Mr Whitehead - his toffee at 4%, sweet and nauseating, - I could not take seriously enough to call a cider. It is interesting that the 115 ciders represented the efforts of little over 20 cider makers. A number had nearly 10 products on offer, many of which I would hesitate at referring to as ciders.

I see in the paper that Chris is looking to stage the Bath Real Ale festival this year after the local CAMRA branch pulled out. I also have spoken briefly to him about his ambition to run a large pub in Bath - it is a question of finding the right premises at the right price. I wish him luck - there is nothing wrong with an entrepreneurial approach - who knows Lilley's Cider Barn may become a physical reality.

Mad Apple Cider

Ian Culleen, Holford Nr Bridgwater. 01278 734870 madapplecidercompany.com

I was on the last weekend of writing up this book and attending a dinner in Taunton listening to National Hunt trainer Paul Nichols speak when someone around the table said to me 'of course you will have covered Mad Apple Cider.' I had a combination of panic and sinking heart - I had never even heard of them.

Early the next morning I investigated on the internet and after a few mistakes around the websites of a Czechoslovakian producer I manage to find a quite exciting website of a cider producer in West Somerset who seems to supply a quite impressive range of pubs in the area.

An email led to quite a quick response with a phone number and after missing each other a few times I eventually spoke to Ian, a delightful sounding chap who I am certainly going to have to search out in the near future but who I also could not bear to leave out of this book.

Ian was a former merchant navy man who first learned to make cider about 14 years ago from a farmer at Chedzoy whose creed for cider making was the very sensible 'take nothing out and put nothing in', make the cider as natural as possible. Ian has followed this creed. He then left Somerset and spent a good number of years in the Channel Islands on Sark where I think he may have run a pub - or at least spent a lot of time in one. Here he started making cider in a relatively small way, some of which found its way into the pub. One evening a friend, Jamie, had been drinking a fair bit of cider and when he went home his wife wondered what was up with him and the next morning told Ian that she thcn rcalised he had been drinking the 'mad apple.' The wonderful name stuck.

Ian had to return to Somerset after his father died to be nearer his mother, though he still has very strong links with Sark and returns a few times each year, including running a charity festival over there. However, at the age of 50 he was faced with the reality that he was not likely to find much of a job, and that he didn't really want to work for anyone else anyway. He decided to take the cider making seriously and set about obtaining some rented premises and identifying some orchards where he could arrange to take the apples.

He only really got going as recently as 2010, which is my excuse for never having heard of him, and is now producing around 5,000 gallons a year. He collects apples from about eight orchards scattered around West Somerset in places such as Lydeard St Lawrence, Halse, Williton, Stogursey, Over Stowey and in particular Halford where he rents the buildings he makes the cider in. Until last autumn he had picked up all the apples by hand but now has taken the very prudent move of using a small apple harvester. This has made harvesting a lot easier though he still has problems with getting his car stuck in the orchards. This was happening so frequently that he equipped himself with a winch to make sure he could get out. He has been delighted to discover that the four wheel drive he has recently obtained has a fixed wheel which should enable him to get out of just about anything - famous last words.

He built himself a wooden press powered -like ours - by a 20 tonne bottle jack. He has had a couple of steel beams inserted into it but as it does 23 gallons per cheese he cannot see the need for anything more expensive. He matures in oak in former red wine casks which gives his cider character.

The first pub he supplied was The Blue Ball at Triscombe and following success there he moved on to others and now lists eight outlets. Bizarrely one of the occasional stockists is The Crown Inn just down the road from me in Pilton. I can hardly imagine it is worth his while to come so far out of his home patch. Most pubs he supplies bag in box, especially where they have a slow throughput, however he also likes to supply in five gallon oak casks to sit on the bar.

I am very much looking forward to meeting up with Ian - and it is really good that the Quantock area, which is really steeped in cider heritage, has a proper cider maker again.

Naish's Cider and Chant Cider

Paul Chant, Piltown Farm, West Pennard BA6 8NQ www.chantscider.com

At the Bath and West Show in 2011 Frank Naish received a lifetime's achievement

award for his contribution to cider. A few people questioned what it was that he had contributed, but most very quickly came around to the view that his contribution is simply through his longevity as a cider maker. He is an institution in himself. At the age of 87 he has been making cider since the 1920's when he first shovelled apples down from the loft to those crushing the apples below at Piltown Farm where he still makes his cider today. And the farmyard today would still be instantly recognisable to anyone who called for some cider in those far off days.

He deserves his lifetime achievement award for being a genuine survival of a past era, a survival of when there were many farmhouse cider makers who saw cider as an essential part of their farming enterprise. I have talked to him of his experiences delivering cider around Shepton Mallet during the Second World War. He is 'living history' in the raw.

He made cider with his brother Harold for many years, but Harold died in the early years of this century. For a couple of years it looked like that would be the end of cider making at Piltown. But fortunately along came Paul Chant, a farming small-holder and jobbing builder, and together with a new squeeze box press Frank start-ed making again. Paul now has his own cider business 'Chant Cider' which has a separate section in the farmyard and HMRC have allowed them to be registered as separate producers. They work totally together in many things. I frequently come across this odd couple out and about the lanes. Paul is often repairing a hedge with Frank standing on and watching. I sometime stop and talk, Frank having a justified moan about the Dirstrict Council refusing him planning permission on a many year derelict house he owns and wanting to return the garden to agricultural land.

There seems little doubt that Frank's hearing, erratic at the best of times, has deteriorated even further recently. When he was guest of honour at the Bath and West he looked a bit bemused by those who wanted to talk to him. I know they had trouble making themselves understood and when he was persuaded to give his opinions on some of today's refined ciders he was quite forthright in his lack of praise! It is best to talk to him via Paul who seems to get through by bellowing at him with his very strong West Country accent. Certainly if you are going to the farm please make sure you contact Paul first.

Frank makes a very traditional cider. It is all stored in old oak pipe barrels (117 gallons) and it tends to vary from barrel to barrel. Sometimes this is because of a difference in the apples and maybe sometimes because it has deteriorated in the barrel. He has a number of traditional orchards with a wide selection of old varieties in them. When it is right the cider is wonderful, rich, dark, fruity and complex. However it is also too dry for the modern tastes of many. If you want a sweeter cider you can buy the dry and sweeten it yourself. For many years this was not a problem but gradually the old clients who liked the sour cider have died out. Although their cider is found at many festivals this is not enough to compensate for the reduction of the farm gate trade - only a pound a litre but a minimum of 5 litres and bring your own barrel. This year Frank had not sold so much and did not have the capacity to make the full threshold allowance as he still had too much left from previous years.

As can be imagined Paul, who I would guess is still in his 40s, is looking to a more enlightened approach. He has boxed up some 20 litre bag in boxes, which at £23.50 are as cheap as you are likely to find anywhere. He has branded his draft as 'Badger Spit' - certainly a different and memorable name. He is talking of going around pubs to try to encourage some to take it. He is also experimenting with some limited bottling and his girlfriend has designed some excellent simple rustic labels.

Some of these experiments are based on their perry which is from the fruit of one Belle de Jersey pear tree. I understand this is possibly the only tree of this variety found in this country. It towers over the rest of the orchard near the house and has quite amazing large fruit which are often more than 1lb in weight. I visited in January on a very breezy day and much of the fruit was still hanging on the tree though being blown around in a violent way. I would not want to be standing underneath if any came down.

I recommend that you get out and visit Frank and Paul and buy some of their very authentic cider. They are a remnant from a time gone by. Go soon while you still have the chance to see this authentic gem of cider making.

Nempnett Cider Company.

Keith Balch, Oxleaze Farm, Nemnett Thrubwell 07861 804711 **SWECA**

Nempnett Thrubwell is one of Somerset's more idiosyncratic village names. Not only is it hard to say but it is also hard to find. It is wrapped in a contorted maze of narrow lanes behind the reservoir at Blagdon. As you follow one of the lanes - of course with grass in the middle - you find Oxleaze Farm where Keith Balch rents a shed as one of our newer cider makers.

Keith started commercially only in 2010 and although he lives 15 miles away at Longwell Green on the edge of Bristol his association with Oxleaze Farm goes back to 1986 when he worked there after he left school. He moved on to an agricultural engineer about two fields away and later became a skilled cabinetmaker. He call his cider Piglet's Choice and during my interview with him the distinctive odour of pigs certainly pervaded the atmosphere. Oxleaze Farm houses a few hundred pigs and there are also some large sheds of free-range broiler chicken so obviously for both health and security reasons general visitors are discouraged.

However, it is the free-range poultry which has provided a major opportunity for Keith. The guidelines suggest that it is desirable for the poultry to have access to woodland cover. I am not sure that this was specifically referring to a cider orchard but it seems a very good fit to me. Over the past few years Keith and the farmer have been planting the paddocks around the large free range poultry sheds with cider trees from the famed propagator John Worle who, although he operates in Herefordshire, actually originates from a few miles down the road in Winford. They have planted one paddock with 196 Dabinett, another with 122 Harry Masters Jersey and another with some of the new varieties that have been released in the past couple of years:Hastings and Gilly's. Keith is looking forward to finding out how these apples perform - the trees certainly look full of vigour. There is one more paddock which he hopes to plant out with Yarlington Mill, a good blend of the traditional and modern.

In the meantime Keith sources apples from nearby villages including Clutton and Chew Stoke. He has also identified a rare Somerset source of perry pears and seemed quite surprised when I guessed first time - but I will keep his secret.

He has set himself up very well with a double bedded Voran press and mill and a pasteuriser. He is experimenting with both apple and pear juice as well as cider and perry. It was good to talk to someone who was still genuinely willing to experiment and see how it turns out. He is keen to learn and improve his technique. The Piglet's Choice Cider I had at a festival in my local pub in Shepton Mallet tasted fine.

He sells through a number of pubs in the Bristol area and some farmers markets. The farmers market at the University of the West of England has been his most successful and he is currently exploring possibilities with the Somerset Farmers Market's circuit.

Still I certainly wish Keith all the best. He is currently keeping just under the 7,000 litre duty threshold but with his enthusiasm to find outlets for his cider I suspect it will not be long before he takes the next step to expand. When all his apple trees come into production in a few years time he will certainly need to.

Orchard Pig

Andrew Quinlan and Neil Macdonald, West Bradley Orchards, Glastonbury, BA4 8LT 01458 851222 www.orchardpig.co.uk *SWECA*

Orchard Pig operates from the orchards of Edward Clifton Brown a delightful man in a delightful setting at West Bradley. These are orchards to which I have been bringing my sons to for pick your own apples for at least 20 years, and I usually now attend the delightful blossom day event which Orchard Pig hold there in late April. My most recent visit was the spring outing of SWECA where we were shown their new orchards of dessert apples for juicing grown on the intensive vine like system, and a sneak preview of their new branding.

Three years ago I referred to Orchard Pig as the new kids on the block as far as commercial cider goes and they are still making rapid progress along that route. However there is a crucial second string to their bow which interests me just as much. Neil Macdonald has a passion for orchards and his subsidiary company Orchard Pig Ground Force now maintain 100 orchards throughout the West Country. They offer a pretty comprehensive package for orchard renovation, maintenance and will even buy the apples. He also runs many courses and gives talks to encourage many people to manage their own orchards. See www.orchardground-force.blogspot.com.

Over Christmas he was on the television on a Winter Watch programme talking to Kate Humble about the very real problems that mistletoe can cause for orchard owners. It is not all about kissing at Christmas; uncontrolled mistletoe will eventually kill the tree it is parasitic on.

It is very important that services like those Neil offers are available to help maintain traditional, or modern, orchards so the heritage can live on. Mind you I had to chuckle at a farmer I was having a drink with the other night. He said Orchard Pig had taken all his apples last autumn yet he discovered that he still owed them over

£200 Knowing the particular problems that Neil had found in that orchard and the remedial work he had to do to correct it I think the farmer will find that in future years the work will have paid dividends many times over. I certainly hope so as Neil was kind enough to let me pick up a couple of sacks of Morgan Sweet from it.

As well as traditional orchards Neil is also very keen on modern plantings. He has costed the system they are now following for intensive planting and growing on wires. Although there is a large capital outlay he reckons payback can be achieved in years eight or nine and over 12 years the return will be 10% per annum - if I have got the figures right. I know one or two of the very traditional cider makers he was talking to looked at him as if he was speaking a foreign language - though the sharper farmers ears pricked up.

Orchard Pig has always made a very nice clean, still cider around the 6.5% ABV strength which I drink quite frequently. They are very much about natural ciders and maintain very high standards of production. Their other ciders tend to be sparkling and they were one of the first to really major on the 4.5% strength ciders both bottled and keg. Rather than adding water and sugars to lower the strength and add the sweetness the public crave they had gone down the route of blending back in apple juice. This certainly makes a very drinkable lower tannin fruity cider - though in my personal view cider and apple juice are not the same products and that adding apple juice tends to flatten the taste which mean a loss of some of its complexities. I know many people who totally disagree with me claiming apple juice is the most natural of all sweeteners. Orchard Pig themselves are quite clear that they are making different product for different markets.

Apple juice is very much a major part of the Orchard Pig business, about 35% of its turnover. It is made on the same belt press as the ciders but is pasteurised in bulk and used as needed throughout the year. They sell a wide range of juices and you will probably see this juice in even more pubs, farm shops, restaurants and delicatessens etc than you do their cider - and that is plenty. With their strong brand they have been very active in succeeding in getting their products out and about. They are now one of the largest of the cider makers outside the big nationals. High profile outlets include, national and regional listings with Waitrose as well as Jamie Oliver, House of Fraser cafes, The Lounge Bar Group, Mitchells and Butler as well as numerous independent on and off trade outlets, as well as a little export to Northern Europe and Singapore.

And now they are looking to step up a gear. At our SWECA visit we were lucky enough to be shown their new brand and range. Why on earth would the cider company with the strongest brand I know want to rebrand? It is to do with the younger market they are looking to appeal to. Their original logo with the apple tree curling round a silhouette of a pig was, they thought, very rural nostalgia, they wanted to evolve the brand to enhance the appeal, giving it character and making it more fun, but maintaining the rural and Somerset connection "Rooted in Somerset" is part of the logo. They also now differentiate the ciders from each other, using colours and names previously it had been Orchard Pig Medium 6.5% sparkling, Orchard Pig Dry 6.5% sparkling, Orchard Pig Medium Still 6.5% etc etc A key objective was better shelf standout. They have now gone for a much more direct contemporary style of logo but very much retaining the pig connection. By the way, the pig connection comes from Andrew who keeps Gloucester Old Spot pigs at his home just a few miles away. The second aspect is their belief that it is the products that need branding differentiating and giving character, much like the beer market, not just the company. There is probably a lot to be said to this but it is not an easy thing to achieve - especially when you are trying to impose an interlinked brand on a whole range at once. Hence, their ciders are now Reveller, Charmer and Truffler - it will take time to get used to the names but they are pleased by initial response from the trade. They have also broadened their range of fruit drinks and put them in small

330 ml bottles to appeal to a totally different market - more the bottles out of chiller cabinets for immediate drinking. They now have names like 'Flower Power', 'Deeply Rooted' and 'Totally Minted' along with 'Apple Tingler' and 'Apple Rambler'. A radical departure from the usual 'apple and...'brands

Orchard Pig also have a lot of tie-ins with other producers, they crush apples for some small producers, they pasteurise and filter for a number of others and bottle and bag in box for others - though due to capacity I understand they are also using others to do bottling for them. There is certainly a tie-up with Brothers Drinks who do their kegging for them. They also market through the national upmarket delicatessen manufacturer and wholesaler Baytree, which was founded by Neil's wife Emma. They store a lot of product at Baytree's premises in nearby Pylle.

I wish them a lot of luck. Both Neil and Andrew are good blokes who I have now known for a number of years. They have needed some major investment from outside backers to move the business forward the way they have - they may well need more over the next few years. They are basically tenants at West Bradley where owner Edward Clifton Brown is now in his 80's and there is limited scope for expansion of the production facilities. It will be very interesting to see where they go with their business.

Parson's Choice Cider

Phil Dolding, Parsonage Farm, West Lyng, Taunton. 01823 490978 **SWECA**

Parson's Choice is one of my favourite spots to buy some cider. It has no pretensions, it is just a straight Somerset cider maker making a straight Somerset cider.

It is run by Phil Dolding and his daughter Jeanette along with help from other members of the family and produces a steady 6,000 gallons a year as it has been for nearly 25 years. Phil is now fully retired as a groundworks contractor but really enjoys his cider business. He is one of those people who it is great to visit and have a chat with whilst having a taste. The chat in particular is liable to last far longer than you anticipate and cover a diverse rang of topics including cider and the rural past of his part of Somerset. I know I was in there one day when a party of cider fans on a tour of the West Country were visiting and they certainly seemed to be having a great time.

A main passion for Phil is his four acre standard tree orchard which he planted out with trees he largely budded and planted out himself with help from former Showerings orchard boss Les Davis OBE. Phil has chosen his advisers well, alongside Les for the orchard his production advice comes from former Long Ashton expert Keith Goverd whose excellent apple juice can be bought through Phil's shop. Apparently the orchard contains 26 different varieties of mainly traditional Somerset bittersweet varieties. In the autumn he prefers to pick up the apples by hand as he gets them a lot cleaner with less debris in them.

Attention to hygiene is a key part of his cider making process. He pays a lot more attention to washing apples and tends to press as he goes so the apples don't hang around to rot. He has used the same standard Voran press for over 20 years and it still has its original set of racks and clothes - Phil believes in thoroughly washing down between each pressing. He ferments in black plastic 1,500 litre containers as he is confident he can get these properly clean. He has used wooden barrels in the past but found however hard you tried to clean barrels out there was always a chunk of dirt left afterwards. After racking and storage to mature the cider he then transfers it into 5 gallon barrels to bring into the shop and sells mainly in gallon containers. As far as I am aware they don't do any bottling and use no chemicals or preservatives at all. They do a sweetened cider for those who want it, the sweetener being added into the 5 gallon barrels. It is a very natural product. Because of that not every barrel will taste quite the same - some will taste fruitier than others, some will retain more natural sweetness. Getting the public to understand that is always a problem, even for someone producing as consistently good cider as Phil.

His cider is mainly sold through their shop where you are as likely to be served by his daughter Jeanette who as she has helped to make much of the cider knows just about as much as Phil but takes no offence at all if you ask to speak to him. She has a very interesting range of things on offer from the inevitable apple juice and pre-serves, through cider mugs to pots and barrels. Outside in the yard they have just about the biggest selection of pots and planters I think I have ever seen, all sorts of shapes and sizes. The shop is open just about whenever you want it to be. I suppose it is really nine to six but I have commented to Phil that quite often when I pass it is early evening and I don't want to disturb him - he says I should come in anyway as there is usually someone there.

They also sell through some of the usual cider wholesalers and one or two local pubs. However ,in the past couple of years they have found that it is increasingly sold to visitors and regulars a gallon at a time.

I am writing this the day after the government has announced it's intention to bring in a minimum charge of 40p per units for any alcohol sold. This would be a disaster for natural cider producers like Phil who are just selling an excellent straight farmhouse product. The 4.4 litre containers he sells cider in, at a strength of about 6% ABV, will contain at a rough estimate 26 units. That suggests that the selling price would have to be at least £10.40 per gallon - and increase of around £4 on his current prices. Will the market stand it? I don't know. Yet I am willing to bet that it is a most unusual occurrence for any of Phil's cider to be used by young people to get tanked up before going out clubbing to cause problems on a Friday night. If the proposals come into force the government risks destroying a very traditional part of our national heritage without achieving anything to sort out the core problem.

Many of the more sophisticated cider producers sell a large proportion of their produce through pubs or as premium bottled products and will hardly be affected by the minimum 40p per unit price. Some producers are in tourist areas where they seem to be able to charge higher prices. However, for our many traditional makers in rural areas it could well be a problem. Please go and buy some cider off of people like Phil. Enjoy the chat and the heritage. Long may it last.

Perry's Cider

George and John Perry, Perry's Cider Mills, Dowlish Wake, Ilminster TA19 0NY, 01460 52681. www.perryscider.co.uk *SWECA*

Dowlish Wake is a quintessentially English setting. You come down the hill, past the church, around the bends, into the small village, cross the ford with a footbridge beside you and turn past the old barns into the attractive former farmyard setting of Perry's Cider. They have been here, making cider, since 1920 and the business is now run by George of the fourth generation with help from his father John, from the third generation, whilst grandmother Marguerite from the second still looks in.

It is a location I know well; with a wife from nearby Crewkerne and a spell working at even nearer Chard I have been buying some cider here for around 30 years. Yes there have been a lot of changes over that time though much stays the same and it is still a very traditional cider making operation but one that has not been slow to embrace modern developments.

Over the past couple of years I have got to know George's father John quite well. He has just about retired from his career as an accountant and is spending more time around the business - though as far as I can see not getting in George's way. His pride is in his orchards where he has planted out an extensive bush orchard just along the lane from the village. I enjoyed a walk around the orchard with John after the SWECA AGM had been held in one of their sheds last September. We had parked our cars in one of their traditional orchards just across the road from the shop. Boughs laden with shining apples and the bright red and green Tremlett's Bitter ready for picking. In John's bush orchard the Morgan Sweet had already been picked and of great interest were some very healthy looking young trees which are

Liz and John flank the author at the 2011 Taste of the West awards at the Eden Project

from the new cider varieties which were the result of the last years of breeding at the Long Ashton research station. Their former pomologist Liz Copas has continued overseeing the project and a number of new varieties have been selected, propagated by John Worle in Herefordshire and are now being planted out. They are nearly all medium tannin bittersweets or bittersharp where traditional varieties such as Dabinett have been crossed with dessert varieties to give earlier harvesting dates to extend the cider making season forward. People like me are waiting to taste some of the ciders from these with interest.

John is the immediate past Chairman of SWECA and we spent a great morning together in 2010 judging the ciders at the Bath and West Show, a fascinating experience. I also spent a wonderful afternoon with him and his wife Liz at the Eden pPoject. We were attending the Taste of the West 2011 awards dinner on a day in early November but sat inside the tropical bio-dome it was like mid summer. The awards were spread over an afternoon of eating a multi-course meal made up of fine West Country produce. I was attending for my employer Old Mill, who had sponsored the 'Best Alcoholic Drinks' award and I was delighted that Perry's had won it with their single variety Dabinet. It has a fine taste and slips down well but the judges also commented on the bottle and its label. Perry's have over the past couple of years developed a very strong modern branding of the 'simple' school which fits extremely well with the mood of the moment especially with discerning younger drinkers.

Perry's make a good clear range of ciders and although draught is still very much part of it - tasting is very well set out in their excellent shop - a lot of their focus is currently on bottled production. A few years back they were lucky enough to get some EU grant funding to put in a superb bottling plant with a through pasteurizer. They not only bottle their own ciders on this line but also bottle for other producers some of the finest ciders the West Country produces, and they produce some white label products for outlets in the South West's holiday markets. We had a demonstration of this bottling plant during our SWECA visit. My only regret is that it is in the barn that was formally used as the shop which was a favourite of mine. However as the excellent new shop and tea room are in another converted barn it would be churlish to comment!

The best feature of all about Dowlish Wake is what a wonderful place it is for people to visit. Attractively set out, you are in a living museum to cider. As well as the orchards you can see the pit for the apples to be tipped into next to the mill and old hydraulic press which is still being used. Next to that is a fascinating museum of two rooms absolutely packed with cider and rural artefacts from a bygone age. There is an old farm wagon or two on display and plenty of wooden barrels. It is the sort of place where you can go yourself, take your mother or your children and there is something to appeal to all.

And of course Perry's do not make a perry!

Pilton Cider

Martin Berkley, Platterwell Lane, Pilton, www.piltoncider.com **SWECA**

When Martin got married to Angela last year he needed to put an occupation on his marriage certificate - and for the first time in his life he completed 'Cidermaker'.

Martin and Angela had first met many years ago at University where they were studying horticulture together - however, they both went off and led different lives until getting back together a few years ago. Martin had worked in computer software whilst Angela was a garden designer. Over recent years the couple have made a big impact on the cultural life of Shepton Mallet with projects like their highly successful Christmas lantern making and parade and the 'Secret Cinema' for a town without one.

However, this book is about cider, which has now taken over a big part of Martin's life. They live in a small cottage just to the south of Shepton, in the Pilton parish and about five years ago Martin asked Roy Trott, a local farmer, if he could have some apples from a pretty extensive orchard nearby. The first year was very much an

amateur communal effort with tubs of apples pounded by sticks to smash them up. The next year he had advance to a heavy old scratter with a concrete roller.

He obtained a large traditional press with a metre square bed which, despite the disaster of having the metalwork stolen from his garden, he is still using. This is powered by a couple of chunky bottle jacks - though he now has now moved on to a modern Speidel mill for the milling.

He and Angela are in the second year of planting out an orchard down the hill at Pylle. With his horticultural background Martin is very interested in some of the orcharding aspects of cider. Nearly all his apples come from either Pylle or Pilton, he feels that if he is using the name Pilton Cider he has to ensure that there is a strong connection between the parish and the product and he mills and presses at his cottage. However, he has now rented premises at the Anglo Brewery in Shepton Mallet - just a mile up the road - where he ferments the juice and carries out the very space consuming functions of bottling and labelling.

Martin has focused on producing one upmarket keeved cider product; chasing the holy grail of natural retained sweetness and natural effervescence. Mastering the process has not been without its problems and failures but the cider he launched on the market in the early summer of 2011 was excellent. I had ordered a dozen bottles for an Old Mill local food and drink reception I was organising in our marquee at the Bath and West Show and even the Partners who are usually rather concerned at my tendency to buy cider when they are expecting champagne admitted that it was absolutely right for the event. Martin sequentially numbers his bottles and as I write in February 2012 is on about 3,200. I was lucky enough to have bottle number 1!

Martin had a stand at the Mid Somerset Show where his cider was a great success on a glorious sunny day when he sold 600 bottles worth of cider and he won a prize for the best label. This really is a good bit of simple but effective artwork. He now sells through a good number of specialist cider off licences, delicatessens, farm shops, restaurants and pubs. His star success so far has been getting Harvey Nichols to stock the product.

Martin is a quietly spoken cidermaker but with a lot of drive. He has a vision of what he wants to produce and is making great strides to get there. It is certainly a product I enjoy drinking. As it has matured in the bottle it has gone a little drier with a more complex taste and he is thinking that this will now be his 'vintage' when he can start selling this winter's produce. I know I will certainly keep on drinking it - and using it to show sceptics what a really good, quality drink cider can be.

Quality English Cider

Keith Goverd, The Bailiffs Cottage, The Green, Compton Dando Bristol. BS3 4LE 01761 490624 *SWECA*

Keith Goverd has a passion to help cider makers raise the standard of cider. He is one of a small number of former Long Ashton research station scientists who still keep very busy with some cider consultancy work. He also makes some very nice produce of his own.

Keith is forthright with his views and is not afraid to let it be known when he doesn't agree with other 'experts.' What Keith is trying to do is to help cider producers do things properly and sometimes he feels that this has to include being practical rather than just following a particular interpretation of the science. He is prepared to talk to any cider maker who wants to phone him. As he says after nearly 45 years he is not rushing around looking for work and for many a phone call can offer considerable help. Where there is a need for further help a day's consultancy work may be appropriate.

He feels one of the issues at the moment is around acidity. Many of the modern cider makers religiously check pH measurements and use this as the determinate of how much sulpher dioxide to add to ensure control of the microflora. Keith is more concerned about getting across that the importance of acidity, titratable acidity, is to do with the taste of the product and that more needs to be done sometimes to correct this. I must confess to being slightly out of my depth with this - I will have to get my son Richie to have a chat with him - he has more of a feel for the science than I do.

His other great mission is to avoid acetification in cider. He has many ways of doing this from adding a bit of sugar to keep fermentation ticking over ,to stretching a thin sheet of plastic across the surface to keep air out. Keith is also a bit critical of many of the judges of cider competitions. This is not only down to lack of genuine expertise, but a failure to agree on what they are judging for. I know he was critical of a very distinguished judge who he felt was judging on the commercial potential of a cider rather than its quality against pre-agreed standards.

He sees this as being an exciting time for the cider industry with so many new producers coming in. He wants to make sure they get the right advice to start with. I hope some of those of you reading this book will be young producers who will feel free to ring Keith up - but make sure you have swotted up on some of the science first!

Keith is also specialises in apple trees and varieties of apple trees and has been involved in a number of projects over recent years including some in Cornwall. He has made single variety apple juice from over 200 varieties of apple and it is apple juice that is the prime concern of his business. He sells his range at the very popular Bath Farmers Market in 75cl bottles. He also sells his own cider, perry and cider vinegar. He is very particular about sourcing his fruit and his ciders are very good. One cider he back sweetens with up to 15% cider apple juice. Please notice the emphasis on the fact that this is juice from cider apples, I confess to finding many ciders that have been back sweetened with dessert apple juice as being rather flat and bland tasting. Bath Farmers Market is every Saturday morning and you can usually find him there. I have also seen his apple juice at Phil Dolding's 'Parsons Choice' Cider but in very few other places.

As I said at the start Keith is passionate about cider producers getting it right. We need to ensure we use his expertise and the few others who were fortunate enough to have had a career in cider science. The big question has to be, where the next generation of advisers will come from?

Rich's Farmhouse Cider

Jan Scott Mill Farm, Watchfield, Highbridge, TA9 4RD. 01278 783651 www.rich-scider.co.uk *SWECA*

These days I mainly see Rich's at the Bath and West Show where they quite often have their bar just along from the Old Mill marquee which I run for the four days. Rich's seem to conveniently forget that they are meant to stop serving at a certain hour and I find it really pleasant having an early evening drink when everything is winding down from a hectic day. The bar is usually run by Jan's husband Brian with support from son George, and Jan usually makes a couple of appearances during the show.

Jan is a very busy woman who has made a huge success of the business since inheriting it from her father Gordon in 1998. I can remember the gaunt Gordon Rich quite well. I used to call in to pick up cider on my way home from work when I did a spell in Bridgwater, I used to drop someone in Highbridge and then take the attractive Wedmore route across country to Wells and Shepton.

Gordon had moved from the Quantocks to Watchfield near Highbridge in the 1950s and had built up a considerable cider business of the old school. Sales from the farm gate from a small cider cellar room which people used to go into for 'tastings'. Their off trade was largely focused around the pubs and clubs and at that time wherever I seemed to go in Somerset, be it for a barbeque, party or drinks after a village cricket match it always seemed to be Rich's cider that was on offer. It has always been quite a light, very sinkable cider which goes down a treat and is very refreshing on a hot day.

However, although they still maintain a pub trade greater than most cider makers,

Martin, George, Russell, Brian, Molly and Jan on the Watchfield Flyer

pub cider is an area that has been slowly slipping away until recent years. Russell Salway has been with the business nearly 40 years since he first started helping after school. He still has his delivery rounds most days of the week delivering to pubs and clubs, though now it is more a case of a barrel or two at a time rather than the 10's and 20's of days gone by. When Jan took over the business she started to focus much more on the potential of tourist trade in Burham on Sea and Berrow. This had long been a target at the bars on the campsites but now there was more of an effort to get the punters to come and visit their farm shop. During the noughties it seemed that every time I visited Rich's, the shop had been expanded and rearranged. A good selection of souvenirs and beers was built up to supplement the cider - though cider tastings and sales remain at the heart of the shop.

In 2008 shrewd business woman Jan took the next step and purpose-built a 60 seat restaurant and tea room. Now it seems that every time I visit the tea room is at least as busy as the shop. There is a carvery serving roasts every day and for the Sunday carvery booking is usually essential. Jan had invited me out to talk about this entry over lunch and the plate full of roast beef was truly delicious. I had to have a second half of their cider to wash it down! All the food comes from as local ingredients as possible and everything is prepared and cooked on the premises.

The family role at Rich's is an essential element of the business. One of Jan's sisters works in the shop and her cousin Martin Rich is the cider maker. I frequently meet him at SWECA meetings usually with his pupil, Jan's son George alongside him. 19 year old George is a strapping lad who is also making a name for himself on the rugby field. I am sure it will not be long before 12 year old daughter Molly finds a role.

The cider choice is usually the basic dry, medium and sweet whether you have it draught in containers or ready bottled in attractive glass flagons of various sizes. They sell some really small 100ml bottles which must contain all of two mouthfuls - though I suspect these sell quite well to tourists looking to take a little novel souvenir back home with them. I wonder how many of these actually get drunk. Martin also likes to make a single variety for their 'Golden Years' range. He selects the best of the ciders and bottles it ups, though it does tend to sell out and only have seasonal availability. For 2012 he potentially has three varieties which look as it they may make it, Lambrook Pippen, Dunkerton Sweet and Yarlington Mill. An interesting selection, I will have to keep dropping in to see when they are ready.

They also sell an extra dry cider. It is amazing how much the taste for sweetness has increased in the public in recent years, where so many foodstuffs are stuffed with unwanted or even suspected sugars. I tasted their dry recently and detected sweetness in it. I asked for the extra dry and there was the Rich's cider I knew of a decade or so ago. They say they still do the extra dry for the old-time drinkers who want it. I was a bit surprised to find myself in that category as I am not usually an extra dry cider drinker.

Rich's Cider Mill is now a good place for the tourist to visit. Very convenient for the M5, you park beside an attractive orchard often grazed by sheep and in summer anyway you are not aware of the problems that this wet land below sea level causes for growing apple trees. As at Perry's you can see the delivery pit for apples and the production process is open to view. There is a delightful small museum with some very old equipment, some of it made just along the road in the next village of Meare. A recent addition to the museum is a restored red Massey 35 tractor affectionately known as the 'Watchfield Flyer'. It was Gordon's and for many a year he and the other staff used it as a workhorse of the business and it was a familiar sight on the roads around the village. Brian had it restored for Jan and it takes pride of place in the museum. There is also a play castle of some sort to keep the children amused, but I must admit I have not paid too much attention to this!

Given its proximity to the M5 they sometimes get some interesting visitors. George had done a spell of work experience when he was 14 at the Highgrove Gardens of Prince Charles. He had taken a box of cider for the gardeners along with some leaflets which got put in the potting shed. It is believed that this led to the arrival of a group of youngsters off to Cornwall and if it had not been for a customer pointing it out they would have been unaware that Prince Harry was amongst the group. Another time Brian was watching with suspicion a group of Irishmen in the shop one Saturday morning - there had been a bit of trouble with some travellers nearby. However, it only turned out to be the boy band Westlife who had been at a nearby party the previous evening.

With Jan at the helm Rich's now looks like a secure family business which knows where it is and what it is doing.

Sheppy's Cider

David and Louisa Sheppy, Three Bridges, Bradford on Tone, Taunton TA4 1ER 01823 461233 www.sheppyscider.com *SWECA*

Sheppy's have been making cider at Three Bridges since 1917 and are now one of the leading manufacturers in the county. They are probably one of the largest of the artisan producers in the country with a genuine national presence, but it is still very much a family business and what I like very much is the effort they are putting into making the cider heritage available to the public - well that and the fact that they make some very fine ciders too!

Sheppys is now run by David and Louisa, a husband and wife combination which seems to work well. David is well known and very popular in the cider industry but last autumn it was no surprise to see that it was Louisa who attended the SWECA AGM. If I want to know anything David usually just refers me to Lousia. Last year they very kindly agreed to help me by putting an advert in my book on the 'History of Cider at the Bath and West Show'. This was particularly appropriate as I have found records of the family competing in the cider making classes at the show from the 1920s and they have been associated ever since. I did meet David's late father Richard Sheppy a few times many years ago when I sold him fertilizer and had to drop the odd thing off at the farm.

The business was built on its location on the main A38 and was a haven for thirsty holidaymakers on their way down to Devon and Cornwall on holiday, and on the way back. However, that trade declined following the building of the M5 in the 1970s. It kept going through its sales to regulars of draught ciders and the range of bottled ciders which they already had established at a time when this was unusual for farmhouse businesses. Their Bullfinch and Goldfinch along with Gold Medal date as brands from the 1930s, certainly innovative marketing for the time.

Bottled ciders have continued to be a major focus for the business and they must be the only farmhouse cider maker to have sold regularly to just about every super-market chain throughout the country. Nowadays they have considerably broadened the range. Their single varieties include Dabinett, Kingston Black, Falstaff, a light dessert cider with no tannin, and Taylors Gold a very nice slightly sweet cider. I drunk a couple of bottles of Taylors recently when I organised a meeting at Barley Mow farm shop near Chard. They also make an Oak Matured Vintage Cider which subtly changes each year with the different seasons but of which David is justifiably proud and indeed is one of my favourites. Add to this an organic cider and a cider made with honey and you will see the extent of the range.

In 2010 David produced a new product - Somerset Draught, a 5.5% blend of cider and dessert apples with a crisp fruity flavour. Not only does he bottle this but he produces it in keg so he can start to challenge in the pub market place where bottles do not make much of an impact. I must admit this is a very refreshing tasting keg product and vastly superior to most of the usual selection available. They have also created a new keg product (4.8% ABV) called Oakwood using one of their former brand names. It is a medium taste cider, based on a vintage quality blend.

This focus on the range of products should not let us forget their cider farm which is amongst the best at making heritage available to the public. They have a shop with tastings which is open most times except low season Sundays - which is when I usually seem to pass it! The shop not only sells cider, after you have tasted to find your favourite, but also includes meat from their herd of Longhorn Cattle which are often to be seen grazing in the orchard. Visitors are also encouraged to have a walk around the orchards and to visit their museum which has an excellent selection of not just cider artefacts but of rural social history. They do offer tours of the cider mill but these need to be booked in advance and are for parties of at least 20.

In the museum you can see the excellent DVD that they had produced for them by Kevin Redpath, a freelance filmmaker from central Somerset. This takes you through the cider making year on the Sheppy's farm. It was played on a non-stop loop in the cider marquee at the Bath and West Show last year. I have a copy with the cultured tones of James Crowden. I also have to mention their wonderful web-site as it was built by my friends Nigel Reece and Paul Stephenson at Cognique in Street who designed the cover of this book.

Currently Sheppy's are growing again. They could not fit any more into their existing range of old farm buildings so they have taken the brave decision to grub up a small area of orchard and build a new pressing shed and warehouse and to plant a new 15 acre orchard in 2013. I am sure this will help to take Sheppy's on to the next level and win even wider recognition for their excellent ciders.

Shepton Cider Mill

Formerly Gaymers. MagnersGB, Kilver Street, Shepton Mallet **SWECA**

It is a difficult time to be writing about the Shepton Cider Mill as no-one - least of all those who work for them - seem to know exactly what is going on.

It is still possibly the second biggest cider mill in the world and three years ago things were going along extremely well. It had been built up over many years from when it was the core part of the Showerings, Babycham empire and the company was one of the top ten companies in the UK. Then there were a succession of sales and purchases. It became part of Allied Breweies, then Allied Domeque, was purchased by Matthew Clark, followed by Constellation Brands and two years ago it was snapped up by C & C Brands, the company that owns Magners.

Over the years the original Showerings business had been added to by the acquisition of medium sized cider producers with a national profile such as R N Coates, Whiteways, Gaymers and finally Taunton Cider in the late 1990s. The company also have their own orchards and have contracts with many growers managing new bush orchards.

At Shepton Mallet they made established leading national brands of cider such as

Dry Blackthorn, Olde English, Natch, and K. They had also established two new brands in Gaymers Original and the cloudy Addlestones and had developed an excellent connoisseur range of the quality bottled ciders Stewley, Newton Vale, Devon and Somerset. For a year after the takeover things carried on much as usual but then these speciality brands became more difficult to find in local outlets with Shepton Mallet losing the level of local autonomy they had gained under the previous regime.

As far as I am aware all these brands are still being produced still but some are very difficult to find. During 2011 it became evident that things were changing. C&C mainly seemed to be interested in promoting keg and bottled Magners Cider. Magners is an Irish cider and I understand that it can only be made in Ireland. Local marketing support was withdrawn and the fantastic regional initiatives that had been developed came to a halt. A large part of the marketing budget for their leading brands like Blackthorn and Gaymers was cut. They pulled out of a number of sports sponsorships and their product was lost in a number of key outlets - interestingly often to be replaced by Thatchers Gold, who thought Christmas had come.

Many pubs and other outlets seem to have been encouraged / forced to change to Magners and the original brands seem to have been relegated to also rans even in the supermarkets. All visible marketing behind the connoisseur ciders seems to have disappeared. C&C seemed to think that they only had to put Magners product into every outlet and sales would switch to it. I fear they have gravely misunderstood the buying public - especially in the West Country.

What the intentions of C&C are now is unknown but a lot of ground has been lost for some of their traditional West Country brands. All I know is that there are currently a lot of disappointed people and a very uncertain future for some dedicated lifelong cider makers.

Meanwhile Thatchers Gold seems to have become the West Country cider of choice.

Stone's Bittersweet Ciders

Richard Stone, Society Road Shepton Mallet. www.bittersweetcider.co.uk www.somersethistory.co.uk *SWECA*

Three years ago when I wrote the Somerset Cider Handbook I recounted my misadventures over many years as a home cider maker and said it was much easier to leave it to the experts. Imagine my surprise when months later my son Richie, then 23, decided that he was going to become a cider maker and started gathering equipment. However, he has a much more scientific approach than me so I thought he may be more successful! He has now made for three seasons and is registered with HMRC so justifies his place in this book. My LinkedIn entry includes the fact that I am 'labourer and marketing' for Stone's Bittersweet ciders.

Richie has approached cidermaking in an interesting fashion. Unlike my slapdash approach he went on training courses run by Peter Mitchell, he insists on cleanliness and sulphites. We have also gone to considerable trouble to source decent bittersweet cider apples. The first year we had too many Michelin in the mix and with inadequate equipment ended up with some drinkable but according to the experts rather 'mousey' cider. The second year was a considerable improvement and this third season tastes even more encouraging.

From the start he has been keen to experiment and as an Early Modern historian doing a Phd his studies of the 17th Century has come up with a number of ideas. We have made hedgerow ciders where apples are fermented with elderberries, wild plums, sloes, raspberries, blackberries and we have flavoured cider with ginger, rosemary, tea, hops, chilli and elderflower. Of course these cannot be sold. According to HMRC they are 'made wines' and would suffer a crippling duty if we wanted to. These of course are full strength ciders and not the watered down fruit ciders which have recently become fashionable. He has made a number of single variety ciders, depending on what apples we can find. The second season we found some marvellous Kingston Black, twice we have made Morgan Sweet to drink over Christmas,

last season we found some Brown's Apple. He has also experimented with Bramley (too acidic) and Ashmeads Kernel, reasonable for a dessert apple.

He has also been keen to experiment with different cider making techniques. He can already claim to be an 'award winning cider maker.' In 2011 he gained a second at the Bath and West in a class for Normandy Style ciders with his experiments at keeving. Then later in the year he won the Supreme Champion Cider at the South West Winter Fair with a naturally sweet cider where he had naturally concentrated the juice through freezing - thanks to Rob and Jane Lunnon at Mendip Moments Ice Cream for loaning a space in their freezer for a few days. He also experimented with a 17th century range of flavoured bottle conditioned cider for an Early Modern history conference he was involved in helping to organise.

This season he has made around 250 litres of a Bath and West 'vintage' with cider apples from the trees planted around the showground in the 1970s. Most of the ground was very rough and the stings from the stinging nettles gained while collecting the apples tingled for a few weeks. Hopefully this will be on sale at the show.

He has provided a lot of cider which has been very well received on the Old Mill hospitality stands I organise at many country shows for my day job. He has also provided cider to a couple of cider festivals including to the Horse Shoe at Bowlish only a few gundred yards down from our house - very few food miles. This little festival is organised by landlady Steph Turner who is a fellow searcher after cider and she can usually be found serving on the SWECA bar at the Bath and West on the Friday.

However, Richie is still hesitating as to how commercial he wants to go. He is currently in his eighth year at Bristol University, writing up his PhD and tutoring on a couple of courses. Where he is going next he is not sure but, he can't yet afford the premises and equipment he would really like for cider making. Of course so far I have totally failed to be able to provide him with the land we would both love to have to plant out our own orchard so we can have even greater control over the apples used.

He is, however, keen to continue with his experiments and I am really excited by some of the quality and innovative craft ciders that he is producing.

Thatchers Cider

Martin Thatcher, Myrtle Farm, Sandford, Somerset, BS25 5RA 01934 822862
SWECA

I had quite a chuckle at a TV advert last year. Thatchers Cider made their debut on our screens and the advert included a pleasantly understated use of an animation of a portly man alongside a taller, slimmer man. Anyone who knows much about Thatchers would have instantly recognised John, doyen of the cider industry alongside his taller son Martin. The inclusion of the scene says more about the friendly family nature of the company than anything else could.

They also adopted a great tag line - 'People who care about Cider.' As a professional marketing person myself I must confess that this type of tag often makes me cringe, there is the real danger of being seen as cynically corrupting peoples views. Here however they are totally justified in its use. Thatchers is a delightful family company who really do care about orchards and cider. Long may it remain so.

It is quite an achievement to have maintained this yet be amongst the top five cider makers in the country. They have been in this group for some time but last year took a major step forward. I first remember coming out to them to collect cider when I was a student in Bristol in the mid 1970's when they were little more than a farm style operation. Now they have a large modern mill and press - probably the most modern of the three national companies' factories I have been around - but standing side by side with 100 year old oak vats used for maturing the cider. They are a genuinely national brand appearing in almost every supermarket and a growing percentage of pubs and yet they retain a very human feel. As well as the introduction of TV advertising last year also saw Thatchers move into sports sponsorship in a significant way capitalising on the unfortunate dislocation within Gaymers following the 'Magners take over'. Thatchers name is now on Bath Rugby shirts, as well as the perimeter boards at the County Cricket Ground in Taunton and at Yeovil Town Football Club. I must admit I was slightly concerned as to whether the company could sustain such an increase in marketing budget but when I recently talked to Martin he confirmed that it was advertising which had produced instant results and they have already booked up to £2.5 million of advertising for 2012.

They could still be doing this and be cynically corporate. But to me this is not the impression they give - they really are 'People who care about Cider'. John is one of the most passionate supporters of English orchards there is, and the company sponsor an award for the best kept orchard at the Bath and West Show. They source English apples from West Country farms and they grow a considerable number of themselves. John has a heritage orchard in the fields beside the mill which contains an extensive library of rare varieties, whilst in the next field but one there is an experimental orchard of intensively planted 'hedgerow' trees.. They are continuing to plant more orchards including some dessert varieties for their premium products - some 50,000 trees have been planted in 2012, at their new land at Shiplake.

Katy is one particular dessert variety which Thatchers major on and they are one of the few people still planting this apple. It makes a very pleasant light cider, especially beloved by women and even more so in Thatchers Rosé where the delicate blush colour apparently comes from the rosy skins of the apples through a process that is a close secret. However it may not be my personal taste as I prefer some tannin in the cider. This is without doubt one of the secrets of Thatchers - their range includes something to suit every shape of cider drinker. For the traditional cider connoisseur, now joined by a new generation of cider drinker, there is the very orange Cheddar Valley - one of the few pints you can still find in pubs at little over £2.00. This is one of a range of traditional draught ciders for pubs. I must confess I find these all taste slightly 'young' but are certainly very drinkable. There is the slightly quirky Green Goblin; originally made for the Hobgoblin Brewery. When they decided they didn't want an own brand cider Thatchers have kept it on in keg and bottles and it is a good tasting cider.

Their best seller however is the now famous Thatchers Gold. Now widely available throughout the country on keg in pubs and in the supermarkets in cans and bottles of various shapes and sizes. It is a vastly preferable alternative certain other national well known brands.

Thatchers also produce a limited number of ciders for other people. Butcombe Brewery make no attempt to hide the fact that their Long Ashton Press Cider - and now their Ashton Still - is produced for them by Thatchers whose farm is only a few miles up the road from the brewery. As Butcombe are now a leading regional brewer this considerably extends the number of pubs you can find their product in. At the Bath and West Show in 2011 Butcombe and Thatchers got together to provide a bar and I understand this will again be present in 2012 though in a different spot and much extended.

Thatchers have a farm shop at their mill at which most of their products can be brought at sensible prices. Rather than a the usual 'farm shop' range their shop just sells cider and Thatchers promotional clothing and products. I do think there is a bit of a missed opportunity here. I also feel Thatchers could be doing more by promoting the heritage of Somerset Cider to visitors to the county if they made it more of a cider visitor centre. However, that is just my view as a marketing man and a 'person who cares about cider'. Perhaps there could be some greater synergy here!

Tricky Cider

Alistair Brice and Steve Watkins, The Old Bakery, Churchingford, Taunton 01823 243129 www.tricky.com

It is nearly 20 years since I first ventured into the heart of the Blackdown Hills accompanying another farm feed rep from a merchants who I was supposed to be helping. I found farmhouses with corrugated iron tin roofs and farmers wives preparing apple turnover and custard for the farmer's lunch in dull white enamelled dishes with blue rims. It was a land that time had forgotten.

Straddling the A303 on the Devon and Somerset border the Blackdown Hills are a wide area of narrow lanes, tiny villages, steep hills, grazing ground, forestry plantations and a number of delightful rural pubs. It is here that you will find Tricky Cider. The name is nothing to do with the deceitfulness that you may suppose but records the fact that the cider was first made at Tricky Warren Farm just outside Churchingford. In the village you will find, on the left hand side of the road, the yard of furniture maker Alistair whilst opposite is the truck and house of Steve a jobbing builder. Both Steve and Alistair come across as laid back guys who are organically attached to a roll-up cigarettes.

They are really keen on their cider and very knowledgeable about both the craft and the local pubs. They now make their cider on a Beare hydraulic press in a 'secret' location a couple of miles up the road. They are just in Somerset though most of the mainly bittersweet apples they use come from just over the border into Devon, though county boundaries do not seem relevant - this is the Blackdowns! They have been making cider since 2004, very gradually expanding their markets. They largely sell through pubs and they have their own mobile cider bar for taking to outdoor events and festivals. Plus Al's yard is open most Sunday afternoons for people who want to come along for a chat, a taste, and to buy some cider.

Their cider can be found in a number of local pubs. The Culm Inn is one well known Blackdown location. I was talking to Keith at Remous, the printers of this book, when finding the latest date I could supply them with the artwork and discovered he had drunk a pint there the previous weekend. But I far more regularly drink Tricky at the Plough Inn in Taunton when it is raining at the county cricket ground just along the road. It is a good clean cider which is made for drinking, usually slightly sweetened. I came across Al in there last summer though he was drinking a real ale. Cider makers do seem reluctant to pay for their own ciders when out, plus you do have to consider that at 6% ABV you can probably only safely drink one and a half pints and remain within the driving limit.

No-one should encourage drinking and driving though it does amaze me how many people think that farmhouse cider is so magically strong that even a couple of sips will jeopardise their licence to drive - even though they happilly drink a couple of glasses of much stronger wine. Basically something that is 6% ABV has six units of Alcohol per litre. A litre is a tad under two pints. Our laws limits are based on a level of alcohol in the blood equivalent to five units in an typically sized person - I believe this is based on 10 stone as an average weight. If you are lighter than this you will not be able to drink so much and remain within the limit. However the converse may well also be true - and there are a number of other factors including time which need to be taken into account. Please do not take my word for it - this paragraph in no way amounts to a defence in court!

Tricky are also to be found inside the large Blackdown Hill Trade Association marquee at the annual Honiton Show at the beginning of August. This is a fantastic country show though it could do with a few more cider makers. I think the show try and tie cider up with their bar franchise which of course discourages smaller makers from taking stands. Still you can often find Tricky there selling by the container if not by the glass.

Last year they had their new line of 500ml bottles on sale. They have taken their straight cider and got a company in another rural backwater area, the Forest of Dean, to gently carbonate and pasteurise. It makes a very refreshing straightforward bottled cider and has allowed them to sell to a much wider selection of farm shops etc. Martin Burroughs recently proudly showed me a bottle at Barleymow Farm Shop at Snowdon Hill west of Chard.

Tricky also have a good website with a blog to tell you about what is going on and a good selection of pictures. You can also order bag in boxes through the website or through the Ciderpunk online shop.

I confess to liking Steve and Al and their cider. Their whole approach seems to really fit in with what I think cider should be about.

Westcroft Cider

John Harris, West Croft Farm, Brent Knoll, Highbridge TA9 4BE. 01278 760752
SWECA

Neither John Harris nor West Croft Cider is that well known even amongst ider fans, but many will have heard of Janet's Jungle Juice. It is just about the only case I am aware of where a product brand from a craft cider maker has become better known than the business itself. Janet's Jungle Juice can often be found across the country both in pubs and at festivals.

Last year it won yet another award - this time at a CAMRA festival in Pendle, which I think is in Lancashire. It is a product that is deserving of winning awards. It is a quite consistent medium dry cider, with the emphasis on the medium. It is made with a blend of good bittersweet apples with perhaps a reliance on the excellent Dabinett apple. John also tries to achieve a level of natural sweetness through prompt racking of the cider which means less need to add sweeteners, if any at all.

I am not on the whole a fan of the funny name school of cider marketing. However, this is one name that has stuck. It came from Janet White who used to help John pick up apples and worked at a very fast pace. John relates that the two of them picked up a ton of apples by hand into sacks within two hours. This is some going. In that time my son Richie and I would struggle to manage half that, and I can certainly vouch that it is back-breaking work. Janet deserves a cider named after her.

John is a quietly spoken family chap who I was really glad to see well on the road to recovery from illness in 2011. He was a farmer's son who left home and became a photographer. However as life goes on he returned home and has now been making and selling cider there for over 20 years. The farm's original orchards were sold for development land but new orchards were planted and are coming into maturity. He now gets most of his apples from his own orchards and some favoured local suppliers.

He makes his cider on a Voran hydraulic press and it is a nice simple operation. Although over the years he has experimented, his range is now restricted to just the dry West Croft Cider and the medium Janet's Jungle Juice. He sometimes makes an occasional single variety, the best tasting sample of Morgan Sweet I have ever had came from here. However, on the whole he keeps the range very simple. He also makes Somerset Cider Vinegar, a product which he says can be hard work but in which there is quite a bit of interest at the moment.

You can buy cider straight from the farm where he is open six days a week - every day apart from Wednesday. There is usually someone around though on the Saturday afternoon I called recently John had slipped out for a couple of minutes which of course encouraged a rush of customers. We were being well looked after by his elderly mother until he returned. Unlike some producers I have seen on my travels John is quite upbeat about how his sales are going. Some producers have been commenting that they were not seeing so much of the wholesalers as in recent years, however they seem to be coming in to John just as regularly if not more so. It is quite interesting to speculate on why that may be. I suspect part of it is that he is relatively convenient to the motorway. I suspect also that the brand 'Janet's Jungle Juice' having built a good reputation is a large part of it. However, we need to understand what has contributed to building that reputation. I feel that this is more to do with the slight sweetness of the cider along with a clean fresh flavour. There can be little doubt that this is what the public want and although I like a dry cider myself there is no doubt that public taste is for a little bit of sweetness. With a product like Janet's Jungle Juice where the sweetness comes partially or totally from natural residual sweetness it gives a freshness to the cider which, to my taste buds, the use of either sugar or artificial sweeteners does not.

As well as the wholesalers for cider to pubs and festivals and farm gate sales to locals and to the many tourists at nearby Burham and Berrow John also sells a steady amount on the internet. He was one of the original suppliers of Cider Punk and also sells through a real ale website in Yorkshire. He often puts his cider in to competitions and is someone who it is always well worthwhile having a chat to.

Wilcox Cider

Richard 'Darren' Wilcox, Wilcox Cider, The Cider Shop, Cheddar Gorge
enquiries@wilcoxcider.com www.wilcoxcider.com **SWECA**

When I first came to Somerset thirty odd years ago I have vague memories of getting some cider from a quarry between Shipham and Cheddar - the base of the legendry 'Lukee' then one of the major characters of the Somerset cider scene. I know I looked for it again when I was researching my first Somerset Cider Handbook but there was a café but no cider. Now even the café is shut.

However the tradition lives on. Allegedly Gerald Lukins (Lukee) tried to take on the Revenue and Customs when he claimed he should not have to pay duty on the water he added to his cider before selling. Although the argument has a certain logic about it he was never going to win and it finished him financially. I have been told his ashes are buried under a cider tree at the Lillycombe cafe. The business was taken over by Arthur - famed for 'Arts Cider shack' at the Great Dorset Steam fair which for many years had been the stamping ground of Lukee before him.

Arthur has now retired and sold the Lillycombe café to Richard Wilcox in 2002 and he sold it on to a non cider maker. But the cider side of the business is still with Richard and his partner Heather who is Arthur's daughter - if I have got it right. Richard still does the Great Dorset Steam Fair every year and it is a major outlet for his cider - as are a number of other steam events and shows. He also sells a bit from the farm at Broadway near Shipham but the vast majority of his cider is sold in their cider shop at the bottom of Cheddar Gorge.

Richard had been making cider on his father's smallholding since he was about 13, just a couple of barrels a year, but it is only in the past decade that it has become his main business - for years he had mainly been a lorry driver. I should have found him when I did my Somerset Cider Handbook - I was aware I had missed a producer in

Shipham and mention it towards the end of the book. It was only in the winter of 2011 that on a drive through Cheddar my son Richie and I spotted the cider shop and went in to investigate and I introduced myself to Richard. On the wall were two certificates for two 2nds in the cider classes at the 2010 Bath and West Show - Jon Perry and I had been the judges but the penny had still not dropped!

I am not surprised Richard's cider won prizes, I have drunk it in a few places now and it is distinctively rich tasting and dark coloured - a really good farmhouse cider. I met him at his father's smallholding. His father is another Richard, basically retired but still keeping busy. It was a dull cold day and I was relieved when they took me into a shed where an improvised stove was burning logs and keeping the place nice and warm. There was a row of wooden barrels, a scattering of dirty cups and glasses and plenty of chairs of various degrees of decrepitude. A traditional cider shed - 'excuse the mess they had a bit of a session last night.'

Richard is now making cider on a considerable scale - about 70,000 litres a year. He has two small orchards of his own and collects a considerable quanty (about 110 tomes) from orchards in Thornbury, north of Bristol and from the orchards of Ron Male at Kingsbury Episcopi in South Somerset. Making on the scale he is, Richard has gradually been mechanising the process but is still making a very traditional product. He used to have a little walk along harvester to pick up the apples but now he has graduated to a larger tractor mounted model. 'I used to like the smaller one but you wouldn't get me going back to it now.' Similarly he has upgraded from his Voran pack press to a second hand belt press. *'It is so much simpler, we can get through eight or nine tonnes a day, pour the apples in one end and get the juice and pomace out the other end. Dad is happy to sit there all day and just needs to give it an occasional prod with a stick if it blocks up. I have even got a special seat for him!"* says Richard pointing out an old milk churn with a bit of sponge foam on top.

He also does a bit of harvesting apples for other people and with the new belt press even has the capacity to do some pressing for others as well.

He mainly makes a straight draft cider from Bittersweet apples. He makes a dry and a medium with some judicious use of sucrelose as the preferred sweetener though he does try to capitalise on natural residual sweetness when he has it. He makes a single variety Dabinet and a Redstreak. He can't understand why Thatcher's have stopped doing a single variety Redstreak, it was a favourite product. He is also experimenting with a Yarlington Mill single variety but is not sure if he is going to sell that yet. He uses Branded Products in the Forest of Dean to bottle some cider for sale in the Shop and other shops. Much of this he calls Cheddar Gold which is the only product he matures in Oak. On the whole he finds plastic or aluminium a lot safer bet and he is currently trying to source those aluminium tanks with the lids that drop down with the cider to keep it airtight.

Richard is the sort of cider producer I like - straightforward, but trying to do a good job and very aware of what he is up to. I hope that even with the introduction of the belt press his cider retains that rich mature, almost macerated, taste. Maybe I can give it another certificate someday if I ever have the honour to be asked to do some more judging.

Wilkins Farm House Cider

Roger Wilkins, Lane End Farm, Mudgely, Wedmore BS28 4TU 01934 712385 www.wilkinscider.com

It is now a considerable number of years since I first searched out Wilkin's cider, they didn't have the home painted signs in the hedges then so it was a lot harder to find, but everything is still very much the same - even the cobwebs. You have to find your way down a series of twisting lanes to no where and find yourself in a genuine farmyard which has made little concession to the number of visitors and the need to park. You have a great view out across the Somerset Moors, or Levels as they seem to be known these days.

Wilkins' is just about the foremost shrine to genuine farmhouse cider and a place of pilgrimage for all cider lovers. That is not particularly for it's range of ciders, Roger makes a very good straightforward clean dry Somerset cider from the apples from the orchards on the steep hill above the farm and elsewhere locally. As Roger says it is a totally natural product - just the juice squeezed from the apples and saccharin. The latter has got him into hot water with some of the cider purists but they are always welcome to drink it dry - as I am most likely to do.

The distinctive feature about Wilkins Cider is that it is a place to go - preferably without having to drive yourself. You arrive and descend into a barn and wait around until someone, usually Roger or one of a number of red-faced locals who are often to be found around the place, offers you a 'taste'. This is half a pint of clear golden cider out of taps at the bottom of a couple of upright wooden barrels. You can have dry, sweet or a mixture of the two - the option most people seem to go for. You stand around sipping and enjoying the ambience of the place. Look at the notice board with old business cards and newspaper clippings about some of the visitors he has had. He has strong ties to music people who have made the trip here, some of whom have lived locally.

On a weekend you may notice parties of people who have booked in for a ploughman's - bread, great cheese and as much cider as you can drink - and in these days of responsible drinking you will only find the odd one or two who may have had a bit too much. For the inexperienced - and those who should know better - cider can creep up on you if it is freely available. One of the unique properties of the drink is that the second pint tastes better than the first and that by the third or fourth it is just sublime. These people will be topping up their half pint glasses on a regular basis - some having come out from Bristol dressed as Wurzels for the occasion.

At the back of the barn is the 'lounge bar'. A cobweb festooned room where a number of chairs and old settees have been set out where the locals and regulars seem to congregate. By now you will be ready for another 'taste.' About now you will need to be buying some cider. They carefully fill whatever size container you choose, knocking it gently on the concrete and tipping it back to make sure every drop of air is got out. This is supposed to help the cider last longer but to be honest unless you put it in fridge it is not going to be at its best after three days. In fact I find that all draught farmhouse ciders always taste at their best straight from the barrel on the farm. They also taste at their best when you are having a sociable chat to others and have a thick jumper and coat on to keep out the cold. I think this is why the tradition of cider barns is still alive and well and, although commercial, Wilkins is the prime example of this.

I realise I have hardly touched on Roger himself. Approaching his mid 60's he is still spry and energetic if a bit greyer haired than the past. He is the busy one who is always finding something to do and is never still for a moment. However he always finds time to chat in his thick Somerset accent about cider issues of one sort or another. Times are always getting worse for farming and cider and he has a host of tales to tell. Roger is very much the heart and soul of Wilkins cider and many people across the county speculate on succession. Roger took over the farm from his grandfather, some wonder if Roger's son really wants the cider business, perhaps history will repeat itself. Idle speculation - let's hope Roger is around for a considerable number of years yet. He obviously sups a considerable amount of his own cider so perhaps that could help to preserve him!

Whist visiting you really must buy some cider. There is also some fruit and veg, a few souvenirs and preserves to buy. And there is some excellent cheese sourced from some of the local farmhouse cheese makers. I particularly like the unpasteurised Westcombe Cheddar from near Evercreech. And there is a good chance you may offered one more 'taste' before you leave.

When visiting Roger about this book I suggested that it was much the same as ever and he confirmed that nothing changes. However times do move on - I have discovered that he has his own website. On it there is a link to a video of a song sung by a folk singer to the tune of 'Hotel California' the Eagles classic. Here it has been altered to 'Welcome to Wilkins Farm House Cider' and the words in combination with the photos will tell you all you need to know and prepare you to get the best out of your visit.

Worley's Cider

Neil Worley 55 Dallimore Lane, Dean, Shepton Mallet, BA4 4SA 07855 51718
Twitter: @WorleysCider Facebook: www.facebook.com/worleyscider
Website: www.worleyscider.co.uk

Neil Worley is one of the new generation of cider makers who has a fascination and passion with all things to do with good food and drink, particularly the influence of *terroir*, custom and provenance. A lot of this was formed by his travels and experiences as a younger man, though he is still quite young now, and I particularly remember him telling me about his discovery of cider in the *Sidre* regions in Spain. When he returned to England and settled with partner Helen and young family at Dean in the East Mendips he was keen to put some of his ideas into practice. Cider is very much a part of this.

Worley's Cider is well worth looking out for - from my experience good clean Somerset cider. He has been making cider commercially for about five years and the business is now at an exciting time of its evolution. He had some early success in competitions at the Bath and West Show and discovered that selecting the right blend and quality of apples is essential to making the right ciders. He sources his apples from local traditional orchards and from some in the south of the county. He is one of those producers who like to look at the natural process of traditional cider and selecting apples that are ripe is part of this. Some commercial producers tend to use unripe apples shaken from trees before they are ready. He has experimented with many blends over the years and has used some traditional varieties such as Yeovil Sours.

He still operates from a large garage on the side of his house and now annually produces about 7,000 litres but is expecting to go above this threshold in the next year or so. He has spent the past few years experimenting with how to produce consistent and repeatable products and at the same time exploring what it is that people want to drink for a cider. In doing so he has spoken to a considerable number of cider makers and learnt a lot about the industry. He is now on the committee of SWECA.

His current ciders tend to fall into two camps. He has traditional full strength dry ciders but he is also producing medium strength 4.5% - 5.5% naturally sweet ciders

- the Holy Grail of cidermaking and many of the new generation are working towards this. The two main methods he uses to achieve this are serial racking and keeving, both of which remove nutrient from the cider giving the natural yeast less to work with. This is producing ciders where the fermentation slows to an imperceptible crawl at around 1.010-1012 SG. He has now found he can achieve this consistently and he is really pleased with his new season ciders. Part of this is also helped by his belief in selling his ciders relatively young and he says many of his ciders tend to still have some natural life in them. He has sold out of his production for the past few years and the pubs he supplies are very pleased with the ciders and the public reaction to them. It was noticable the Worley's barrel was one of the fastest to empty at the Horseshoe Cider Festival at Bowlish recently.

Neil's focus is on producing a very natural cider based on the selection of apples. He wants to deliver products that excite and inspire through flavour and provenance, avoiding the use of artificial sweeteners, dilution, pasteurisation and other tampering wherever the market allows him to do so. He currently outsources the milling and pressing of his fruit to other cider makers with the capacity to take on the work. This in no way takes away from his control of his final product and is indeed part of a long tradition. In many parts of the area - Dorset, Dartmoor and Cornwall have been suggested; cider making was often a semi-communal operation with one farm having the press and everybody bringing their own apples. Where heavy stone crushers where used this was often essential. There is also a tradition both in England and France of travelling presses which would travel from farm to farm to crush and press the apples. In fact the use of 'outsourced' functions is widespread from contract apples growing to contract bottling. Virtually any stage can be outsourced but it is important that, as in Neil's case, the cider maker retains control over his ciders throughout the process. Neil assures me he will get his own mill and press when finances permit, and sees this as an important acquisition that will have been informed by his experiences of the results from different pressing formats and processes he's seen amongst the contractors he's used.

Neil gets the freshly pressed juice back to his home in Dean and the fermentation takes place over the winter. As mentioned he currently sells out of his annual production, usually in nine months. Festivals are an important element to his sales, giving both volume to sales and publicity to his products but he also sells through events, pubs and farm shops mainly in the local area. I am currently trying to support his application to have a cider bar at the Mid Somerset Show.

He makes good use of modern media to get the message out about his cider and his philosophy for cider making. He has one of the more constructive blogs for a cider maker and uses a combination of well written articles about his cider with articles about good food. He is also a fan of Twitter and I learnt the other week that his children were excited about his getting some Tamworth weaners, it is all part of building up relationships and gaining publicity and puts my rather functional tweets to shame!

I am certainly looking forward to seeing how Worley's Cider develops over the next few years, and finding more places I can drink it.

Other Somerset Producers

Somerset still has by far the greatest number of cider producers. It has not been possible to get around them all for full interviews. In this section I look at some of the others. Some are in here because I couldn't find them, a few because they are too small to warrant a full profile, one or two who are not conventional cider makers and quite a few who I covered at greater length in my Somerset Cider Handbook but really could not find much new to say about them. I have also updated on a few who I have no longer included.

Andrew Ritchie, Fitzroy Farm, Taunton 07808 611273

Andrew is a solicitor with a small traditional orchard whose hobby of making fine cider has just about grown into a small business now he is registered with HMRC. He had an amazing success last year when he won the medium class of the Farmhouse Cider competition at the Bath and West Show. I can remember the consternation that no one knew who he was!

I am not surprised his cider won. From my experience I know that when the judges are tasting dozens of very similar ciders it is quite easy to spot the ones that are not going to win but with so many fine ciders you are looking for something stands out to win. The cider of Andy's I tasted had just a little bit more apple fruitiness than most.

This probably comes from the fruit in his orchard but he is also very particular as to how he makes it. Fruit is picked up as it ripens and falls throughout the season from September until the end of November. He blends what is ready a wheelie bin full at a time and washes, mills and presses in his 30 litre basket press. He fills 30 litre fermenters and lets it ferment out whilst it stands perfectly still. When he needs cider to drink he siphons off of the lees being very careful not to disturb them and puts the cider into plastic lined Manucubes - though bag in boxes would probably have the same effect.

He prefers a medium cider so he then adds some sugar to slightly sweeten and puts in the fridge to pull off as he needs, very pleasant it is too. Last season he made about 800 litres of this fine golden cider. Obviously this is one of those ciders that you will not find out and about much. If you are interested it is probably best to phone Andrew direct to find out where you can taste some.

Gurt Dog Cider

Somewhere near Langport

I have tasted Gurt Dog Cider in two different pubs but have been unable to track down the maker. Some other makers I have asked are aware of him but can't remember his name. I strongly suspect it is from somewhere on the moors near Langport, where the legend of the Gurt Dog is part of cider lore.

I must admit I was very alarmed when I had my first taste of this cider. It tasted very distinctly of horses, quite unlike anything I had ever tasted before and indeed ever wanted to taste again. I did mention this on a cider web forum and the redoubtable expert Andrew Lea informed me that it was a perfectly natural cider taste resulting from the actions of a particular lactobacillus. Personally I am not quite sure that is enough of a reason to inflict it on an unsuspecting public without a warning.

When I tried it in a second pub it was not so bad - just a very basic dry Somerset Farmhouse cider. Here I was intrigued by the marketing technique. Apparently he had left a demijohn on the bar and told the landlord to see if it sold and been around to refill it when the landlord was out. I think it only lasted the two demijohns. The pub already sold a very good Somerset cider made only a few yards up the road.

Wood's Traditional Cider

Drayton, Langport Somerset. 01458 251246

I know this cider exists but it is another one I have been unable so far to track down. It comes from the moors just outside Langport near Muchelney and it may be the same traditional cider maker as one I have been told about in that area for some years. I heard from another producer that they were having a real go at getting their product out and about just before last Christmas and had been selling at markets.

I recently read a report in a small local newspaper that their cider is for sale at the King Alfred pub at Burrowbridge so of course I had to drop in on a recent trip to Taunton. When I asked for it they insisted on giving me a taste in case it wasn't my taste. The hand pump said it was a still cider but there was some life in the glass and an element of sweetness. I suspect it was this seasons cider and not quite finished - but as such was quite nice. They said it varied from delivery to delivery and was often much sharper. I have tried ringing their phone number on a number of occasions and left messages on their telephone answering service but so far no one has come back to me to enable me to tell you any more - the search goes on. Stop press - met them at the North Somerset Show on 7 May - the day before this goes to the printers - they seemed a very genuine couple.

Mathew Bryant. Hinton St George

Matthew is not really a cider producer - he makes a quantity of very traditional dry cider for his own pleasure which I have tasted both at Powerstock and at the early September festival which Matthew organises in the village hall at Hinton St George to raise money for the village. A very nice event which I was delighted to attend last year.

Kitty and Dicky, Middle Chinnock. 01935 881109

Again not sure if this has yet made it to the ranks of a HMRC registered cider maker. Richard Macey works part time for Nigel Stewart of Bridge Farm and can frequently be found working on his stands at a number of shows. A few years ago he decided to make some cider of his own which has appeared at various events and festivals. He produces with his partner Kitty who bubbles over with enthusiasm.

At Powerstock last year they won a couple of placings with some very nice Kingston Black cider that had retained a lot of residual sweetness. It had still retained some of that sweetness when I tasted it at Hinton St George in September - a very nice cider.

Bath Ales - Bounders Cider

Bath Ales Limited Units 3-7 Caxton Business Park, Crown Way, Warmley Bristol BS30 8XJ 0117 947 4797 hare@bathales.co.uk

Bath Ales really do make some smashing beer. Brews like Gem or Wild Hare are always a great sight when you see them in pubs - you just know they are going to be good every time you drink them.

Like many breweries they felt the need to have a cider in their range and came up with Bounders. As beer and cider do not really mix in the same manufacturing plant they outsourced production. After an initial wrong direction I was delighted to be informed by them at the Bath and West in 2011 that they were now sourcing from one of our finest craft cider makers - it fits so well with their ethos as a craft brewer. No names were mentioned, but I was asked to look behind me where I was delighted to see the Sheppy's stand. Bounders is a fine high juice, refreshing keg cider made in the traditional way from Somerset cider apples. I see from their web-site that they are now also selling a still version in polypins.

So if you see Bath Ales Bounders Cider on your travels please be assured this is well worth drinking.

Brothers Drinks Co Ltd

Matthew Showering Anglo Trading Estate, Shepton Mallet, BA4 5BY 01749 344446. www.brotherscider.co.uk

Brothers Drinks have a great heritage in Shepton Mallet for innovative drinks. The four brothers are great nephews of Francis Showering the inventor of Babycham and a member of a family who had been brewing beer and making cider in Shepton Mallet since the early 19th Century. Brothers Drinks was founded in the early 1990s when the brothers were unable to buy back their former business.

Their flagship from the start was a strong perry to compete with some of the strong ciders which were popular at that time. However, it was only a moderate commercial success and the company focused on bottling alcoholic drinks for others through the alcopops boom. They have become probably the biggest bottler of alcohol in glass in the UK in their factory in Shepton Mallet. Alongside this they had always had a bar selling their strong perry at the nearby Glastonbury Festival - along with Julian Temperley's 'Cider Bus' it is one of my must visit points of call. It was there that they were amongst the first to coin the term 'Pear Cider' after getting fed up explaining to people that perry was like cider but made with pears. It was also there that they started putting shots of concentrate of other juices into the perry. Strawberry 'Cider', Lemon 'Cider', Toffee Apple 'Cider' and a number more were invented and a whole fashion started for fruit ciders.

No one, least of all the Showerings themselves, are going to claim they are making ciders in the old traditional way. They import concentrate of conference pears from Spain and manufacture a product with glucose syrup, waters and alcohol. As a cider purist I am supposed to be offended by this type of commercial product, in some instances I very much am, but not with Brothers. They make no pretence that it is anything else. They are competing in the alcopops edge of the cider market and their excellent brand, image and promotion, including TV advertising, is clearly aimed at the youth market. This approach has changed very little since the innovative marketing of their great uncle when he targeted another strong perry, Babycham, specifically at women and caused a social revolution which made it acceptable for women to go to pubs.

Their products can be found in very many supermarkets, pubs and clubs through out the country.

Cider Lakes Farm

Ian Gibson, Doubonni Farm, Wick Road, Lympsham, BS24 0HA 01278 751593
www.ciderfarmlakes.co.uk

Although I have not been back here for about three years I believe this business is still going. Ian Gibson is a very interesting businessman and has developed an unusual 'attraction' near Burnham on Sea. It has a conference facility, fishing lakes and a shop which sells cider to the tourists in the area. All set in a few acres of attractive cider orchards.

According to his website he still makes cider in the traditional way although he uses a modern press. It has been suggested to me that that press is in fact Thatcher's who take most of the apples from the orchard. Other cider producers I have talked to do tend to speculate how much the cider is that comes back and which the public are invited to taste is based on his own juice.

I am not sure of the long term proposition at Cider Lakes Farm. Ian is certainly not as young as he used to be and I heard rumours from a local producer that one of the fishing lakes has now been filled in. Still it may be worth your while to search out for yourself.

Ermie and Gertie's

Ian Sinclair, Pitney House. Pitney, Langport. TA19 9AR 01458 252308
www.ermieandgertie.com

One of the problems with websites is that it is often very difficult to tell what is currently happening to a company. Ermie and Gerties is a case in point as the last news article on there is about the release of their bottle conditioned cider in February 2009 - which is over three years ago.

Ian Sinclair took early retirement from a career in the city in 2007 and set up this very pleasant lifestyle business aiming high to sell produce into up market deli-catessens - which he has done quite successfully. They have a wonderful brand based around a pair of their Guernsey cows. Their productrange is focused on Ice Cream from Guernsey Milk, sorbets, apple juices and meat. They also have a nice cider orchard and produce some pleasant ciders.

Their local outlet is the farm next door where an old acquaintance of mine from times selling to farmers, Rob Walrond and his family run an excellent farm shop. It is from here that I have purchased Ermie and Gertie's cider in the past and it is definitely where I will have to go soon to check it out. www.pitneyfarmshop.co.uk

Long Ashton Cider Company

c/o Butcombe Brewery, Cox's Green, Wrington, BS40 5PA 01934 863963 www.butcombe.com

The Long Ashton Cider Company is a wholly owned subsidiary of Butcombe Brewery. Butcombe was one of the early, new breweries following the return to favour of real ale in the 70s and 80s. They make a fine range of beers and now also run a considerable number of pubs and are a genuine regional brewer.

Long Ashton Cider is their cider brand and full marks to them for keeping the name of the former Long Ashton Research station alive and in front of cider drinkers. There is no secret about the fact that their ciders are made for them by near neighbours Thatchers and as you would expect from Thatchers they are very good commercial ciders.

Ashton Press is a 4.8% keg cider which will be found in many pubs up and down the country. It is a pleasant medium dry, just a bit drier than Thatchers Gold. In 2011 I think, or it may have just been 2010 they introduced Ashton Still a 4.9% draught cider to appeal to the more traditional cider market. The closest known brand would be Addlestones out of Shepton Cider Mill. It is slightly cloudy, though in the case of Ashton Still I would have said only very slightly. It is a very refreshing drink, quite pleasant with a bit of a tingling after taste. Not a 'real cider' but a very welcome addition to the limited range of okay ciders you can find in multiple pubs.

Natterjack Cider

Steve Gillham, Natterjack Cider, Currypool, Cannington.

I was very sceptical as to whether the name Natterjack cider was still being used. However research on the internet showed them as being among the exhibitors at a food festival in the East Midlands less than a year ago. I am far more familiar with their 'Somerset Cider and Apple Juice Bar' which appears at a number of shows. Gillingham and Shaftesbury is one and they have also been at Frome Show the past few years but Steve himself has not been manning the stand.

Steve is an experienced cider maker and is the former husband of Gill Gillham at Torre Cider. He says that most of his activity is outside Somerset and he visits some bigger events around the country. Last autumn I also noticed a sign pointing off the Taunton - Watchet Road for Somerset Cider and Apple Juice. There was something about the terminology and the red writing on a white background that made me wonder if this is connected, although it is not the same location as the address above which could well have come from an outdated internet reference.

The ciders themselves are acceptable, though as at Torre, they tend to have gone for high strength with a suspicion that they may have had sugar added to increase the strength.

The Original Cider Company - Broadoak

Clutton Hill Industrial Estate, Clutton, BA39 5QQ

There have been rumours flying around the internet over that past few weeks that there has been a change of management / ownership at The Original Cider Company. This would not be the first time that there have been changes there.

Brian Brunt set up Broadoak Cider about 20 years ago and has run it from a former feed mill and pig farm at the top of Clutton Hill ever since, through a few changes of set-up and ownership. Brian is a chirpy character with a strong love of making cider and blending. At one time they did a lot of crushing of apples and supplying the juice into Gaymers however it is many years since cider apples were seen at the factory. Brian has cider apples crushed for him in Herefordshire and the juice tankered in, along with quite a lot of apple concentrates, not all of it cider apple concentrate, which he blends with glucose, water and industrial alcohol etc to produce his colourful range.

They are most famous for the Broadoak range of ciders but also produce a wide range of other drinks there. They make the popular keg product Pheasant Plucker and various other keg products for other people. I understand they produce all the products for Chris Lilley and a number of other people. Their biggest market is to the independent grocery trade where they do a huge number of cheap brand ciders, some with very low fruit content in the two or three litre PET bottles. They are also famous for their product 'Moonshine' a sweet white cider of considerable strength. This may be one of the cider producing companies that the government is targeting with the 40p per unit minimum price idea.

They are now one of the largest cider makers in the country outside the top five. They were producing over a million gallons three years ago when I last visited and their landlord has told me they have expanded very considerably since then. There is room in the cider market for all types of producers and competition is usually a good thing. My biggest gripe about these ciders is partly that they encourage the impression that they are genuine traditional farmhouse ciders and more   particularly that the Real Ale organisation CAMRA get these ciders in to their festivals and promote them as 'Real Ciders'. It is difficult to know who is fooling who here because they quite blatantly do not fit the quite stringent standards that CAMRA themselves put on this definition, a matter of constant debate on internet forums.

Pennard Wines and Ciders

Dr Hugh Tripp, Pennard Wines and Cider Avalon Vineyard, East Pennard, Shepton Mallet 01749 860393 www.avalonvineyard.co.uk

Tucked away off the lane from Wraxall to West Bradley you can find Avalon Vineyard, an organic wine and cider maker who is something different. He is perhaps best known for his extensive range of fruit wines which can be found in many farm shops and delicatessens and Hugh is quite often out and about doing tastings at shows and exhibitions.

Very much as a second string he also makes organic cider. As he himself says this is largely organic by neglect. His own and some neighbours orchards had nothing done to them for many years so he was quite easily able to register them as organic. In fact there is nothing from the fruit point of view that is at all different about his cider than any other traditional Somerset cider.

He presses his cider on a big hand cranked old press and presses through straw. I am certainly not always a big fan of pressing through straw and have only come across a few like Mark Venton in Devon who seem to do it well. The straw needs to be very clean and fresh otherwise there is a lot of undesirable bacteria which can get into the juice. Sometimes it can lead to a heavy dirty taste.

Hugh ferments his cider out dry but customers have the option of buying a sweet version where the sweetening is by saccharin which he points out is definitely not organic. I last went to Avalon Vineyard in the autumn when they had some pick you own Raspberries which Richie and I pressed in with some of our cider and touch wood seems to have made a very palatable drink.

Avalon Vineyard is usually open and there are some trails around the orchards that can be followed. It may well be worth your while to taste some of the interesting organic fruit wines.

Torre Cider Farm

Gill Gillham, Torre Cider Farm, Washford, Watchet TA23 0LA 01984 640004. www.torrecider.co.uk

I was disappointed not to find time to renew my acquaintance with Gill at Torre Cider in my current round of searching out ciders. It is right up on the North Somerset coast between the Quantocks and Exmoor in a part of the county with a considerable cider making tradtion but with very little of it surviving.

At Torre Cider Farm Gill has built up a very pleasant little tourist attraction, using the better connotations of that phrase. There is a very nice tea room and shop, there are some farm animals for children to look at and tractors for them to play on. There is a small cider museum and video, and of course there is the cider.

She has her own orchard which was planted out about 20 years ago and she also get apples from some other local traditional orchards. The cider is made in the traditional way with a Voran press. The cider seems to be made with the tourist in mind - which is not surprising considering that is her prime market. It has developed some 'silly' names for brands. Nothing wrong with Farmhouse at 6.5% ABV, but there is then the sweet Howzat at 7%; Sheepstagger, dry at 7.4%; and Tornado, described as 'mind-blowing extra dry' at 8.4% ABV the highest legally allowed for it to be sold as cider. To me the latter especially tastes as if the strength has been built up through chaptelisation, the adding of sugar. My personal view is that this takes away from the true cider taste.

Anyway if you are on the North Somerset Coast and fancy a cider, Torre is well worth going to. It is just a shame it is the part of the country where they don't seem to have built the roads yet!

Bradley's Juice

Miles Bradley, Box Bush Farm, Box Bush Lane, near Hewish, BS24 6UA 01934 822356 www.bradleysjuice.co.uk

I first met Miles a few years ago at North Somerset Show. He was selling his own range of apple juices and also helping sell someone's box scheme for organic vegetables. He seemed a nice chap who, as I was at the show for Old Mill on business, I gave a business card to. I have bumped into him once or twice since then including in March at a SWECA meeting, so I asked the obvious question.

Yes, he has started to make a bit of cider. As you use the same equipment to make apple juice as you do cider it would seem a very sensible thing to do. He is making a totally natural cider with no sulphites and only using the natural yeast. According to his website his new cider is called Bradders and has a very attractive logo in colours and design that support Somerset Cricket Club. As a member that can be no bad thing. His website also reports that he is planting some more Kingston Black Trees, to boost cider production, in a new 'red' orchard with red apple varieties.

I look forward to trying some of the cider if there is any left by the time I get to it.

I don't think they are there any longer

A few producers from my 2009 Somerset Cider Handbook who I don't think are still there - though please check out for yourselves!

Wattles Cider, Wells. Paul was trying to make a fine quality Kingston Black based cider to sell to the French. His website still appears live but I was told that he was selling his orchards and I can no longer see the small Wattles Cider sign that used to be on the gate to his house. The main part of the business was his wife's sheep for meat which is part of the Level's Best syndicate.

Valley Farm. I most recently saw my friend Brian Mead at the Frome Show. I told him I had seen that his smallholding and very nice house was on the market. He said he is looking to downsize. I understand he has sold his press. He is a great character who I have known for   nearly 30 years and I certainly hope to see him around.

Whitney Farm Cider. This was a young couple who had taken on the tenancy of a council farm near Ilminster which included a small orchard. They had plans to make cider but talking to the chap's father I don't think they have yet got around to making the cider - too many other things to do.

Wrington Press. They made a small amount of 'Yellow Toad Cider' as part of an organic vegetable growing concern. I heard that they had shut down - I hope not as it was a nice set up.

In addition there is Rosy Pearce at Perry Tree Farm, Chew Stoke. I mentioned in my last book that I thought she was there and later went and found her. She produced some very nice cider and some even better perry from a former Long Ashton Perry orchard they have on their farm. The main reason she had started making cider was as they could not get anyone to take the fruit. However, with the upturn of interest in Cider and perry this is no longer a problem and she was finding it a drag to have to sit in to sell cider on Thursday afternoon and Saturdays when she wanted to get on with other work on the farm.

My friend Roy Trott who farms near Shepton Mallet is still expecting to go back into cider production 'next year', as he has been for the past four years! Each autumn he has been waiting for a bit of building to be finished or a bit of kit to be made or repaired and has never yet quite got around to it. I am not complaining as we have had some apples from him.

New style orchards for Orchard Pig, West Bradley

Index by Producer

Bibliography

Whilst writing this books there have been a number of books which have influenced me and provided snippets of valuable information. Although any errors will be my own I am indebted to the following:

Ted Bruning   *Golden Fire - the Story of Cider* 2012 Bright Pen

Liz Copas   *A Somerset Pomona, The Cider Apples of Somerset*
                           2001 The Dovecote Press

James Crowden   *Cider - The fogotton miracle* 1999 Cyder Press 2

James Crowden   *Ciderland* 2008 Birlinn Ltd

Mark Foot   *Cider's Story Rough and Smooth* 1999 privately published

R K French   *The History and Virtues of Cider* 1982 Robert Hale

Carol Trewin   *The Devon Food Book 2010* Flagon Press

E V M Whiteway   *Whiteway's Cider - A Company History* 1990 David and
                           Charles

Picture Credits

The cover photo comes from a disk I was sent a number of years ago by the Somerset Strategic Partnership which were free to use for promoting Somerset business. As I am promoting 50 plus Somerset business in this book I hope they think that is proper use.

The vast majoriy of the photographs are all too obviously snapshots I have taken on my searches. A good number, the better ones, are by my son Richard and one at least is by either my wife Christine or my other son James - the fact that both Richard and I are in it is a bit of a giveaway.

A few producers have sent me some of their own photographs - these are probably quite easy to spot as the standard is a lot higher. Martin Inman of Lulworth Skipper also provided some other photographs of people like Rose Grant. Many thanks to all